So All Israel Shall Be Saved

So All Israel Shall Be Saved

*Donald Robinson and Biblical Theology
at Moore Theological College*

Nathaniel Parker

WIPF & STOCK · Eugene, Oregon

SO ALL ISRAEL SHALL BE SAVED
Donald Robinson and Biblical Theology at Moore Theological College

Copyright © 2025 Nathaniel Parker. All rights reserved. Except for brief quotations in critical publications or reviews, no part of this book may be reproduced in any manner without prior written permission from the publisher. Write: Permissions, Wipf and Stock Publishers, 199 W. 8th Ave., Suite 3, Eugene, OR 97401.

Wipf & Stock
An Imprint of Wipf and Stock Publishers
199 W. 8th Ave., Suite 3
Eugene, OR 97401

www.wipfandstock.com

PAPERBACK ISBN: 979-8-3852-3584-1
HARDCOVER ISBN: 979-8-3852-3585-8
EBOOK ISBN: 979-8-3852-3586-5

VERSION NUMBER 01/24/25

Unless otherwise indicated, all Scripture quotations are taken from the King James Version (KJV) and are in the public domain.

Scriptures marked GNB are from the Good News Bible © 1994 published by the British and Foreign Bible Society. Good News Bible © American Bible Society 1966, 1971, 1976, 1992. Used with permission.

Scripture quotations marked NEB are taken from the New English Bible, copyright © Cambridge University Press and Oxford University Press 1961, 1970. All rights reserved.

Abstract

This book examines the reception of Donald Robinson's legacy in Moore Theological College's biblical theology program. It answers the question, Is it feasible to speak of a Moore School of Biblical Theology? What is distinctive about its teachings, and how has it been shaped by the scholars who have contributed to it? The biblical theology program at Moore Theological College can be traced back to Donald Robinson. One unique contribution of Robinson to Moore College's biblical theology program was his distinction theology concerning the role of Israel in redemptive history as an alternative to dispensationalism and covenant theology. By examining Robinson's view of Jew and gentile in the New Testament church and by tracing how his view has been affirmed, revised, rejected, or ignored by biblical theologians at Moore College who were influenced by or who followed Robinson (including Graeme Goldsworthy, Lionel Windsor, D. Broughton Knox, and William Dumbrell), this book seeks to clarify the reception of Robinson's legacy at Moore College as well as offer an assessment on the plausibility of a distinct Moore School of Biblical Theology.

Dr. Nathaniel Parker

Advisor: Dr. Craig Blaising
School of Theology, Southwestern Baptist Theological Seminary, 2023

I dedicate this book to my mother, Faye Parker, who has been there for me during my entire life and studies; to Dr. Craig Blaising, my PhD supervisor, who guided me through my PhD program; and to Jesus Christ, my Lord and Savior, who gave me the gift of everlasting life.

Contents

Preface | xi
Acknowledgments | xiii
List of Abbreviations | xvi

1. Introduction | 1
2. A Historical Survey of Israel's Role in Redemptive History Within Anglicanism | 8
3. A Brief History of Moore College and Donald Robinson's Distinction Theology | 36
4. Departing from Robinson: Graeme Goldsworthy's Christocentric Biblical Theology and Goldsworthy's Successors | 73
5. Fully Departed from Robinson: D. Broughton Knox, William Dumbrell, and Their Successors' Reformed Redemptive History Approaches to Biblical Theology | 103
6. Toward a Robinson Revival: Lionel Windsor's Evangelical Post-Supersessionist Theology and Additional Scholars | 126
7. Summary and Conclusion | 142

Afterword | 149
Bibliography | 151

Preface

THE SEEDS FOR THIS dissertation (and this book) were planted in my first biblical theology research seminar under Dr. Craig Blaising at Southwestern Baptist Theological Seminary. Dr. Blaising handed me an article from William Dumbrell and wanted to see how well I could write a research paper on Dumbrell's position on the Abrahamic covenant. This led to further exploratory research on various scholars at Moore Theological College. My goal was to determine if it was plausible to speak of a Moore School of Biblical Theology shaped by Donald Robinson's unique distinction theology concerning the role of Jew and gentile in the New Testament church. The results of that labor comprise this book. What I have determined is that the biblical theology that was mostly associated with Moore College appears to have been more in line with the redemptive-history approach commonly associated with Geerhardus Vos and those who followed him at Westminster. However, Robinson's distinction theology has begun to see a revival among later scholars in Moore's biblical theology program (such as Lionel Windsor), and scholars who originally ignored Robinson's unique contribution (such as Graeme Goldsworthy) later began appreciating some aspects of it.

Robinson's distinction theology concerning Israel and the gentiles in God's plan, contrary to his claims, does not fully eliminate all forms of supersessionism. Robinson's concept of an eschatological *new man* that eliminates the distinction between Jews and gentiles still retains a modified form of supersessionism. I disagree with Robinson's distinction theology and believe that Robinson did not go far enough in his theology to properly retain a distinction between Israel and the gentiles in God's eschatological plan. While Robinson should have taken the conclusions of his distinction theology further, he is a useful dialogue partner with those within progressive dispensationalism who, like Robinson, also include a distinction between Jew and gentile within the New Testament church. Robinson also rejected Christian restorationism and advocated that God's promises to Israel are fulfilled through the spreading of the gospel from Jewish believers to gentiles and reciprocally back to other unbelieving Jews. I affirm the importance of the gospel as going from Jewish believers to gentiles and reciprocally back to other unbelieving Jews to fulfill the Bible promise "so all Israel shall be saved" (Rom 11:26). However, I disagree with Robinson's rejection of Christian restorationism and believe that God's promises to Israel are to be fulfilled literally (including God's land promise as a literal fulfillment in the nation of Israel) in addition to the gospel being given back to the Jews. While Robinson was incorrect in his rejection of Christian restorationism, he also makes a useful dialogue partner for those within Anglicanism who advocate for a positive theological interest in Israel (such as those within New Christian Zionism).

It has been quite a journey up this Australian Anglican mountain, no less difficult than a climb up Ayers Rock. It has been rewarding to finally reach the summit and enjoy the view at the top. I pray that my efforts will be a useful contribution to the theological discussion concerning Israel's role in redemptive history. As a Christian believer who is also one of Abraham's Jewish physical offspring, and as one who loves the nation of Israel and her people (and my fellow people), this research subject was dear to my heart personally. Like Paul, I can now say that "I have fought a good fight, I have finished my course, I have kept the faith" (2 Tim 4:7).

Acknowledgments

THE JOURNEY THROUGH A PhD program, dissertation, and book publication does not happen in isolation, and I want to thank everyone who has accompanied me on this journey through my years of study. I want to first of all thank my mother, Faye Parker, who has been there for me throughout my entire life and alongside my studies the entire time. I want to thank my late father, Bruce Parker, who provided for my family and my studies over the years. I want to thank my PhD supervisor, Dr. Craig Blaising, who guided me through the majority of my program, seeing me through until the end. I want to thank my dissertation committee members Dr. Jeffrey Bingham and Dr. Robert Caldwell for guiding me through the completion of my dissertation and being there when I crossed the PhD finish line. Thanks also goes to my initial supervisors, Dr. Dongsun Cho and Dr. John Yeo, who oriented me through the first year of my program and allowed me to smoothly transition to Dr. Blaising as my supervisor. I also want to thank all of the additional professors I attended classes with at SWBTS during my program, including: Dr. David Dockery, Dr. Eric Mitchell, Dr. Terry Wilder, Dr. Malcolm Yarnell, and those on my comprehensive exam committee, including Dr. Madison Grace. I want to thank the SWBTS PhD and Registrar's offices, including those who served during my program and who previously served (such as Wynette Taylor) for answering all my questions throughout the program. Thank you all for guiding me through each course and each stage.

I want to thank my fellow students at SWBTS who read over drafts of my dissertation, helped resolve some humorous typos, and provided feedback, including: Sherrie Moore, Gayla Parker, and Joel Wright. I also want to thank my fellow MDiv student from my time at Luther Rice College and Seminary, Jonathan Ray, who also read a draft of my PhD dissertation and provided useful feedback. Special thanks also goes to others who provided feedback, including: John Greathouse, Ryan Marks, and the Ohm family (Judge Ralph, Derrie, and Ashlyn). Thanks goes out to Luther Rice College and Seminary where I completed my bachelor of arts and MDiv, which laid the foundation for my PhD program at SWBTS, including professors such as Dr. Scott Moody, who prayed for me every step of my PhD program.

Special thanks goes to the individuals who assisted me during the research and writing stages of my dissertation. Thanks to SWBTS libraries (especially Dr. Craig Kubic) and Moore Theological College Library (especially Erin Mollenhauer) for providing me with research materials to utilize in my dissertation, as well as the Church of England Library. Thanks also to: Patrick Cates, Chrissy Coblentz, Paul Hames, Alex Jacob, Philip Kern, Meredith Lake, Gerald McDermott, Marlon Patterson, Russell Powell, Rory Shiner, Vincent Williams, and Lionel Windsor, and anyone else I have communicated with during the research stage of this dissertation. Thanks also to Michele Bozzacco Wormell at Accordance Bible Software; Rick Mansfield, Todd Cullop, and Fern Anderson at Logos Bible Software; John Fallahee at LearnLogos.com; Anne Putnam and Steve Siebert at Nota Bene; and Ori Redler at Mellel for providing me with resources, training, and the technology necessary to complete this dissertation.

I want to thank my colleagues at my employers, Earth Networks/Davis Instruments/AEM and Accordance Bible Software, for graciously working with my study schedule so I could balance my work and studies. I especially want to thank my manager at Earth Networks/Davis Instruments/AEM at the time of my PhD dissertation, Amanda Long; my current manager, Brett Lane; and my former manager, Chris Sloop, for giving me the opportunity to serve the customers at Earth Networks over the years of my studies, and I look forward to continuing to do so in the future. I also want to thank my colleague at Earth Networks/Davis Instruments/AEM Steve Prinzivalli, who prayed for me during the duration of my PhD program and provided some useful study materials during my program (which were vital in helping me pass my comprehensive exam!). I also want to thank my manager at Accordance Bible Software, Richard Perry, and his wife, Linda Perry, and owners Troy and Michelle Wormell, and the rest of the Accordance Bible Software family, for giving me a chance to begin my new job at Accordance while I wrapped up my PhD dissertation. Thanks to Chris Kirkland and Doug Gould at Cyber Team US for providing me another job opportunity while I finish my first major academic publication.

ACKNOWLEDGMENTS

I want to thank the team at Wipf and Stock for providing me the opportunity to publish my first academic work and finally add the title of *published author* to my CV. Special thanks goes to George Callihan for getting my submission through the door, Matthew Wimer for assisting me every step in the publishing process, and the rest of the editorial team for all the work you did in transforming this PhD dissertation into a published book. I would not have succeeded without you!

Finally, I want to thank my Lord and Savior Jesus Christ, the One who gave me everlasting life and the One who called me into the years of studying that allowed me to complete this PhD, all for his glory. This dissertation would have never made it across the finish line if it were not for the daily grace of Jesus Christ.

Abbreviations

ANF	*Ante-Nicene Fathers*
BSac	*Bibliotheca Sacra*
BZNW	Beihefte zur Zeitschrift für die neutestamentliche Wissenschaft
Chm	Churchman
CMJ	Church's Ministry Among the Jewish People
ECF	Early Church Fathers
ETS	Evangelical Theological Society
EvQ	*Evangelical Quarterly*
Exp Tim	*Expository Times*
IFES	International Fellowship of Evangelical Students
Imm	*Immanuel*
IVF	InterVarsity Fellowship
JBL	*Journal of Biblical Literature*
JETS	*Journal of the Evangelical Theological Society*
JMES	*Journal of Middle Eastern Studies*
JTS	*Journal of Theological Studies*
LMS	London Missionary Society
LSJ	London Society for Promoting Christianity Among the Jews
Neot	*Neotestamentica*
NPNF[1]	*Nicene and Post-Nicene Fathers*, Series 1
OTL	Old Testament Library
RTR	*Reformed Theological Review*

ABBREVIATIONS

RTRSS	Reformed Theological Review Supplement Series
SBJT	*Southern Baptist Journal of Theology*
SESU	Sydney University Evangelical Union
SNTSMS	Society for New Testament Studies Monograph Series
SWBTS	Southwestern Baptist Theological Seminary
SwJT	*Southwestern Journal of Theology*
TDNT	*Theological Dictionary of the New Testament*. Edited by Gerhard Kittel and Gerhard Friedrich. Translated by Geoffrey W. Bromiley. 10 vols. Grand Rapids: Eerdmans, 1964–76.

1

Introduction

THE AUSTRALIAN INSTITUTION MOORE Theological College offers a vibrant biblical theology program.[1] By all accounts, the biblical theology program at Moore can be traced back to Donald Robinson. Moore's biblical theology program has been carried forward through the students who have been given the opportunity to study there.

Is it feasible to speak of a Moore School of Biblical Theology? What is distinctive about its teachings and how has it been shaped by the scholars who have contributed to it?

One of Robinson's unique contributions to Moore's biblical theology program was his distinction theology concerning the role of Israel in redemptive history. He provided a different and provocative answer on the fulfillment of Israel's promises in redemptive history (different from typical covenantal and dispensational answers on the same question), and thus provided a distinctive interpretation of the shape and framework of redemptive-historical biblical theology in Moore's biblical theology program that developed around his core course. By examining Robinson's view of Israel and its relation to the church in redemptive history and by tracing how his view has been affirmed, revised, rejected, or ignored by biblical theologians at Moore College, this book provides a historical survey on the reception of Robinson's legacy in Moore's biblical theology program, as well as offers an assessment on the plausibility of a distinct Moore School of Biblical Theology.

---

1. *Moore Theological College* will be abbreviated as *Moore* or *Moore College* throughout most successive uses in this book.

Survey of Literature

At the 2011 conference of the Evangelical Theological Society (ETS), Constantine Campbell read a paper by Graeme Goldsworthy titled "Origins and Guiding Principles" as one of a three-part series on "Biblical Theology at Moore." In his paper, Goldsworthy alluded to a Moore School of Biblical Theology. While defining the Moore College School of Biblical Theology as an annual conference held by Moore College, Goldsworthy implied that the conference stems from an underlying Moore School of Biblical Theology founded by Donald Robinson. Goldsworthy was one of Robinson's students and successors in further developing and carrying on some of Robinson's teachings. He also brought greater attention and popularity to Moore's biblical theology program. Richard Gibson also presented a paper examining what Moore's present-day teaching of biblical theology comprises (specifically concerning Goldsworthy's contributions to the program). Brian Rosner finished off the conference presenting a paper that examined one scholar's (Rosner's personal) reflection on biblical theology at Moore College, attempting to uncover major themes within biblical theology, the relationship between the Old and New Testaments, and the relationship between continuity and discontinuity (with one brief mention regarding the role of Israel in redemptive history) in biblical theology.

Donald Robinson's writings concerning the relationship between Jew and gentile and Israel and the church can be accessed in the recently published edition of his writings, which includes many that were formerly unpublished.[2] Robinson's student and successor, Graeme Goldsworthy, carried some of Robinson's teaching to the masses (while ignoring Robinson's distinction theology in his earlier writings) in a series of works.[3] Lionel Windsor contributed to a revival of Robinson's distinction theology with his evangelical, post-supersessionist understanding of the relationship between Jew and gentile and Israel and the church.[4]

---

2. Robinson, *Donald Robinson: Selected Works*. See especially "Jew and Greek," 1:79–109.

3. Goldsworthy, *According to Plan*; *Christ-Centered Biblical Theology*; *Gospel and Kingdom*; *Gospel in Revelation*; *Gospel-Centered Hermeneutics*; *Jesus Through the Old Testament*; "Kingdom of God"; "Lecture 1"; "Lecture 2"; "Lecture 3"; *Preaching the Whole Bible*; and *Son of God*.

4. Windsor, "Formation of Gentile"; *Paul and the Vocation*; and *Reading Ephesians and Colossians*.

INTRODUCTION

Other publications from Robinson's contemporary D. Broughton Knox, as well as Robinson's successors, will be examined. Some of Robinson's successors or scholars who studied at Moore whose contributions are useful for examination include: Barry Webb, William J. Dumbrell, Peter O'Brien, Michael P. Jensen, Robert Banks, Vaughan Roberts, Richard Gibson, Paul Williamson, Kevin Giles, David Peterson, John Pryor, Malcolm Richards, Glenn Davies, and Phillip Jensen.[5] These publications contribute to how well Robinson's distinction theology concerning Israel's role in redemptive history has been received by post-Robinson scholarship at Moore.

Additional literature that has contributed a better understanding of these issues include publications by scholars who have studied Robinson's legacy (such as Chase Kuhn and Rory Shiner), who provide additional context to the history of Moore College from its founding through Robinson's tenure (such as John McIntosh, Edward Loane, Peter Bolt, F. B. Boyce, and T. C. Hammond), or who provide a critique of Moore's biblical theology program (such as Barry Horner).[6]

In order to better understand the theological context within Anglicanism in which Donald Robinson made his unique contribution, research literature concerning the role of Israel in redemptive history within Anglicanism will be examined. Contributions from Donald Lewis, William Hechler, Enzo Maass, Benzion Netanyahu, David Furse-Roberts, Roland Ward, J. M. Yeats, Yaakov Ariel, Gerald McDermott, and Sarah Lebner Hall contribute to the discussion on Christian restorationism within Anglicanism.[7] Publications from W. D. Davies, J. I. Packer, R. Newton Flew,

---

5. Knox, "Church and the People"; Webb, *Message of Zechariah*; "Role of OT and of Biblical Israel"; Dumbrell, *Covenant and Creation*; "Covenant with Abraham"; *End of the Beginning*; *Faith of Israel*; "Paul and Salvation History"; *Search for Order*; O'Brien, "Church as a Heavenly"; O'Brien and Peterson, *God Who Is Rich in Mercy*; Jensen, *Sydney Anglicanism*; Banks, *Paul's Idea of Community*; Roberts, *God's Big Picture*; Gibson, *Interpreting God's Plan*; Williamson, "Abraham, Israel and the Church"; "Covenant," in *New Dictionary of Biblical Theology*; "Covenant," in *Dictionary of the Old Testament*; *Sealed with an Oath*; Giles, *What on Earth Is the Church?*; Peterson and Pryor, *Fullness of Time*; Richards, "New Israel"; Davies, "William John Dumbrell"; and Jensen, "Israel's Future."

6. Kuhn, *Ecclesiology of Donald Robinson*; Shiner, "Reading the New Testament"; McIntosh, "Anglican Evangelicalism in Sydney"; Loane, vol. 2 of *Donald Robinson: Selected Works*; Bolt, *Cross from a Distance*; *Portrait in His Actions*; Boyce, *Thomas Moore*; Hammond, *In Understanding Be Men*; and Horner, *Eternal Israel*.

7. Lewis, "Evangelicals and Jews Together"; *Origins of Christian Zionism*; *Short History of Christian Zionism*; Hechler, *Restoration of the Jews to Palestine*; Maass, "Forgotten Prophet"; Netanyahu, *Founding Fathers of Zionism*; Furse-Roberts, "Victorian Evangelical

and John Stott provide examples of a typical covenant theology that exemplified a form of supersessionism that was prevalent within Anglicanism.[8] The writings of John D. Hannah, W. H. Griffith Thomas, William Lawton, Larry Crutchfield, J. N. Darby, C. Bass, Donald Durnbaugh, C. Norman Kraus, C. I. Scofield, Charles Gallaudette Trumbell, Craig Blaising, and Darrell Bock provide a history of dispensationalism from Darby through Scofield.[9] Franz Rosenzweig and James Parkes are two additional examples besides Hechler that contribute to the discussion on two-covenant theology.[10] J. Y. Campbell was a contemporary of Robinson who interacted with Flew concerning how to interpret the use of ἐκκλησία throughout the New Testament.[11] R. Kendall Soulen and Craig Blomberg provide some additional background material for studying Windsor's evangelical, post supersessionist position.[12]

Research Question

How was Donald Robinson's view concerning the role of Israel in redemptive history received by his successors at Moore College? Did it shape Moore's biblical theology program and contribute to the distinctiveness of its biblical theology program? Is it feasible to speak of a Moore School of Biblical Theology?[13]

Shaftesbury"; Ward, "Passion for God"; Yeats, "To the Jew First"; Ariel, "Israel in Contemporary"; "Unexpected Alliance"; McDermott, "Can Evangelicals Support"; *Israel Matters*; *New Christian Zionism*; and Hall, "Anglicans and Israel."

8. Davies, *Gospel and the Land*; Packer, "Basic Christian Doctrines"; *Concise Theology*; *"Fundamentalism" and the Word of God*; "Introduction: On Covenant Theology"; *Knowing God*; "Nature of the Church"; "One Body in Christ"; Flew, *Jesus and His Church*; "Some Outstanding New Testament Problems"; Stott, *Basic Christianity*; *Cross of Christ*; *Message of Romans*; *One People*; "Place of Israel"; and *Understanding the Bible*.

9. Hannah, "'Thomas' in the Memorial Lectureship"; Thomas, "Great Facts"; *St. Paul's Epistle to the Romans*; Lawton, "Winter of Our Days"; Crutchfield, *Origins of Dispensationalism*; Darby, "Considerations"; Bass, *Backgrounds to Dispensationalism*; Durnbaugh, *Fruit of the Vine*; Kraus, *Dispensationalism in America*; Scofield, *Rightly Dividing the Word of Truth*; Trumbull, *Life Story of C. I. Scofield*; Blaising, "Future of Israel"; Blaising and Bock, *Dispensationalism, Israel and the Church*; and *Progressive Dispensationalism*.

10. Rosenzweig, *Star of Redemption*; and Parkes, *Foundations of Judaism and Christianity*.

11. Campbell, "Origin and Meaning."

12. Soulen, "Post-Supersessionism"; and Blomberg, "Freedom from the Law."

13. *School* in this book refers to a *school of thought* consisting of a coherent theological

INTRODUCTION

Thesis

Donald Robinson's distinction theology concerning the role of Israel in redemptive history was his attempt at offering a mediating position between dispensationalism and supersessionism. His distinction theology can be summarized as "God's distinctive promises to Israel are in the New Testament fulfilled, not to all believers, but to Jewish believers who constitute the restored remnant of Israel and that gentile believers are the inheritors of other promises altogether, that is, the promises made in the Old Testament to the nations who should come to Israel's light."[14] Robinson's distinction theology was initially ignored by scholars who followed Robinson, brought attention to, and popularized Moore's biblical theology program (such as Graeme Goldsworthy and William Dumbrell). However, Robinson's distinction theology reentered the biblical theological discussion at Moore College by an appreciation of Robinson's contribution in some of Goldsworthy's later writings, as well as through the contribution of scholars such as Lionel Windsor. In its current state, a Moore School of Biblical Theology would fall within a Reformed redemptive-historical biblical theology in the Westminster tradition following the teachings of Geerhardus Vos. With the revival of an interest in Robinson's distinction theology concerning the role of Jew and gentile within the New Testament church, the teachings that comprise a Moore School of Biblical Theology could potentially be shaped by Robinson's unique contribution through the scholars who have brought attention to Robinson's distinction theology back into the theological discussion.

Survey of Chapters

Chapter 2 will survey a brief history of the role of Israel within Anglicanism. Various positions concerning Israel's role in redemptive history and the relationship between Jew and gentile in the church were prevalent

---

interpretation that carries forward distinctive features of a founding figure. An example of this use of *school* can be found in Klink and Lockett, *Understanding Biblical Theology*, 67. A helpful definition of *biblical theology* from a Moore Theological College scholar is provided by Brian Rosner: [Biblical theology] "proceeds with historical and literary sensitivity and seeks to analyse and synthesize the Bible's teaching about God and his relations to the world on its own terms, maintaining sight of the Bible's overarching narrative and Christocentric focus." Rosner, "Biblical Theology," 10.

14. Robinson, "Jew and Greek," 81.

throughout Anglican theology. There was a general position of supersessionism that the church was a new Israel (held by Anglican covenant theologians). There was also a positive theological interest in Israel that developed into a position of Christian restorationism advocating for Jewish evangelism and for restoring a Jewish nation in the land of Israel. Dispensationalism was another position that developed out of a positive theological interest in Israel and shared some aspects of Christian restorationism. Each of these differing theological positions frame the discussion for examining Robinson's unique distinction theology as his attempt at an alternative, mediating position.

Chapter 3 will survey the history of Moore College from its founding through Robinson's tenure, as well as Robinson's establishment of Moore's biblical theology program. The chapter will also examine Robinson's distinction theology concerning Israel's role in redemptive history, his attempt at a mediating position that was neither a supersessionist covenant theology nor dispensationalist, and whether Robinson fully eliminated all forms of supersessionism in his distinction theology. Robinson's theological position as a response to Christian restorationism will also be discussed.

Chapter 4 will examine how Graeme Goldsworthy and his successors (Vaughan Roberts, Richard Gibson, Brian Rosner, Peter O'Brien, and Paul Williamson) began to depart from Robinson's distinction theology. Goldsworthy's development of the three epochs of the kingdom of God in a Christocentric biblical theology, his initial ignoring of Robinson's distinction theology, and his later appreciation of some aspects of it (without fully incorporating it into his biblical theology) will be discussed.

Chapter 5 will examine D. Broughton Knox, William Dumbrell, and their successors (Peter Bolt, Barry Webb, Kevin Giles, and Malcolm Richards) as additional examples of scholars who largely ignored Robinson's distinction theology and, like Goldsworthy, popularized a Reformed redemptive-historical biblical theology into Moore's biblical theology program. The contributions of Knox, Goldsworthy, and Dumbrell form the plausibility of a Moore School of Theology that primarily followed the Westminster tradition of Geerhardus Vos.

Chapter 6 will survey a revival of and interest in Robinson's distinction theology in the biblical theology contributions of Moore scholars in later scholarship. With Lionel Windsor's evangelical, post-supersessionist position, one can begin to see the return of an emphasis on Robinson's distinction theology to Moore's biblical theology program. Additional scholars (Robert Banks, George Athas, Phillip Jensen, Anthony Nichols, Martin Pakula, Ma'afu Palu, Jeff Read, and W. H. Salier) provide further examples of scholars who have expressed a revival of interest in Robinson's distinction theology.

Chapter 7 will offer a summary and conclusion. It will also recommend future study, research, and theological developments that resulted from this study.

2

A Historical Survey of Israel's Role in Redemptive History Within Anglicanism

Introduction

A BRIEF HISTORICAL SURVEY concerning Israel's role in redemptive history within Anglicanism is necessary to frame the discussion for Donald Robinson's distinction theology in chapter 3.[1] The general position of supersessionism (that the church has become a new Israel) has been dominant throughout church history and Anglican ecclesiology (examples during Robinson's time include the covenant theologians R. Newton Flew, J. I. Packer, and John Stott).[2] There was also a broad positive theological

---

1. This historical survey is not exhaustive but covers some significant theological positions that frame the context for Donald Robinson's contribution in chapter 3. The arrangement of the theological positions is not necessarily chronological. This chapter places each position in a logical arrangement that allows for response and dialogue among the proponents of each position. Robinson did not necessarily respond to (or dialogue with) each *theologian* represented in this chapter. As shown in chapter 3, he responded to each theological *position* covered in this chapter.

2. *Supersessionism*, also known as replacement theology, views the church as the replacement of Israel. The church has become a new Israel. One such work which summarizes this viewpoint is Robertson, *Israel of God*.

Supersessionism occurs across a wide range of theological systems within Christian theology. Covenant theology is one form within Christian evangelical theology in which supersessionism is prevalent. For more information on *covenant theology*, see Lillback, "Covenant Theology"; Horton, *God of Promise*; and Vos, "Doctrine of the Covenant."

Helpful works that contrast dispensationalism with covenant theology include: Fuller, *Gospel and Law*; Brand et al., *Perspectives on Israel*; and Gentry and Wellum, *Kingdom Through Covenant*.

8

interest concerning Israel within Anglican theology that taught various ways of viewing the fulfillment of Israel's promises in redemptive history and the relationship of Jew and gentile in the church. The position of Christian restorationism that developed into Christian Zionism was a philo-Judaic movement that included members within the Anglican communion (such as Lord Shaftesbury and William Hechler in the nineteenth century) that resulted in the practical applications of evangelism to the Jewish diaspora and the advocating of the reestablishment of a modern-day Jewish nation in the land of Israel.[3] The teachings of some leaders within Christian restorationism (such as Hechler) further developed the concept of a two-covenant theology (separate ways of salvation for Jews and gentiles).[4] Some traditional evangelical Anglican leaders (such as Stott) criticized two-covenant theology as an extreme position.[5]

The position of dispensationalism (that Israel and the church are distinct in redemptive history) shared some aspects of Christian restorationism's positive theological interest in Israel.[6] It was developed in

---

3. The term *Christian Zionism* began to be used in the same context as *Christian restorationism* around March 10, 1896. See Merkley, "Zionists and Christian Restorationists." Robinson primarily used the older term *restorationism* in his essay "Biblical Understanding of Israel," 182, 184, although he also used the newer term *Zionism* to describe the movement in its later developments. This book primarily uses the term *Christian restorationism* to refer to the movement, but will occasionally use the term *Christian Zionism* in places where Robinson himself used it. A helpful definition of *Christian Zionism* (which is also an accurate definition of *Christian restorationism*) is provided by Donald Lewis: "The belief that the Jewish people were destined by God to have a national homeland in Palestine and that Christians are obliged to support the Jewish state." Lewis, "Evangelicals and Jews Together," 2. For a brief history of Christian Zionism, see Lewis, *Short History of Christian Zionism*. For a discussion on the current theological orientation of Christian Zionism as a nondispensational response to critics who have alleged Christian Zionism as theologically dispensational, see McDermott, *New Christian Zionism*.

This book uses *philo-Judaic* as expressing affinity or care for the Jewish people.

4. See the discussion later in the chapter on the origins and development of *two-covenant theology* (also known as *dual-covenant theology*). A brief definition of two-covenant theology is: Jews are saved through the religion of Judaism, whereas gentiles are saved through Christ. This book uses the term *one-covenant theology* in contrast to two-covenant theology to refer to Jews and gentiles as both being saved through Christ. See also the discussion on two-covenant theology in Blaising, "Future of Israel."

5. Stott was also critical of Christian Zionism in general, not only the two-covenant theology that emerged from the movement.

6. Robinson considered dispensationalism as one form of Christian restorationism in his essay "Biblical Understanding of Israel," 180–81, although he also recognized there were nondispensational Christian restorationists.

reaction to Anglican ecclesiology by theologians who left the Anglican communion (such as J. N. Darby) and formed the nucleus of the Brethren movement.[7] However, dispensational theology influenced some within Anglicanism who embraced many of its theological points short of ecclesiological separation (such as W. H. Griffith Thomas). Both Christian restorationism and dispensationalism were developed in the context of Anglican theology but pushed beyond it while simultaneously exercising influence upon members of the Anglican communion.

Each of these differing theological positions frames the discussion for examining what Robinson proposed as a distinction theology as his attempt at an alternative, mediating position concerning the role of Israel in redemptive history.

Supersessionism

The various ways of relating Israel and the church have been part of theological discussion throughout church history.[8] Supersessionism was a general position that considered the church a new or true Israel. It developed early in the church's teaching and was the default position in patristic, medieval, reformation, and post-reformation theology.[9] It is the dominant umbrella

---

7. For more on the early development of dispensationalism in the life of J. N. Darby, see Crutchfield, *Origins of Dispensationalism*. For historical works on the origins of the Brethren, see Stoffer, *Background and Development*; and Durnbaugh, *Fruit of the Vine*. For more on the history of the Brethren in Australia, see Newton, "History of the Brethren in Australia."

8. Three works that examine the theological discussion concerning the relationship between Israel and the church throughout church history are Diprose, *Israel in the Development*; Charlesworth, *Jews and Christians*; and Daley, *Hope of the Early Church*.

9. Justin Martyr (ca. 105–ca. 165) was one of the first church leaders to call Christians the true Israel. See Justin Martyr, "Dialogue of Justin," 261. See also Richardson, *Israel in the Apostolic Church*, 1.

Irenaeus (ca. 135–ca. 202) believed that the true seed of Abraham was the New Testament church, although he also believed there would remain an end-time literal city of Jerusalem. See Irenaeus, "Against Heresies."

Origen (ca. 185–ca. 253) began to popularize the view that the true Israel must be interpreted spiritually to refer to Christ's followers. See Origen, *On First Principles*, bk. 4, 299–301; and "Commentary on John," 104.

Augustine (354–430) and his followers further popularized the view that the New Testament church is the new Israel. Augustine refers to the elect as the "truer Israel of God" in "Letter 149." See also Augustine, *Expositions*, 550; Fredriksen, "*Secundum Carnem*," 29–30; and Dubois, "Jews, Judaism and Israel."

position that informs most of the theological discussion apart from theologians who seek to find a positive theological interest concerning Israel.

In his essays on Jew and gentile, Robinson interacted with works that exemplified supersessionism. Two examples (one general and one specific to Robinson's context) are Earle Ellis's (1926–2010) book *Paul's Use of the Old Testament* and *The Faith of the Church*, a report of the Joint Commission on Church Union of the Congregational, Methodist, and Presbyterian Churches of Australia.

Robinson referenced Ellis's *Paul's Use of the Old Testament* in his essay "Israel and the Gentiles in the New Testament" and the chapter "Jew and Gentile in the New Testament," originally in *Faith's Framework*, as an example of supersessionism. Under "The True Israel," Ellis stated that Paul considered the Christian church the "faithful remnant of Israel, the true people of God."[10] He elaborated that "Christians are the true 'Jews' . . . Israel . . . Israel after the Spirit . . . the seed of Abraham . . . the Israel of God . . . the circumcision . . . the peculiar people." He considered the church to be the "continuing body of OT [Old Testament] Israel," in which the gentiles were considered part of the true Israel.[11] Robinson's collection of essays on Jew and gentile provided his alternative position in that Jewish (not gentile) believers comprise the true Israel, the seed of Abraham, and the circumcision in the New Testament.

The *Report of the Joint Commission on Church Union of the Congregational, Methodist, and Presbyterian Churches of Australia* is one example of supersessionism within Robinson's context. Robinson began his essay "The Salvation of Israel in Romans 9–11" by stating it is commonplace throughout theological discussion to consider the church as the new Israel, referencing the language of the *Report of the Joint Commission* when he summarized that the report "speaks of the 'continuity' of the church 'with the history and life of Israel' and of its being in reality 'the true

---

For a brief historical sketch on Justin Martyr, Irenaeus, Origin, and Augustine, see also McDermott, *Israel Matters*, 3–10, 33–34.

Two additional works that survey supersessionism throughout church history (while offering critiques of supersessionism) are Soulen, *God of Israel*; and Vlach, *Church as a Replacement*.

10. Ellis, *Paul's Use of the Old Testament*, 136–39. See also Robinson, "Israel and the Gentiles," 7–8; and "Jew and Gentile," 412–13.

11. Ellis, *Paul's Use of the Old Testament*, 136–39 (bracketed text added).

Israel.'" In his next paragraph, he responded to the report by stating: "This theological question I believe to be mistaken."[12]

Covenant Theology

Supersessionism is found across a wide range of theological systems within Christian theology. One form within Christian theology in which supersessionism is prevalent is covenant theology.[13] In his essay "On Covenant Theology," J. I. Packer (1926–2020, an Anglican covenant theologian during Robinson's time) surveyed the history and position of covenant theology. Packer began his survey of covenant theology as a theological development of the Reformation (including contributors such as Huldrych Zwingli, Henry Bullinger, John Calvin, and Zacharias Ursinus). He then discussed how Johann Koch (Cocceius) developed a biblical-theological position of covenant theology consisting of three covenants (the covenant of works, the covenant of grace, and the new covenant) in redemptive history. Since he wrote the article as an introduction to Herman Witsius's *The Economy of the Covenants Between God and Man*, Packer concluded his history of covenant theology by elaborating on how Witsius modified and further developed Cocceius's position of the three covenants (Witsius taught that the three covenants are: the covenant of works, the covenant of redemption, and the covenant of grace).[14]

Packer began his survey on the position of covenant theology by defining a covenant as "a voluntary mutual commitment that binds each party to the other," particularly a mutual commitment between God and man.[15] He defined covenant theology as a biblical hermeneutic in which the concept of God's covenantal relationship with mankind throughout redemptive history was Scripture's unifying theme. He elaborated on the threefold covenantal arrangement in Scripture developed by Witsius and

---

12. Robinson, "Salvation of Israel," 47. See also Shiner, "Reading the New Testament," 85.

13. For overviews on covenant theology, see Lillback, "Covenant Theology"; and Vos, "Doctrine of the Covenant." For an extensive study on covenant theology, see Witsius, *Economy of the Covenants*. William Dumbrell also overviews covenant theology throughout his work *Covenant and Creation*.

14. Packer, "Introduction: On Covenant Theology," 20–21. English Puritans (including John Owen and Francis Turretin) taught covenant theology. See Gentry and Wellum, *Kingdom Through Covenant*, 73.

15. Packer, "Introduction: On Covenant Theology," 10–11.

taught by many post-Witsius covenant theologians. God made a covenant of works between Adam and Eve that would have granted them eternal life, conditioned on their obedience to God not to partake of the fruit of the forbidden tree. Adam and Eve disobeyed God, and sin entered the world and mankind through Adam (as mankind's representative). God provided salvation to mankind through his eternal covenant of redemption with Christ (as the mediator and second Adam). Christ fulfilled mankind's redemption through his birth, obedience, death, and resurrection. Believers (the elect) are saved through the covenant of grace in Christ (which rests upon the covenant of redemption). Scripture presented various covenants (such as the Abrahamic and Mosaic covenants), each covenant is subsumed under a single covenant of grace.[16] Packer defined the elect who are saved through the covenant of grace as comprising a single covenantal community from "Abel, Noah, and Abraham through the remnant of Israel, to the worldwide New Testament church of believing Jews and Gentiles."[17] He taught that the elect who partook in the covenant of grace comprised a continuity in which God's promise to Old Testament Israel that he "will be your God, and ye shall be my people" (Lev 26:12) carried over to the New Testament church (both believing Jews and gentiles together comprising one elect people).[18] Only Jews and gentiles in Christ were in a covenant of grace with God and could be considered the people of God.[19] He interpreted the olive tree (Rom 11) as representing the New Testament church, comprised of both believing Jews and gentiles, without their ethnic distinctions. Unbelieving Israel were the branches that were broken off after the death of Christ and replaced by the branches of believing Jews and gentiles who were grafted into the olive tree. Christ represented the seed of Abraham. Gentiles partook of Christ in their salvation and became the recipients of the promises of the Abrahamic covenant.[20] Believing gentiles and Jews together comprised one group of people who are Abraham's seed, a new Israel, and a new chosen people of God, the New Testament church.[21] The new covenant

---

16. Packer, "Introduction: On Covenant Theology," 12–16.
17. Packer, "Introduction: On Covenant Theology," 14.
18. Packer, *Concise Theology*, 87–88, 199.
19. Packer, *Concise Theology*, 89.
20. Packer, *Concise Theology*, 88–89, 200.
21. Packer, "Basic Christian Doctrines," 886–87.

people of God, the New Testament church, have inherited God's promises to Old Testament Israel.[22]

Shiner noted that Robinson was impressed by an article Packer wrote concerning the centrality of covenant as Scripture's unifying theme. However, Robinson, as well as his successors in Moore's biblical theology program, gave less emphasis to the concept of covenant as Scripture's central theme (see chapters 3 and following).[23] Robinson also rejected the position of covenant theologians that the church comprised of believing Jews and gentiles without ethnic distinctions inherited the promises of Israel. He instead taught that it was believing Jews in the New Testament who were the recipients of God's promises to Israel and that believing gentiles were the recipients of God's other promises to the nations. He took issue with the olive tree (Rom 11) as representing the New Testament church, instead viewing the root of the olive tree as representing the blessing of Abraham in which believing Jews and gentiles shared without eliminating their ethnic distinctions.

R. Newton Flew (1886–1962) was a fellow student alongside Robinson in C. H. Dodd's New Testament seminar at Cambridge.[24] He is an example of a covenant theologian Robinson interacted with during his education. Flew placed the origin of the church, not in the New Testament event at Pentecost in the book of Acts, but in the Old Testament at the call of Abraham in Gen 12. He argued that Scripture taught a continuity between Old Testament Israel and the New Testament church, with the New Testament church being the "true inheritors of God's promises to Old Testament Israel."[25] In *Jesus and His Church*, Flew traced a biblical theology of the church as the new Israel and true Israel throughout the New

---

22. Packer, *Concise Theology*, 200.

23. Shiner, "Reading the New Testament," 56.

24. Shiner, "Reading the New Testament," 65.

25. Flew summarized his argument concerning the continuity between the Old Testament Israel and the New Testament church: "It is true to say that for the early Christian the Church goes back to the time of Abraham. It is hardly correct even to say that Jesus founded the Church. He reconstituted it. The proud consciousness of being the true inheritors of God's promises in the Old Testament to Israel is manifest in St. Paul, in the Epistle to the Hebrews, in the First Epistle of St. Peter, and finds a quainter expression in the Epistle of Barnabas. In the Apostolic Tradition of Hippolytus the ordination prayer for the bishop has the following for its second sentence: 'Thou hast appointed the borders of Thy Church by the word of Thy grace, predestinating from the beginning the righteous race of Abraham." Flew, "Some Outstanding New Testament Problems," 217.

Testament.²⁶ He began by stating that only one true religion offers salvation, Christianity, through belief in Christ as one's Messiah. It was Christ who purged and reconstituted Old Testament Israel through Christ's choosing a little flock who comprise a remnant of Israel, the apostles. After the death and resurrection of Christ, those who responded to the preaching of Peter and the apostles (the remnant of Israel) throughout the book of Acts became a new community, a new people of God, and a new Israel. His interpretation of the olive tree (Rom 11) was that it comprised a single people of God, the New Testament church, in which unbelieving Jews were broken off and gentile believers (and later Jewish believers) were grafted in. The New Testament church, the new and true Israel, is comprised of a believing Jewish remnant and gentile believers, together who comprise one people of God without any ethnic distinctions. Throughout his biblical theology, Flew drew a continuity between the use of the term קָהָל about Old Testament Israel and ἐκκλησία as referring to the New Testament church, viewing both as representing the same reality and equating the New Testament church with Old Testament Israel.²⁷

J. Y. Campbell (1887–?) was another contemporary of and fellow student with Robinson and Flew in Dodd's New Testament seminar at Cambridge.²⁸ Campbell wrote and presented a paper (likely in response to Flew) in which he argued against the use of the term ἐκκλησία as referring to the New Testament church as a new Israel or new people of God in continuity with Old Testament Israel. Campbell taught that the term ἐκκλησία referred to an assembly, not the group of people the assembly represented.²⁹ The Old Testament use of the term קָהָל did not refer to the people of God but merely referred to a generic assembly of people.³⁰ The term ἐκκλησία was never used in any key biblical texts that presented a continuity between Old Testament Israel and the New Testament church or that taught

---

26. Flew, *Jesus and His Church*, 14.

27. Flew, *Jesus and His Church*, 14, 30, 35, 88, 100–104, 125, 150–51, 158–59, 166, 169, 172–73, 181–82. Like Flew, Packer performed a similar exegesis which linked the use of the term ἐκκλησία in the Septuagint (which referred to the congregation of Old Testament Israel) to the use of ἐκκλησία referring to the New Testament church. He considered the ἐκκλησία of Old Testament Israel and the New Testament church as one continuous "covenant people of God." See Packer, "Nature of the Church," 886.

28. Shiner, "Reading the New Testament," 65.

29. Campbell, "Origin and Meaning," 130, 132.

30. Campbell argued that עֵדָה would have been a more likely term used to refer to the people of God. See Campbell, "Origin and Meaning," 133, 136.

the New Testament church is the true Israel of God.³¹ The use of the term ἐκκλησία in the New Testament was a logical choice to refer to a general assembly of New Testament Christians without technical or theological significance. The term would later refer to local church congregations in a similar sense that the term συναγωγή referred to local Jewish synagogue congregations. The term later referred to the universal church as comprising a grouping of various local churches, not to be construed as a universal church in continuity with Old Testament Israel.³² Campbell summarized his position concerning the use of the term ἐκκλησία throughout the New Testament by stating: "We must conclude, therefore, that there is no good evidence for the generally accepted view that in using the word ἐκκλησία the early Christians were borrowing an Old Testament term in order to express their claim to be the true people of God, the legitimate successor of the Israel of the Old Covenant."³³

Robinson likely followed the Flew/Campbell dialogue while in Dodd's seminar. Like Campbell, Robinson reached a similar exegetical conclusion concerning the use of the term ἐκκλησία in the New Testament as referring to a general assembly of Christians, not a continuity with Old Testament Israel. He would also propose an alternative position to Flew in that it was the Jewish remnant of believers in the New Testament who comprised the true Israel, excluding gentile believers who responded to the preaching of the apostles. While gentile believers would come alongside Israel, they would not be equated with Israel.

Introducing a Positive Theological Interest Concerning Israel

A positive theological interest concerning Israel was introduced into theological discussions around the 1580s–1590s. Protestants began rethinking the Augustinian teachings of the medieval church that equated the church with Israel. Theodore Beza (1519–1605) was a reformed (Calvinist) theologian who interpreted Israel in Rom 11 as referring to literal Jews, not the church. This position was reflected in the notes of later editions of the Geneva Bible. By the middle of the seventeenth century, the belief that

---

31. Two examples provided by Campbell are 1 Pet 2:4–10 and Paul's discussion of the relationship between Christians and Israel throughout the book of Romans. See Campbell, "Origin and Meaning," 138, 140.

32. Campbell, "Origin and Meaning," 42.

33. Campbell, "Origin and Meaning," 141.

a mass evangelization of Jews would occur in fulfilling Rom 11:26 (that "all Israel shall be saved") became popular, especially among Puritans.[34] Donald Lewis (1950–2021) argued that Puritanism's popular interpretation of Israel as literal Jews "resonated with the idea of the divine 'election' of the Jews" and further advanced the necessity of Jewish evangelism.[35] Within the writings of Anglicanism, John Foxe's (1516–1587) *Book of Martyrs* (1563), while critiquing the religion of Judaism throughout the work, taught the validity of God's covenant with the nation of Israel.[36] John Bale's (1495–1563) *The Image of Both Churches* (1570), while a work from a supersessionist view, advocated evangelizing the Jewish diaspora and taught an eschatological role for the Jewish people.[37]

The belief that following their mass evangelization, the Jews would also return to the land of Israel became popular between 1585 and 1640.[38] This belief (like the belief in the mass evangelization of the Jews) became popular among Puritans. Britain was considered a chosen nation to lead the Christian world of the present age while protecting and restoring God's Old Testament chosen nation as God's first nation, Israel.[39] Within the writings of Anglicanism, Thomas Draxe's (?–1618) *The Worldes Resurrection* (1618) advocated for the restoration of a Jewish nation in and the return of the Jews to the land of Israel, rebuked the church's treatment of the Jews throughout history, and argued that God had providentially preserved the Jewish diaspora.[40] Two later works that reinforced the theological discussion advocating for a restoration of a Jewish nation in the land of Israel were

---

34. Lewis, *Origins of Christian Zionism*, 26–29. See also Vreté, "Restoration of the Jews," 15; and McDermott, "Can Evangelicals Support," 257. Puritanism's evangelization of the Jewish diaspora was also considered a means to combat Roman Catholicism's influence in Britain. Jewish converts to Christianity could align with the Puritans in a battle against Roman Catholicism's infiltration of Britain. See Lewis, *Short History of Christian Zionism*, 62.

35. Lewis, *Origins of Christian Zionism*, 66, 68, 156.

36. McDermott, *Israel Matters*, 36.

37. In Lewis, *Origins of Christian Zionism*.

38. Lewis, *Origins of Christian Zionism*, 27–29.

39. Hall, "Anglicans and Israel," 170. See also Lewis, "Evangelicals and Jews Together," 6–7; and *Short History of Christian Zionism*, 58.

40. Lewis, *Origins of Christian Zionism*, 29. See also Draxe, *Worldes Resurrection*, 37, 56; and Vreté, "Restoration of the Jews."

Thomas Scott's (1747–1821) *Commentary on the Bible* (1804) and Thomas Newton's (1704–1782) *Dissertations on the Prophecies* (1825).[41]

In addition to interpreting Israel as referring to literal Jews, a popular theological shift from postmillennialism to premillennialism occurred during the 1820s among many Anglicans who later became involved in Christian restorationism. Prior to this shift, many Anglicans involved in Jewish evangelism were postmillennialists.[42] The popular shift to premillennialism began in post-Reformation Christianity through a renaissance of a literal reading of a future millennial kingdom in Rev 20. The medieval church's failure to fulfill its role of ushering in the kingdom of God (a position held by some Reformers) opened the door for premillennialism to return as a popular position.[43] The deterioration of international affairs (such as the French Revolution) also caused some Anglicans to reexamine their eschatological position in line with a premillennial interpretation of Rev 20 and believe an imminent, literal return of Christ would occur.[44] As some Anglicans began to accept a premillennial eschatology, a greater appreciation of the prophetic role concerning the nation of Israel, the Jewish people, and the importance of advocating for a restoration of a future Jewish nation in the land of Israel became popular in theological discussions.

By reexamining the teachings of the medieval church that the church is Israel with the alternative position that Israel in Rom 11 is the Jewish people, coupled with the popular theological shift from postmillennialism to premillennialism, some Anglicans began accepting a positive theological interest in Israel and the Jewish people. Two theological positions

---

41. McDermott, *New Christian Zionism*, 65.

42. McDermott, *Israel Matters*, 38. See also Lewis, "Evangelicals and Jews Together," 6.

Premillennialism is the position that interprets Rev 20 as Christ returning to earth before a literal, one-thousand-year millennium. Christ establishes a literal kingdom during the millennium. *Postmillennialism* is the position that interprets Rev 20 with Christ returning to earth after a *millennium*, which is defined as an indefinite time period in which the church is active, the gospel has spread throughout the earth, and that evil on the earth has diminished.

For a discussion on the differences between premillennialism and postmillennialism (and amillennialism), see Blaising et al., *Three Views on the Millennium*.

43. Blaising, "Premillennialism," in *Three Views on the Millennium*, 176–77. For a brief history of premillennialism and how it allowed for a greater appreciation of a positive theological significance of Israel in Anglican evangelicalism, see the section "An Overview of Millennialism" in Yeats, "To the Jew First," 209–12.

44. Lewis, *Origins of Christian Zionism*, 67–68, 88. See also Furse-Roberts, "Victorian Evangelical Shaftesbury," 125–26; and Hall, "Anglicans and Israel," 171–72.

further built upon this interest. The first was a position of Christian restorationism that later developed into Christian Zionism. The second was dispensationalism (which shared some aspects of Christian restorationism, such as a literal future for the nation of Israel).[45]

Key Anglican Figures in Nineteenth- and Twentieth-Century Christian Restorationism

Christian restorationism was a position that built upon the positive theological interest in Israel by first popularizing Jewish evangelism (in fulfillment of the Rom 11:26 teaching that "all Israel shall be saved"). It later expanded to include advocating for a restoration of a Jewish nation in the land of Israel (believing that God's land promises to Israel await a future fulfillment, including returning the Jewish people to their land).[46]

David Bogue (1750–1825) preached a sermon before the London Missionary Society (LMS) in 1806 to spur British interest in Jewish evangelism.[47] His sermon led to the formation of the largest evangelical missionary society to the Jews, the London Society for Promoting Christianity Among the Jews (LSJ).[48] The society was formed by Joseph Frey (1771–1850), a Jewish convert to Christianity, who evangelized Jews in Britain (and later America). Frey previously served at the LMS before branching off to form the LSJ. The LSJ began as an interdenominational missionary society. It was later realigned as an Anglican missionary society after Frey departed from England to become involved in missions to American Jews.[49] The LSJ was formed in 1809 to fulfill the Pauline mandate that the gospel should be given to the Jew first. Its members considered Jewish evangelism to be at the forefront of Protestant evangelicalism's global missions activity.[50] Members of the LSJ also applied God's Abrahamic covenant promise in Gen 12:3

---

45. Hall, "Anglicans and Israel," 171–72.

46. During this later expansion, Christian restorationism began to develop into the position of Christian Zionism.

47. Yeats, "To the Jew First," 208.

48. Different scholars abbreviate the London Society for Promoting Christianity Among the Jews as either LSJ or LJS (or utilize other alternative abbreviations). Donald Lewis uses the abbreviation LSJ in *Origins of Christian Zionism* and his journal articles. This book will use Lewis's abbreviation LSJ to refer to the society.

49. Lewis, "Evangelicals and Jews Together," 4–5.

50. Hall, "Anglicans and Israel," 172.

to their work in Jewish evangelism. They believed that by evangelizing Jews, Britain would be blessed, leading to an expansion of its political empire.[51] The LSJ later branched out into an evangelistic society to Jews worldwide instead of primarily focusing on the evangelization of British Jews. This new international focus caused some members of the LSJ who wished to remain focused on evangelizing British Jews to break away from the LSJ to form a new Anglican society fulfilling the LSJ's original mission, the Philo-Judaean Society (in 1827).[52] At its peak, the LSJ was the largest producer and distributor of English material concerning the Jews and Jewish evangelism.[53] The work of the LSJ continues to the present age through the Church's Ministry Among the Jewish People (CMJ).[54]

As Christian restorationism began to expand its focus to include advocating for a restoration of a Jewish nation in the land of Israel, one key nineteenth-century Anglican political figure in the movement was Lewis Way (1772–1840). Way was a wealthy attorney and philanthropist (who inherited £300,000 from John Way).[55] He donated £10,000 to the LSJ in 1814, leading the way in its restructuring in 1825. He was a premillennialist and wrote extensively defending premillennialism. He believed there was a need for Jewish evangelism and advocating for restoring a Jewish nation in the land of Israel.[56]

Another key nineteenth-century Anglican political figure involved in Christian restorationism was Anthony Ashley-Cooper, Lord Shaftesbury (1801–1885).[57] Shaftesbury was a contemporary of Edward Bickersteth (1825–1906) and witnessed Bickersteth's theological shift from postmillennialism to historic premillennialism.[58] Bickersteth was involved in the

---

51. Yeats, "To the Jew First," 207–8. Yeats offered a helpful summary of the mission work of the LSJ and the positive theological interest concerning the Jewish people that was circulating throughout Britain during the nineteenth century: "the Jews were construed as the theological axis upon which all of theology, missiology, and eschatology turned" (212–13).

52. Hall, "Anglicans and Israel," 172.

53. Yeats, "To the Jew First," 212.

54. CMJ UK, "Our History."

55. John Way was unrelated to Lewis Way but left Lewis the inheritance due to their shared surname.

56. Lewis, *Short History of Christian Zionism*, 78–79.

57. Lewis, *Origins of Christian Zionism*, 10. Lord Shaftesbury was the seventh Earl of Shaftesbury. His previous title was Lord Ashley.

58. Lewis, "Evangelicals and Jews Together," 7. For further discussion on *historic*

LSJ and, together with Shaftesbury, contributed to establishing an Anglican bishopric in Jerusalem.[59] While Bickersteth was involved with Jewish evangelism, he believed that a mass evangelization of the Jewish people would primarily occur after their return to the land of Israel.[60] Like other members of the British aristocracy, Shaftesbury was a member of the Clapham Sect, a group of Anglicans involved in Jewish evangelism who also influenced British politics and contributed to the Anglican Church's mission activity. Shaftesbury agreed with the popular position among Puritans concerning advocating for a restoration of a Jewish nation in the land of Israel and assisting in the return of the Jewish people to their land.[61] He was involved in numerous philo-Judaic activities as a member of the British aristocracy, serving as the president of the LSJ and petitioning the British government concerning restoring a Jewish nation in Israel.[62] He wished to right Britain's past wrongs when it banned Jews in 1920. He noticed how Britain and Holland later prospered when they began taking in and assisting Jews into their nations, whereas Spain went into decline after expelling Jews from theirs. He believed national prosperity or decline resulted from how nations treated the Jews (in fulfillment of God's promise to Abraham in Gen 12:3 that he would bless those who blessed Israel and curse those who cursed Israel).[63] He wished to reform British society by assisting various groups of people he considered to be victims of persecution. He considered the Jewish people one of the most persecuted victims throughout history. He wished for Britain to lead the way in assisting the Jewish people through Jewish evangelism, through advocating for a Jewish nation in the land of Israel, and for returning Jews to their land, in order to receive God's promised blessings (in Gen 12:3) back upon the British empire.

One key nineteenth-century Anglican clergy figure who contributed to developing Christian restorationism into a position of Christian Zionism was William Hechler (1845–1931). Hechler (who, like Shaftesbury, served in the LSJ) believed that the land of Israel still belonged to the

---

premillennialism, see Ladd, *Blessed Hope*; and Blomberg and Chung, *Case for Historic Premillennialism*.

59. Furse-Roberts, "Victorian Evangelical Shaftesbury," 127.

60. Lewis, *Short History of Christian Zionism*, 108–10.

61. Furse-Roberts, "Victorian Evangelical Shaftesbury," 121. See also Lewis, *Origins of Christian Zionism*, 115; and Thiselton, *Thiselton Companion*, 246.

62. Ward, "Passion for God," 20–21. See also Ariel, "Unexpected Alliance," 74.

63. McDermott, *Israel Matters*, 38–39.

Jewish people based on God's promises to Abraham throughout the book of Genesis.[64] He wrote a pamphlet in 1882 titled *The Restoration of the Jews to Palestine*.[65] In it, he argued that it is the role of Christians to love the Jewish people and to labor toward advocating for restoring a Jewish nation in the land of Israel to usher in the second coming of Christ. He also believed there was an ethnic distinction between Jew and gentile that went beyond Jewish assimilation into gentile culture, considering the Jewish diaspora a distinct and separate people from the gentiles.[66] Hechler's development of Christian restorationism into a position of Christian Zionism originated when he was introduced to the father of political Zionism and Jewish Zionist leader Theodor Herzl (1860–1904).[67] Hechler read Herzl's work *Der Judenstaadt*, eventually becoming a valuable adviser to Herzl and introducing Herzl to the Grand Duke of Baden to further advocate for restoring a Jewish nation in the land of Israel.[68] Herzl called for the assembly of the First Zionist Conference, with Hechler playing a role in securing philo-Judaic Christians to attend. The conference was to be held in Munich but was transferred to Basel due to opposition in Munich by its Jewish population. The conference occurred on August 28, 1897, in which Herzl was elected president of the newly formed World Zionist Organization. The organization's goal was to unite and resettle the Jewish people in the land of Israel, to strengthen a Jewish national movement within the land of Israel, and to work with other foreign governments to fulfill Zionism's goals.[69] While Herzl was the architect of the World Zionist Organization, without the assistance of Hechler, Herzl would not have had access to prominent foreign dignitaries to help launch his political Zionist agenda, and Herzl's role in bringing philo-Judaic Christians into a movement of Zionism helped to further Herzl's political Zionist goals.[70]

Shaftesbury and Hechler's efforts helped contribute to the eventual drafting of the Balfour Declaration in the twentieth century, which was

64. Maass, "Forgotten Prophet," 161, 185.
65. Maass, "Forgotten Prophet," 162.
66. Hechler, "II. Dispersion Fulfilled," in *Restoration of the Jews to Palestine*.
67. Ariel, "Israel in Contemporary," 463. See also Maass, "Forgotten Prophet," 165. For more on Herzl, see the chapter "Theodor Herzl" in Netanyahu, *Founding Fathers of Zionism*, 57–90; and JewishHistory.org, "Crash Course."
68. Klinger, "Reverend William H. Hechler." See also Ariel, "Unexpected Alliance," 78. *Der Judenstaadt* is also available in an English translation, *The Jewish State*.
69. Jewish Virtual Library, "Zionist Congress."
70. Gerrish, "Christians Remember Zion."

Britain's most important development concerning the land of Israel between the First Zionist Conference and the 1948 establishment of a modern-day Jewish nation in the land of Israel.[71] The Balfour Declaration was written by British foreign secretary Arthur James Balfour (1848–1930), writing to Baron Lionel Walter Rothschild (1868–1937) to support establishing a Jewish nation within the historic land of Israel.[72] While there were political motives in Britain and advocates from secular Zionism that contributed to the drafting of the Balfour Declaration, the efforts of Christian restorationists (which further developed into Christian Zionism) also contributed toward Britain's support of the restoration of a Jewish nation in the land of Israel.[73] Lord Balfour's Christian background included respect for the Jewish people. He wished to give back to the people who birthed the foundation of Christianity, and he did so by drafting the Balfour Declaration.

Hechler eventually ventured into theological territory that conservative Anglicans would consider extreme. As he attached himself to Herzl's Zionist efforts, he prioritized advocating for a restoration of a Jewish nation in the land of Israel and assisting Jews returning to their land over Jewish evangelism. He believed that Jews would only fully embrace Christ as their Messiah after they returned to their land. He eventually ceased all efforts concerning Jewish evangelism, assisting in developing a two-covenant theology within Christian Zionism. He believed there were two differing salvation covenants, one for gentile Christians and a separate one for Jews, that nullified any need for Jewish evangelism. Two-covenant theology was also proposed in *The Star of Redemption*, the work of Jewish author Franz Rosenzweig (1886–1929). In his work, Rosenzweig argued that Jews are already born in a relationship with God through a Jewish salvation covenant. In contrast, gentile Christians are made instead of born in a relationship with God in a Christian salvation covenant.[74] He used the illustration that in the star of redemption, Judaism (the Jewish salvation covenant) is its core, whereas Christianity (the Christian salvation covenant) is its rays.[75] Anglican minister James Parkes (1896–1981) proposed a similar two-covenant theology to Hechler's. In his work *The Foundations of Judaism and Christianity*, he argued against any attempt or need for evangelizing Jews, viewing Judaism

---

71. Lewis, *Origins of Christian Zionism*, 1.
72. Klinger, "Reverend William H. Hechler," 72.
73. Ariel, "Israel in Contemporary," 79.
74. Rosenzweig, *Star of Redemption*, 396.
75. Rosenzweig, *Star of Redemption*, 397.

and Christianity as comprising two separate and parallel salvation tracks, in which neither religion should replace the other.[76]

Two-covenant theology was rejected by many within Anglicanism as an extreme theological position. Anglican minister and covenant theologian John Stott (1921–2011) provided a clearly articulated refutation of two-covenant theology. Stott considered both Jew and gentile as being under a single calling of God (the covenant of grace) and that the "covenant of God is the same throughout, from Abraham to Christ."[77] Only those in Christ are genuinely saved. There are no ethnic barriers or ethnic distinctions in salvation.[78] In his commentary *The Message of Romans* he refuted two-covenant theology's position concerning different salvation tracks for Jews and gentiles. He appealed to the olive tree (Rom 11) as one olive tree comprised of both Jewish and gentile believers, without their ethnic distinctions. Nonbelieving Jews were broken off from the olive tree because they rejected Christ as their Messiah. The only way for Jews to become grafted back into the olive tree is through salvation in Christ.[79]

Like Packer, Stott is an Anglican covenant theologian. Those Stott deemed as in Christ are not only the individuals who are genuinely saved, but they also comprise Abraham's seed.[80] They are the "heirs of the promises God made him" (Gal 3:29).[81] Israel (according to Stott) is comprised of "neither Jews nor Israelis, but believers in the Messiah."[82] He considered both believing Jew and gentile, without their ethnic distinctions, to "belong to the covenant people of God."[83] Israel's national failure to accept Christ as their Messiah opened the door to the gentile nations, with a new spiritual Israel becoming the true inheritor of the promises of God.[84] The calling to a physical, national Israel has now been extended to all gentile nations, fulfilled by one new humanity that eliminates ethnic distinctions.[85] The New

---

76. Parkes, *Foundations of Judaism and Christianity*, 330.

77. Stott, *One People*, 21; and *Understanding the Bible*, 144.

78. Stott, *Cross of Christ*, 188–89.

79. Stott, *Message of Romans*, 304–5. Stott believed there would be a widespread salvation of the Jews as they turned to Christ as their Messiah. See Stott, "Place of Israel," 170.

80. Stott, *Basic Christianity*, 155.

81. Stott, *Understanding the Bible*, 144.

82. Stott, "Place of Israel," 167.

83. Stott, *Message of Romans*, 55–56.

84. Stott, *Message of Romans*, 266–67.

85. Stott, *One People*, 24.

Testament church is the true children of God and spiritual descendants of Abraham.[86] Not only did he refute two-covenant theology as an extreme position, but he (unfortunately) extended his critique to Christian Zionism in general on multiple grounds. First, he believed that the New Testament lacks any discussion concerning the restoration of a Jewish nation. Second, he believed that Christ fulfilled Israel's promises, and the new international community in the New Testament, comprised of believing Jews and gentiles (without any ethnic distinctions), are the inheritors of Israel's promises.[87] Finally, he believed that the church is the fulfillment of the Abrahamic covenant's blessing concerning all the families of the earth, with a future land promise not fulfilled in a literal (Jewish) nation of Israel but in an eschatological, heavenly reality (a New Jerusalem).[88]

Christian restorationism began with a focus on evangelizing the Jewish diaspora. Believing Jews joined gentile churches. Eventually, its focus expanded to include advocating for a future Jewish nation in the land of Israel and returning the Jewish diaspora to their ancestral homeland in Israel to fulfill biblical prophecy. Hechler ventured further by eliminating a need for Jewish evangelism in his two-covenant theology. Robinson interacted with Christian restorationism in his essay "Biblical Understanding of Israel." He summarized Christian restorationism's position concerning the restoration of a Jewish nation in the land of Israel. He also noted the role of key nineteenth-century figures in the movement (such as Lord Shaftesbury), as well as the efforts of the LSJ concerning Jewish evangelism. He was comfortable with efforts to evangelize Jews. However he (unfortunately) disagreed with Christian restorationism's position concerning the restoration of a modern Jewish nation in the land of Israel and in assisting the return of the Jews to their land as the fulfillment of God's land promises to Israel. He believed there was a difference between God's plan of not abandoning the Jewish people (including Jewish salvation in Rom 9–11) and the Christian restorationist position that the Jews continue to have a God-promised right to the land of Israel in the present age. He rejected Christian restorationism on four grounds. First, he believed the Old Testament land promises to Israel extended further than the modern nation of Israel. He cited Gen 15:18–21 as evidence that the land promises to Israel included Syria, Lebanon,

---

86. Stott, *Cross of Christ*, 188–98, 249.
87. Stott, "Place of Israel," 170–71.
88. Stott, *Understanding the Bible*, 58–59.

Jordan, and northern Sinai.[89] In contrast to Christian restorationism, he did not consider the current modern nation of Israel as fulfilling the Old Testament land promises. Second, he believed the land promises to Israel were conditional upon obeying God's laws. Due to their disobedience, the Jews forfeited their land promises, according to Robinson. Third, he did not believe the New Testament contained any explicit language concerning the carrying forward of any Old Testament land promises concerning the nation of Israel. Finally, he considered Jewish salvation (what Robinson referred to as their heavenly inheritance) as the fulfillment of God's promises to them. He did not consider God's promises to the Jews requiring a literal land promise. He would agree with covenant theologians that no future return of the Jewish people to the land of Israel is biblically warranted. He would modify the position that the church, comprised of both a Jewish nucleus and gentile believers, together comprise a new Israel. He limited the true Israel to the Jewish nucleus and instead labeled the church (composed of Jews and gentiles) a new Adam (see chapter 3). He also rejected two-covenant theology, believing instead that Jews and gentiles shared a common salvation in Christ. He did believe that the one gospel of Christ was presented in two distinct missions (aspects) to Jews and gentiles. Jews and gentiles would each be given a different presentation of the same gospel of Christ based on their prior knowledge of God.[90] While Robinson did not directly mention the term *two-covenant* theology in his writings on Jew and gentile, he did teach that Jew and gentile share a common salvation in Christ. However, the gospel presentation should be different for Jews and gentiles (depending on their prior knowledge of God).

Dispensationalism

Dispensationalism also developed from a positive theological interest in Israel. It shared some aspects of Christian restorationism (such as a belief in a literal future for the nation of Israel). Dispensationalists were also premillennialists and disagreed with a supersessionist view that the church was a new Israel.[91] Dispensationalism was developed in reaction to Anglican

---

89. Other passages Robinson cited for evidence include Num 13 and 34; Josh 10–19; 1 Kgs 4:21–24 and 8:65; 2 Kgs 14:25; Amos 6:13; Ps 72:8; Ezek 47; and Zech 9:10.

90. Robinson, "Biblical Understanding of Israel," 182, 184–86; and "Jew and Greek," 81–85.

91. Robinson included dispensationalism as a form of Christian restorationism in

ecclesiology by theologians who left the Anglican communion (such as J. N. Darby) and formed the nucleus of the Brethren movement (during the nineteenth century in Britain and expanding into other countries including the US).[92] John Nelson Darby (1800–1882) was an Anglican priest in Ireland who became dissatisfied with the Church of England. He had issues with what he believed was the Anglican Church's failure to teach salvation by grace, as well as the Anglican Church's establishment religion from its uniting with the state. He believed Anglican Church ecclesiology was a visible,

---

"Biblical Understanding of Israel," 182, 184–86. For more on dispensationalism as a form of premillennialism, and the relationship between dispensationalism and Christian Zionism, see Blaising and Bock, *Progressive Dispensationalism*, 21: "One of the most well-known features of the dispensational tradition is the belief in a future for national Israel. That future includes at least the millennial reign of Christ and for some dispensationalists, extends into the eternal state as well. Because of this strong belief, some early dispensationalists, such as W. E. Blackstone, played a key role in garnering support for the Zionist movement."

See the comments of "Dispensationalism, Classical," in Hays et al., *Dictionary of Biblical Prophecy and End Times*, 118: "Its adherents make a sharp distinction between Israel and the church. God made an unconditional covenant with Israel, and they will always be his special people. Even in the New Testament 'Israel' means ethnic, national Israel and should never be spiritualized to refer to the church. The church is a parenthesis in God's plan, coming into existence after Israel rejected the kingdom. When the time of the Gentiles is fulfilled, God will offer the kingdom again to Israel. The purpose of the millennium in Revelation fits into God's plan at this point. During the millennium, God's unconditional promises will be kept and other prophecies will be fulfilled through the restoration of Israel."

Blaising noted that dispensationalism "is especially noted for strong rejection of certain forms of supersessionism or replacement theology—that is, rejection of the belief that the church fulfills and replaces Israel in the divine plan. . . . Dispensationalists did not believe that the dispensation with Israel was simply a 'shadow' of reality revealed in the church; rather, Israel and the church revealed distinct purposes in God's plan. The dispensation with Israel set forth an earthly, political purpose, whereas the dispensation with the church set forth God's spiritual, heavenly purpose in which there is no ethnic distinction. These two purposes not only account for structural differences between the two dispensations but also give rise to distinct sets of promises, each pointing to its own form of eschatological fulfillment. Consequently, dispensationalists expect a future dispensation in which these promises can be distinctly fulfilled. Since promises from the last dispensation concern Israel specifically, there must be a future for Israel in a dispensation to come." See Blaising, "Dispensation, Dispensationalism," 248.

92. For more on the early development of dispensationalism in the life of J. N. Darby, see Crutchfield, *Origins of Dispensationalism*; and Bass, *Backgrounds to Dispensationalism*. For historical works on the origins of the Brethren, see Stoffer, *Background and Development*; and Durnbaugh, *Fruit of the Vine*. For more on the history of the Brethren in Australia, see Newton, "History of the Brethren in Australia."

worldly, and man-made form of church government.[93] Believing that the church had failed, he joined a group of believers who referred to themselves as the Brethren and taught that all believers shared a common unity in Christ, and they are led by the Holy Spirit.[94] The Brethren were critical of denominational divisions throughout churches and the failure of various churches to attempt such a common unity.[95] They rejected the divisions of denominations and the establishment religion of churches who united with the state (such as the Anglican Church). They rejected the ordained clergy's role in the ministry and emphasized lay believers.

Darby's belief concerning the church as a failure resulted in his placing the church and Israel into separate dispensations. He made a distinction between the heavenly people (the church) who would be taken up to heaven in order for the earthly people (Israel) to take part in a literal restoration during Christ's return and reign.[96] The heavenly people are the saints throughout the ages (the true church is heavenly and invisible) who are resurrected and receive their heavenly blessing. The earthly people (the visible people, primarily Israel, plus gentiles on the earth during Christ's reign) occupy Christ's kingdom and partake in literally restoring the earth (lost during the sin of Adam). God restores the earth and grants

93. Erich Geldbach made the comment that Darby's position concerning unity in Christ "lay outside all the denominations and involved a rejection of everything hierarchical, institutional, liturgical, and sacramental. It would come to expression every Sunday in the breaking of bread at the Lord's Table, where 'two or three' (Matt. 18:20) would gather together." See Geldbach, "Plymouth Brethren," 247.

94. Galli and Olsen, "John Nelson Darby," 98–99; and Hoffecker, "Darby, John Nelson," 228.

Galli and Olsen observed that "Darby saw history as a 'progressive revelation,' and his system sought to explain the stages in God's redemptive plan for the universe. There was nothing especially radical about dividing history into periods. What separated Darby's dispensationalism was . . . the absolute separation of Israel and the church into two distinct peoples of God." Galli and Olsen, "John Nelson Darby," 99–100.

Craig Blaising noted that "the church is supposed to know that she has a heavenly future and is called to a heavenly way of life. The failure of this dispensation comes when the church thinks that it has an earthly purpose, when it begins to think of itself as an earthly people and becomes preoccupied with earthly things. Such preoccupation has brought about what is called 'Christendom'—that political cultural phenomena of the Western 'Christian' nations. Classical dispensationalism viewed Christendom as a perversion of sinful humanity which tries to substitute itself for the real church of God. Christendom, the human failure of this dispensation, will be judged at the return of Christ." See Blaising and Bock, *Progressive Dispensationalism*, 25–26.

95. Darby, "Considerations."

96. Dickson, "Darby, John Nelson," 179.

immortality to the earthly people. The heavenly people will not participate in the earthly people's fulfillment of God's promises during Christ's reign, nor will the earthly people participate in the heavenly people's blessing in heaven.[97] Darby's separation of the earthly and heavenly people taught an eternal duality in which the church would eternally occupy heaven whereas Israel would be physically restored and eternally occupy earth. One critical element missing from Darby's theology was Jewish believers within the New Testament church. One can infer that Jewish believers within the church would be considered part of the heavenly people and not participate in the restoring of Israel or the earth.

The Bible conference movement shared some aspects of the Brethren movement (such as members of multiple denominations freely studying the Bible together under a common unity in Christ led by the Holy Spirit) while supplementing the work of existing denominational ministries (unlike the Brethren, the Bible conference movement did not reject the role of ordained clergy or existing ministries).[98] The Niagara Bible Conference in the late nineteenth century was an American Bible conference that contributed to the development of the position of dispensationalism.[99] Various teachings resulted from the Niagara Bible Conference. One was that Christ (the one who unites believers) is the focal point of interpreting Scripture. Another was that postmillennialism (the popular eschatological position during its time) did not emphasize the centrality of Christ as the one who would usher in the kingdom (postmillennialism believed that Christ returned after the kingdom arrived through the preaching of the gospel and the Christianizing of society). In its place, members of the conference began to repopularize the position of premillennialism (that Christ would return before the kingdom in order to usher in the kingdom). Various teachers at the conference outlined numerous dispensations (usually

97. Spencer, "Dispensationalism," 854.

98. Craig Blaising noted one difference between the Brethren movement and the Bible conference movement: "While the Brethren had focused their attention on the local church, the leaders of the Bible conferences sought to draw out the practical significance of the universal church, that one body of Christ which transcended local churches and denominations. The Bible conference was a visible, tangible Christian communion based solely on the reality of the universal church. It could not and did not try to replace local church communion and ministry." See Blaising and Bock, *Progressive Dispensationalism*, 17–18.

99. For more on the Niagara Bible Conference, see Kraus, *Dispensationalism in America*; and Sandeen, *Roots of Fundamentalism*. See also Niagara Bible Conference, "Declaration of Doctrinal Belief," 509–11.

seven).[100] One teaching of the conference that further developed Brethren theology and dispensationalism was the distinction between the heavenly and earthly people. The heavenly people (the church) will eternally occupy heaven so that the earthly people (primarily Israel but also including gentiles during the millennium) will occupy Christ's earthly kingdom and eternally occupy a literally restored earth.[101] There is a positive theological significance for Israel in dispensationalism concerning a literal restoration of Israel on the earth (similar to Christian restorationism). However, what is absent is any distinction between Jewish and gentile believers within the New Testament church. One can infer that Jewish believers comprise the heavenly people along with gentile believers without an ethnic distinction between the two, whereas the Jews that comprise the earthly people are an entirely distinct reality.[102]

Dispensationalism was made popular by C. I. Scofield's (1843–1921) Scofield Reference Bible, produced in 1909.[103] Scofield was a member of the Niagara Bible Conference, and the notes in his reference Bible helped to circulate the teachings of a Bible conference (such as the Niagara Bible Conference) to readers.[104] Scofield came from an Episcopal background and in 1882 began pastoring a congregational missional church in Dallas, Texas.[105] During his pastorate, he became friends with James H. Brookes

---

100. See Parsons, "Dispensations," in *Truth* 11 (1885) 460–66; and "Dispensations and the Second Coming of our Lord," in *Truth* 11 (1885) 314.

101. Blaising and Bock, *Progressive Dispensationalism*, 10, 14–15, 23–26. Blaising defines *a dispensation* as "a particular arrangement by which God regulates the way human beings relate to Him. Dispensationalism believes that God has planned a succession of different dispensations throughout history, both past, present, and future. Furthermore, dispensationalists believe that these dispensations are revealed in Scripture, in both biblical history and prophecy" (11). See also Blaising and Bock, *Dispensationalism, Israel and the Church*, 16–17, 19–20.

102. See Rowdon, "Dispensational Theology," 259: "Dispensationalists accept that believing Jews—as individuals—find their place in the church during the dispensation of grace, but the promises made to the natural seed of Abraham await the premillennial return of Christ with his church for their fulfilment. Then will be initiated the dispensation during which the material blessings promised to Israel will be bestowed and will be characteristic, though not to the exclusion of the spiritual dimension."

103. For more on the life of C. I. Scofield and the development of the Scofield Reference Bible, see Trumbull, *Life Story of C. I. Scofield*.

104. Blaising and Bock, *Progressive Dispensationalism*, 10–11; and *Dispensationalism, Israel and the Church*, 21–23.

105. He was ordained as a Congregationalist in 1883 but later transferred to the Presbyterian Church in the US in 1910. See Spencer, "Scofield, C(yrus) I.," 906.

(1830–1897; Brookes read Darby extensively) who introduced Scofield to dispensationalism and premillennialism. Scofield wrote *Rightly Dividing the Word of Truth* (a work from a dispensationalist and premillennialist view) in 1888, later offering his own correspondence Bible study course. He also pastored a congregational church in Northfield, Massachusetts, in 1895, later becoming the president of Northfield Bible Training School.[106] He returned to Dallas in 1902, where he began work on the Scofield Reference Bible. Based on the King James Version text with footnotes clarifying the meaning of some biblical texts, the reference Bible utilized a chain reference system to allow Scripture to interpret Scripture and organize all of the Scripture passages on particular biblical themes. It defined major doctrines of Scripture (such as atonement, kingdom, and church) and outlined each book of the Bible. It also incorporated a dispensational interpretation of Scripture similar to Darby. The Bible conference movement and Scofield Reference Bible were instrumental in popularizing dispensationalism among American fundamentalists, especially among Presbyterians, Baptists, and Congregationalists.[107]

Like Darby, Scofield taught a distinction between the heavenly people (the church) and the earthly people (Israel). The church would be removed from the earth in order to fulfill God's promises to Israel concerning the Abrahamic covenant in a literal restoration of Israel and the earth after Christ returns to usher in his kingdom.[108] Scofield also offered the clearest language concerning dispensationalism's position on Jewish believers

---

106. Hankins, "Scofield, Cyrus Ingerson," 589–90.

107. Hankins, "Scofield, Cyrus Ingerson," 590–91; Fackler, "Scofield, Cyrus Ingerson," 616; Blaising and Bock, *Progressive Dispensationalism*, 10–11; Kerr, "Scofield, Cyrus Ingerson," 787.

108. Scofield, *Rightly Dividing the Word of Truth*, 15–19. Craig Blaising noted that "Classical dispensationalists saw God's covenant with Abraham (in Gen. 12 and following) as the foundational covenant in Scripture." Classical dispensationalists applied the Gen 13:16 promise of "I will make your descendants as the dust of the earth" to the earthly people, first to the physical offspring of Abraham (Israel) who would then bless the Gentile nations. They also interpreted the Abrahamic covenant spiritually, citing the Gen 22:17 promise of "I will greatly multiply your seed as the stars of the heavens" as referring to the heavenly people, the church, as Abraham's spiritual offspring. Scofield differed with Darby in his interpretation of the new covenant. Darby taught that the new covenant (Isaiah, Jeremiah, and Ezekiel) applied to Israel, the earthly people, not the church, the heavenly people. Scofield interpreted the new covenant as he did the Abrahamic covenant, both literally applying to Israel, the earthly people, and spiritually applying to the church, the heavenly people. See Blaising and Bock, *Progressive Dispensationalism*, 27–30.

within the New Testament church. S. R. Spenser noted that Scofield's distinction between Jew and gentile is lost in the church:

> The anthropological distinction of Jew, Gentile and the church of God, involving a heavenly (church) and earthly (Jew) dichotomy of their character and destiny, characterizes Scofield's thought, echoing J. N. Darby. Israel is God's national people, but in the church the distinction between Jew and Gentile is "lost" (Scofield 1965, 12) or "disappears" (Scofield 1965, 14). For Scofield "Israel stands connected with earthly and temporal things" but the church "with spiritual and heavenly things." (Scofield 1965, 12)[109]

In his essays on the relationship between Jew and gentile, Robinson primarily interacted with Scofield as a representative of dispensationalism, sometimes referring to the position of dispensationalism as the *Scofield position* or *Schofield position*.[110]

In addition to his interactions with Scofield, Robinson also interacted with dispensationalists through members of the Brethren who were involved in the Katoomba Convention (a Bible teaching convention that began in the Blue Mountains of Australia in 1903) and the Sydney University Evangelical Union (SESU, formerly known as the Sydney University Bible League).[111] While Anglicans primarily comprised the membership

109. Spencer, "Scofield, C(yrus) I.," 908.

110. Robinson, "Jew and Greek," 81–85. Robinson's interaction with Scofield was likely due to his observation outlined in Robinson, "Origins and Unresolved Tensions," 9, that the Scofield Reference Bible was "familiar to many Australian evangelicals, not least when its sale was subsidised by a Sydney businessman prominent among the Brethren." As he was discussing his "three stages" of redemptive history in "Origins and Unresolved Tensions" (see chapter 3 for further elaboration on Robinson's "three stages"), he also made the following comment on page 10 concerning dispensationalism: "However, I do not think this kind of Dispensationalism [referring to the Scofield Reference Bible] had any influence in the circles that were looking for biblical structures in the 1940s and 1950s" (bracketed text added).

Spencer noted that "Scofield so effectively distilled American dispensationalism that it was often called Scofieldism." See Spencer, "Scofield, C(yrus) I.," 910. Craig Blaising also noted that the term *dispensationalism* was first used concerning the Scofield Reference Bible's interpretations, so Robinson was not the only one who referred to dispensationalism as the *Scofield position*. See Blaising and Bock, *Progressive Dispensationalism*, 22.

111. Shiner, "Reading the New Testament," 34, 86. Shiner cited Marcia Cameron, "Interview 10 with Bishop D. W. B. Robinson," May 16, 2007, 11, as evidence that dispensationalism was "the atmosphere I [Robinson] was brought up in," (bracketed text added). Shiner also noted: "According to Robinson, the influence was largely through the Brethren, and when he was growing up 'about half' of the Katoomba Convention was dispensationalist. Robinson felt that his own father was probably 'betwixt and between'

ISRAEL'S ROLE IN REDEMPTION HISTORY WITHIN ANGLICANISM

of the SESU, members of the Brethren still taught in the SESU and comprised about half of the members of the Katoomba Convention.[112] Howard Guinness (1903–1979) was an Anglican ministry leader who came from a Brethren background and a contemporary of Robinson in the SESU and Katoomba Convention. Guinness was a premillennialist, and Shiner labeled him in agreement with many of dispensationalism's teachings.[113] The majority of his ministry service focused on student mission activity. He frequently preached that the return of the Jews to the land of Israel would usher in the second coming of Christ.[114]

W. H. Griffith Thomas (1861–1924) was another Anglican minister who was a premillennialist and moderate dispensationalist.[115] He began his ministry serving as a lay curate in London. He was ordained as an Anglican deacon in 1885, later becoming a senior curate at St. Aldate's Church, Oxford, in 1889. Beginning in 1896, he served at St. Paul's, Portman Square, London. He became principal of Wycliffe Hall, Oxford, in

---

on the issue, though he never talked about it." For more on the Katoomba Convention, see Braga, *Century Preaching Christ*. For more on the SESU, see Lake, *Proclaiming Jesus Christ as Lord*.

112. Shiner, "Reading the New Testament," 34, 86.

113 Shiner cited Lawton, "Winter of Our Days," 24, commenting: "Lawton claims Howard Guinness as an Anglican who held to the position [dispensationalism]," (bracketed text added). Shiner's label seemed to stem from Lawton's paragraph: "Howard Guinness expounded the same prophetic imagery. He told the gathering for the 66th Anniversary of the Methodist Central Mission that nuclear warfare was the fulfilment of Jesus' prophecy about the end of the age. The signs of that end were upon them as they witnessed the return of the Jews to Palestine, the growth of the missionary movement, and anxiety and world calamity 'in which the forces of nature would become out of control.' . . . His reference to Jewish nationalism binds him into a long tradition of evangelical eschatology. Many Protestant Christians believed that a return of the Jews to Palestine would herald the second coming of Jesus." Guinness's exposition on the Jews return to Palestine, coupled with him coming from a Brethren background, is what Shiner considered as sufficient grounds to label Guinness a dispensationalist. Shiner asserted that those are the grounds by which many Australian Anglicans would label one a dispensationalist. However, with the exception of Guinness's coming from a Brethren background and his belief in premillennialism, there does not seem to be an explicit statement concerning if Guinness would consider himself a dispensationalist or if he agreed with a dispensational view of the church.

114. Lawton, "Winter of Our Days."

115. See Hannah, "'Thomas' in the Memorial Lectureship," 12–13. See chapter 3 on Thomas's interactions with John Davies, a principal at Moore College who was also a premillennialist. Davies would later nominate Thomas as a candidate for the archbishop of Sydney in 1909.

1905. He was also one of the editors of *The Churchman*.[116] He wrote a series of articles in popular periodicals (including *The Churchman* and *The Sunday School Times*) arguing for a personal, premillennial second coming of Christ that included a future national salvation for Israel during Christ's second coming.[117] In his work *St. Paul's Epistle to the Romans*, Thomas taught that the olive tree (Rom 11) was the nation of Israel. He defined spiritual Israel as believing Jews (from natural, national Israel). The fulfillment of "all Israel shall be saved" (v. 26) would occur during a future national salvation of Israel at Christ's second coming.[118] God's promises to Israel await a future fulfillment. They were not limited to Jewish believers within the New Testament church.[119]

Robinson agreed with dispensationalists that the church was not a new Israel. However, he did not fully accept all of the theological conclusions taught by dispensationalists. He differed with dispensationalists concerning the composition of Jew and gentile in the New Testament church. He believed that dispensationalists taught no significance for Jewish believers in the New Testament church since dispensationalists considered all believers in the church (including Jewish believers) as separate from Jews who comprise Israel.[120] As an alternative, he believed that the New Testament

---

116. Cragoe, "W. H. Griffith Thomas," 68–70.

117. One example is Thomas, "Great Facts About Our Lord's Coming."

118. Thomas, *St. Paul's Epistle to the Romans*, 298. See also Hannah, "'Thomas' in the Memorial Lectureship," 250–51.

119. Thomas, *St. Paul's Epistle to the Romans*, 238–39, 289. On page 313, Thomas, citing Scofield, elaborated: "A clear distinction is made throughout between Jew and Gentile. Although in the present Christian dispensation, individual Jews and individual Gentiles combine to form one church, the body of Christ, yet in the great future to which the Apostle [Paul] looks, national distinctions will remain, and the Jew, the Gentile, and the Church of God will be kept separate until that day when 'God shall be all in all,'" (bracketed text added).

120. Robinson, "Jew and Greek," 81–85.

Shiner referred to dispensationalism as the "joker in the pack" in Australian evangelicalism (See Shiner, "Reading the New Testament," 34) by observing that Anglicans viewed dispensationalism negatively due to the disruptive nature of dispensational eschatology to Anglicanism's establishment religion and established eschatology. Australian Anglicans such as Robinson, while rejecting the theological system of dispensationalism, dialogued with dispensationalism's position concerning Israel's role in redemptive history.

Robinson critiqued Scofield's dispensational interpretation of James's speech in Acts 15 in "Jew and Greek" by discussing that Scofield reversed the missions of restoring Israel through a Jewish remnant and offering the gospel to the gentiles, plus Scofield placed the rebuilding of the temple in a future millennial kingdom. See Robinson, "Jew and Greek," 88.

church consisted of a believing Jewish nucleus distinct from gentile believers in the church. The Jewish nucleus of believers constituted the true Israel (see chapter 3). Like his disagreements with Christian restorationism, he also disagreed with dispensationalism's position concerning a future fulfillment of Israel's Old Testament land promises.[121]

Conclusion

Various positions concerning Israel's role in redemptive history and the relationship of Jew and gentile in the church were prevalent in Anglican theology. There was a general position of supersessionism that the church was a new Israel held by Anglican covenant theologians (such as Packer, Flew, and Stott during Robinson's time). There was also a positive theological interest in Israel that developed into a position of Christian restorationism that advocated for Jewish evangelism and restoring a Jewish nation in the land of Israel (through the efforts of the LSJ and nineteenth-century leaders such as Shaftesbury and Hechler). Dispensationalism (through the works of leaders such as Darby and Scofield) was another position that developed from a positive theological interest in Israel. Supersessionism and dispensationalism shared a similarity in that both failed to give a distinction between Jew and gentile within the New Testament church. It is within this theological context that Robinson proposed his unique distinction theology as an alternative, mediating position.

F. F. Bruce (1910–1990) is a contemporary of Robinson who came from a Brethren background but rejected dispensationalism. See Grass, *F. F. Bruce: A Life*.

121. In the 1950s and 1960s, revised dispensationalism was popularized by Charles Ryrie (1925–2016). Revised dispensationalists dispensed with the eternal dual states of the heavenly and earthly people and also dispensed with the terms *heavenly people* and *earthly people*. They used the terms *Israel* and *the church* to refer to the two groups of people. Revised dispensationalism retained the loss of a distinction between Jew and gentile within the New Testament church, as believing Jews were considered part of the church, but not Israel. While there is no interaction between Robinson and revised dispensationalists, Robinson would have likely taken a similar issue with revised dispensationalists as he did with Scofield and classic dispensationalists. See Ryrie, *Dispensationalism Today*; and Blaising and Bock, *Progressive Dispensationalism*, 31–32.

3

A Brief History of Moore Theological College and Donald Robinson's Distinction Theology

Introduction

MOORE COLLEGE'S BIBLICAL THEOLOGY program began to develop under Donald Robinson. One of his unique contributions to Moore's biblical theology program was his distinction theology concerning Israel's role in redemptive history as his attempt to provide an alternative between supersessionism (particularly covenant theology) and dispensationalism. It is useful for readers to first briefly survey Moore College's history from its origins to Robinson's tenure to set the stage for his contribution to Moore's biblical theology program.

A Brief History of Moore College from Its Origins to Robinson's Tenure

Moore College was founded in 1856 by Bishop Frederic Barker (1808–1882), the second bishop of Sydney, after the death of its namesake, Thomas Moore (1762–1840).[1] The roots of Moore College originated from Bishop William Broughton's (1788–1853) desire to found an

---

1. McIntosh, "Anglican Evangelicalism in Sydney," 2, 129. Moore died on Christmas Eve in 1840. See Loane, "Thomas Moore Early Life," 36; and "Thomas Moore of Moore Bank," 75. For additional history on Thomas Moore, see Bolt, *Portrait in His Actions*.

Anglican college.[2] Like Broughton, Moore expressed his desire to found a college (stating the desire in his will). He wanted a college "for youths of the 'Protestant persuasion . . . according to the principles of the United Church of England and Ireland.'"[3]

Moore was one of the first colonists to arrive in Australia, arriving at Sydney in 1792.[4] He was best known for his shipbuilding work, becoming a master boat builder in Sydney in 1796.[5] He later relocated to Liverpool in order to help establish the town.[6] He served as the town's magistrate in 1810. He was involved in the funding of numerous building projects throughout Liverpool, including his estate Moore Bank, the town's first school, courthouse, and three churches: a Roman Catholic Church, a Presbyterian Church, and an Anglican Church (St. Luke's Church, the church he attended).[7] He was involved in other philanthropic contributions throughout Liverpool over the years, including donating a pipe organ to one of Liverpool's churches in 1831 (the organ was eventually sold to Moore College in 1970 for their chapel use). In his later years, he moved into a house on Elizabeth Street in Liverpool (where he passed away), as he wished Moore Bank to be left to the Anglican Church to house Australia's bishop (a wish never fulfilled). His namesake continues through his Moore Bank estate, Moore Street, and his most lasting legacy, Moore College.[8]

Moore College began in Moore's Elizabeth Street house in Liverpool, with the goal of training ministers, one specific area of education not covered by the University of Sydney.[9] The goal of the college was to become the primary college for training ministers in the Diocese of Sydney.[10] The college

---

2. One previous attempt was St. James College at Lyndhurst, a short-lived college founded in 1846.

3. Boyce, *Thomas Moore*, 13. Moore had wished to call the college St. Thomas College. See Loane, "Thomas Moore and the Early Life," 36–37.

4. Boyce, *Thomas Moore*, 3. See also Campbell, "Biblical Theology at Moore."

5. He was one of the carpenters of the ship *Britannia*. See Loane, "Thomas Moore and the Early Life," 39, 46.

6. Boyce, *Thomas Moore*, 8.

7. The estate's name, Moore Bank, was eventually revised to Moorebank. This book will use the original *Moore Bank* for consistency. For additional history on Moore's time in Liverpool, see Boyce, *Thomas Moore*, 10; and Loane, "Thomas Moore of Moore Bank," 76–77.

8. Loane, "Thomas Moore of Moore Bank," 75–79.

9. Loane, "Thomas Moore of Moore Bank," 76.

10. McIntosh, "Anglican Evangelicalism in Sydney," 2.

relocated to Newtown in 1891.¹¹ Moore left an endowment including a series of farms he hoped would raise enough income to help start and fund the college during its early years. However, Moore College would need to postpone its official launch until its leadership raised additional funding.¹² When Moore College had enough funding to launch, Dean Cowper (1810–1902) served as the college's interim principal. William Hodgson (1809–1869) served as the college's first full-time principal, a position he served in for eleven years (until 1867).¹³ Marcus Loane (1911–2009) noted that during Moore's early years, the curriculum primarily comprised instruction in the Old and New Testaments, the third through seventh centuries of church history, evidence for the Christian faith (such as Butler's *Analogy* and Paley's *Evidences*), the Thirty-Nine Articles, and the Book of Common Prayer.¹⁴ The town of Liverpool demolished Moore College's original building, and the property is now part of the town's hospital.¹⁵

In 1897, Nathaniel Jones (1861–1911, who attended Oxford for his MA) became principal at Moore. Like Robinson, Jones participated in the Katoomba Convention. He interacted with dispensationalists in the convention (primarily members of the Brethren). He was a premillennialist and introduced premillennialism into the curriculum at Moore through his work *The Teaching of the Thirty-Nine Articles*.¹⁶ Under "The Return of Christ," he taught that Christ's second coming is literal not figurative, and he appealed to Rev 20 as support for Christ's judgment of the nations after his return.¹⁷ Jones was also a close friend of W. H. Griffith Thomas. He nominated Thomas as a candidate for the archbishop of Sydney in 1909

---

11. Bolt, "Family Correspondence of Thomas Moore," 279.

12. Boyce, *Thomas Moore*, 13–14. The series of farms Moore left as part of the endowment did not produce enough income (due to a recession occurring throughout Australia) to successfully start and fund Moore College. See Loane, "Thomas Moore of Moore Bank," 79.

13. Boyce, *Thomas Moore*, 14–15.

14. Loane, *Centenary History*, 36. Loane briefly elaborated on some of the minor adjustments to Moore's curriculum under various principals on pp. 49–50 and 92–93. Absent from Moore's early years was any course on biblical theology or any course that taught a unity between both testaments.

15. Loane, "Thomas Moore of Moore Bank," 81.

16. McIntosh, "Anglican Evangelicalism in Sydney," 124, 169. McIntosh considered Jones a "historicist premillennialist" as defined by A. R. Fausset, not a futurist or dispensational premillennialist.

For more on the Katoomba Convention, see Braga, *Century Preaching Christ*.

17. Jones, *Teaching of the Articles*, 30–33.

(due to Jones and Thomas sharing a common belief in premillennialism), a position for which Thomas failed to win the election.[18] There is no evidence that Thomas taught or lectured at Moore (even during Jones's tenure), but Jones and Thomas did correspond with each other.[19]

John Davies (1879–1935) became principal at Moore in 1911 until he died. He studied at Alderman Davies School, Cambridge University, and Ridley Hall Cambridge. According to Stephen Judd's (1957–) biographical sketch on Davies, the goal of the new principal was to increase Moore College's academic standards by strengthening Moore's partnership with the University of Sydney (a nearby college where many students began their education before completing their ministry training at Moore) and adopting some of the curriculum requirements of the Australian College of Theology (a network of Bible colleges throughout Australia and a partner of the Australian Anglican Church).[20] Judd (in his biographical sketch) and John McIntosh (1935–, in his dissertation) labeled Davies as somewhat theologically liberal. For example, McIntosh argued that Davies considered the Bible a record of revelation. He also argued that Davies believed the Bible should be studied the same as other literature.[21] In terms of Davies's position on eschatology, McIntosh argued that, contrary to Jones, there was no evidence that Davies accepted premillennialism.[22] Moore College suffered funding issues during Davies's time as principal, during which the board of trustees appointed a committee of management and control to oversee the college. However, the committee went beyond managing Moore College's finances and weakened Davies's authority by becoming involved in student admissions. Instead of students being admitted based on the principal's decision, the committee ruled that the archbishop, not the principal, held

18. Dickey, "Jones, Nathaniel," 192; and McIntosh, "Anglican Evangelicalism in Sydney," 184.

19. See Samuel Marsden Archives, "Griffith Thomas, W. H."

20. Judd, "Davies, David John," 88–89. For more on the Australian College of Theology, see "About—History." While Moore College adopted some of the Australian College of Theology curriculum requirements, it did not become a member of it. For more on the life of John Davies, see West, "D. J. Davies: A Principal Embattled."

21. Judd referred to Davies as "a protestant in churchmanship but a liberal in scholarship" in "Davies, David John," 88–89. McIntosh referred to Davies as an "evangelical liberal." In "Anglican Evangelicalism in Sydney," 384, he cited Davies's manuscript "Interpretation of Scripture" concerning Davies's position on the Bible as a record of revelation. He discussed the theologically liberal education Davies received in chapter 7, "Liberal Evangelicalism Embraced," 295–334.

22. McIntosh, "Anglican Evangelicalism in Sydney," 296–97.

the final approval of all student admissions.[23] The committee included members Judd labeled more conservative evangelicals (in contrast to Davies). Judd considered their involvement in student admissions a vote of no confidence against Davies's liberal scholarship.[24]

In 1936, T. C. Hammond (1877–1961) became principal at Moore under the appointment of Archbishop Howard Mowll (1890–1958), a position Hammond held until 1953. Hammond received philosophical training at Trinity College, Dublin, later studying theology at the divinity school. He raised Moore from its financial and enrollment slump under Davies. During his time as principal, the college trained over two hundred students, constructed three new building wings, and constructed a chapel. He was also respected throughout Australian Anglicanism and spoke at the Katoomba Convention.[25] Shiner considered Hammond to be theologically a centrist who avoided either fundamentalism or liberalism. For example, Rory Shiner (1975–) argued that Hammond affirmed the doctrine of the inspiration of Scripture in the words of Scripture but that he denied the necessity of the doctrine of inerrancy.[26] In Hammond's *Inspiration and Authority*, he stated that Scripture was preserved with "substantial accuracy" and that "it is essential that the existent book in any translation should be in a real sense the Word of God."[27] However, he summarized his position on inerrancy as follows: "No particular text or translation of the Sacred Scriptures is wholly free from error. Every honest text and translation contains the message of God in such purity that the errors scarcely dim its lustre and do not at all impair its life-giving quality."[28]

Hammond used W. H. Griffith Thomas's work *The Principles of Theology* as one of Moore's theological textbooks.[29] However, unlike Jones and Thomas, he was not a premillennialist, with eschatology only briefly

---

23. Loane, *Centenary History of Moore*, 122–23.
24. Judd, "Davies, David John," 88–89.
25. Nelson, "Hammond, T(Homas) C(Hatteron)," 152.
26. Shiner, "Reading the New Testament," 22. Shiner cited Hammond, *Inspiration and Authority*, 32–33. McIntosh presented Hammond's position on the doctrine of Scripture in "Anglican Evangelicalism in Sydney," 446–56, using a similar description to Shiner concerning Hammond's theologically centrist position on page 467.
27. Hammond, *Inspiration and Authority*, 37.
28. Hammond, *Inspiration and Authority*, 38.
29. McIntosh, "Anglican Evangelicalism in Sydney," 594; and Shiner, "Reading the New Testament," 27.

mentioned in his work *In Understanding Be Men*.[30] The work comprised his theological textbook, geared initially to introduce students in other academic fields to Bible doctrines. It quickly became a standard textbook for theological education in Bible colleges, which helped to provide structure to the students' Christian faith.[31] While Robinson did not study directly under Hammond, he regularly communicated with Hammond.[32] Hammond left Robinson an academic legacy which allowed Robinson to question traditional interpretations of the biblical text and become a pioneer of various theological innovations. His distinction theology concerning Israel's role in redemptive history was one area in which Robinson would pioneer one of his well-known theological innovations.[33]

Marcus Loane became the principal of Moore in 1953 as Hammond's successor.[34] Loane's main leadership goal was the spiritual formation of Moore's student body, a role in which Loane was personally involved. He would directly visit with individual students at Moore, praying for and with them.[35] Robinson began serving at Moore while Loane was principal. Moore's biblical theology program began under Loane's leadership and Robinson's supervision (this will be discussed later in the chapter).

Biographical Sketch on Donald Robinson

Donald Robinson (1922–2018) laid the foundation for the biblical theology program and theological methodology that scholars and students at Moore College utilize today. During his time at Moore, Robinson began as an Old Testament lecturer. He also served as a senior New Testament lecturer in 1954 and as the college's vice principal in 1959 (when D. Broughton Knox became principal). Robinson spent time with T. C. Hammond at Moore when he was a child. In addition to his ministry service, he also served in World War II.[36] Concerning his education, Robinson first attended the

---

30. McIntosh, "Anglican Evangelicalism in Sydney," 433; and Hammond, *In Understanding Be Men*, 188–89.

31. Nelson, "Hammond, T(Homas) C(Hatteron)," 151.

32. Shiner, "Reading the New Testament," 26.

33. Thompson, "Donald William Bradley Robinson," 5.

34. Loane later became the first Australian-born Archbishop of Sydney. See Goldsworthy, "Lecture 2," 17–21.

35. Shiner, "Reading the New Testament," 52–53.

36. Thompson, "Donald William Bradley Robinson," 4; and Shiner, "Appreciation of

University of Sydney, studying under G. P. Shipp (1900–1980).[37] Robinson was indebted to Shipp's course on the semantic differences between the vocabulary of Mark in contrast to Matthew and Luke. In his *Reformed Theological Review* (*RTR*) article "'The Church' Revisited," he mentioned that Shipp's course taught him "how to assess the actual semantic value of words as they are used by individual writers and in particular contexts, without simply importing a dictionary meaning into them with a heavy hand."[38] He noted that "commentators and theologians tended to read more into the meanings of words than either context or usage warranted, and did not allow for subtle changes of meaning of words from one writer to another or even from one context to another in the same writer."[39] Robinson graduated from the University of Sydney in 1946. While a student there, Robinson was a member of (and later president of) the SESU.[40]

After graduating from the University of Sydney, Robinson attended Cambridge University (graduating in 1950).[41] He studied under scholars comprising what Chase Kuhn referred to as the "Cambridge evangelical tradition," including C. F. D. Moule (1908–2007, who sharpened Robinson's eye for linguistic details in the biblical text) and C. H. Dodd (1884–1973, who taught Robinson a biblical theology concerning the concepts of promise and fulfillment and introduced Robinson to the doctrine of ecclesiology).[42] It was in Dodd's seminar that Robinson would learn of the theological dialogue between R. H. Newton Flew and J. Y. Campbell concerning the use of ἐκκλησία (see chapter 2), and Robinson would reach similar exegetical conclusions to that of Campbell (discussed later in the chapter).[43]

Robinson served at St. Matthews, Manly, and St. Philips, Sydney, at the beginning of his ministry service. It was in this ministry context that

---

D. W. B. Robinson," 11.

37. Loane, "Richard Johnson Faithful Minister," 11.

38. Robinson, "'Church' Revisited," 261.

39. Robinson, "'Church' Revisited," 262.

40. Shiner, "Reading the New Testament," 21. For more on the SESU, see chapter 2 of this book, and Lake, *Proclaiming Jesus Christ as Lord*.

41. Loane, "Richard Johnson Faithful Minister," 11.

42. Kuhn, *Ecclesiology of Donald Robinson*, 50, 52–54. Kuhn notes that the foundation for the "Cambridge evangelical tradition" began with scholars such as B. F. Wescott, J. B. Lightfoot, and F. J. A. Hort, later carried forward by their successors. See also Shiner, "Appreciation of D. W. B. Robinson," 12.

43. Kuhn, *Ecclesiology of Donald Robinson*, 53–55.

MOORE THEOLOGICAL COLLEGE & ROBINSON'S "DISTINCTION THEOLOGY"

Robinson began teaching at Moore College from 1952 to 1982.[44] While at Moore, Robinson became the second bishop of Parramatta in the diocese of Sydney in 1973. After serving at Moore, Robinson became the ninth archbishop of Sydney from 1982 to 1993, retiring as archbishop in 1993 and returning to teach part-time at Moore.[45]

Robinson's first published work was on the semantic range of the term παραβολὴ throughout the Synoptic Gospels in the 1949 edition of the *EvQ*. Contrary to Loane, Robinson argued for Markan, not Matthean priority. Shiner summarized Robinson's work that "the common modern English understanding of the word 'parable' as a short story illustrating a specific point needs to be tested against actual usage in the Synoptic Gospels," and that the word παραβολὴ shifts usage "from Mark to Luke, and finally to Matthew. Matthew emerges as the 'first Form critic' with novel usage of παραβολὴ as meaning something like the modern definition of a didactic story."[46] Robinson also wrote nine academic articles on the relationship between Jew and gentile in redemptive history, his most substantial work being his 1961 article "Jew and Greek: Unity and Distinction." While most of Robinson's published writings were a collection of articles, many academic in tone, Robinson made a single substantial written contribution for both an academic and nonacademic audience in his 1985 publication of *Faith's Framework*, the text of his 1981 Moore College Annual Lectures.[47]

As an Anglican living in Australia, Robinson pioneered scholarship that shaped Anglicanism.[48] In contrast, Anglican Church leaders in the United Kingdom (UK) tended to make the majority of their contributions within the existing, established theological boundaries of the Anglican Church.[49] Shiner contrasted Robinson's work with UK Anglicans: "Whilst

---

44. Loane, "Richard Johnson Faithful Minister," 11.

45. Thompson, "Donald William Bradley Robinson," 5–6; and Shiner, "Appreciation of D. W. B. Robinson," 9.

46. Shiner, "Reading the New Testament," 54.

47. Shiner, "Appreciation of D. W. B. Robinson," 10, 15.

48. One example is Robinson's work on reviving the Anglican prayer book for an Australian context. See Shiner, "Reading the New Testament," 25.

49. Two examples of UK Anglicans covered in chapter 2 are J. I. Packer and John Stott. Shiner noted that UK Anglicans tended not to innovate theologically in their writings but kept their theological writings within the context of the established theology of Anglicanism. Australian Anglicans (such as Robinson) tended to attempt various theological innovations (such as Robinson's distinction theology concerning the relationship between Jew and gentile) in their writings while remaining within the Anglican communion. See Shiner, "Reading the New Testament," 25.

UK evangelicals were working *in* the Church, figures like Donald Robinson were also working *on* the Church."⁵⁰

Donald Robinson's Understanding of Ecclesiology

Robinson developed most of his theological positions concerning ecclesiology while he taught at Moore. Robinson's first course on ecclesiology concerned the use of the term ἐκκλησία throughout Acts. He later took over Moore's special doctrine course and taught on the topic of ecclesiology. This course taught ecclesiology in light of promise and fulfillment as Scripture's unifying theme and the church's role in redemptive history.⁵¹ This course developed into a course on a biblical theology of the church, which laid the foundation for Robinson to further establish Moore's robust biblical theology program (see next section, "Robinson's Efforts in Establishing Moore's Biblical Theology Program"). Robinson also contributed numerous theological developments concerning the doctrine of ecclesiology throughout his writings. One area of focus that began in his writings and was developed during his work in establishing Moore's biblical theology program was his distinction theology concerning the relationship between Jew and gentile in redemptive history.⁵²

Robinson read various scholars who contributed to his understanding of ecclesiology. Robinson appreciated F. J. A. Hort's (1828–1892) *The Christian Ecclesia*, stating that it "set the lines" of his study on the doctrine of the church and considered it a "classical exposition of what the word *ekklesia* means in the Bible."⁵³ Robinson cited Hort's argument that the English term *church* "carries with it associations derived from the institutions and doctrines of later times" and does not "convey the full and exact force which originally belonged to *ekklesia*."⁵⁴ He appreciated Hort's historical development of ἐκκλησία throughout Scripture, particularly that Hort "concentrated

---

50. Shiner, "Reading the New Testament," 25 (italics added). A helpful explanation to Shiner's comment is that UK Anglicans remained within the boundaries of an established Anglican theology in their service to the church and their writings. However, Australian Anglicans served as theological pioneers in developing innovations in their writings and shaping the direction of the Anglican Church in Australia.

51. Kuhn, *Ecclesiology of Donald Robinson*, 62–63.

52. Thompson, "Donald William Bradley Robinson," 5.

53. Robinson, "'Church' Revisited," 260.

54. Hort, *Christian Ecclesia*, 1.

attention on the biblical understanding of *ekklesia*."⁵⁵ Edwin Judge (1928–, a friend of Robinson's) wrote an article titled "Contemporary Political Models for the Interrelations of the New Testament Churches" which compared a universal church to the local church. He applied the term ἐκκλησία to the local church (as did Robinson): "Everything that can be said about the *ecclesia*, can be said equally and fully of each [local] *ecclesia*, and that there will be no other way of using the term, except by deliberate and conscious extension of the self-evident meaning."⁵⁶ K. L. Schmidt's (1891–1956) article on ἐκκλησία in the *Theological Dictionary of the New Testament* was a helpful research work as Robinson thought through his exegesis of the term ἐκκλησία as used throughout Scripture, although Robinson had issues with Schmidt attempting to find a single definition for the term ἐκκλησία.⁵⁷ J. Y. Campbell's position concerning how the term ἐκκλησία primarily meant *assembly* or *gathering* and does not theologically link the ἐκκλησία of the New Testament church to the ἐκκλησία of Old Testament Israel was a valuable work that Robinson consulted in his exegesis of ἐκκλησία. As Robinson traced the exegetical data concerning the use of the term ἐκκλησία, he reached a similar position to that of Campbell.⁵⁸

At Moore College, Robinson served closely with D. Broughton Knox, whom Kuhn has summarized as "the greatest theological influence on Robinson."⁵⁹ While Robinson was more of a New Testament exegete and biblical theologian, and Knox was more of a systematic theologian, the two were complementary to each other's work to the point where scholars have considered the ecclesiologies of Robinson and Knox as comprising

---

55. Robinson, "'Church' Revisited," 260. Hort traced the term ἐκκλησία throughout the Septuagint (comparing it with the Hebrew terms קָהָל and עֵדָה and the Septuagint term συναγωγή) and New Testament (particularly how ἐκκλησία was used to describe the early church). Kuhn noted that Hort "noticed a distinction of usage between *ekklesia/qahal* as exclusively descriptive of a human gathering and *synagoge/edah* which is often descriptive of a gathering, but also used to describe the Israelite people as whole, particularly as their representative heads gathered," and Hort differed from Robinson and considered the "later usage of *ekklesia* in the New Testament is used to describe more of the new society that had been created in Christ, the singular church on earth, than exclusively describing singular (local) congregations." See Kuhn, *Ecclesiology of Donald Robinson*, 53.

56. Judge, "Contemporary Political Models," 74 (bracketed text added).

57. Karl Ludwig Schmidt, "Ἐκκλησία," TDNT 3:502–36; and Robinson, "'Church' Revisited," 261.

58. Kuhn, *Ecclesiology of Donald Robinson*, 54–55.

59. Kuhn, *Ecclesiology of Donald Robinson*, 61.

a Knox-Robinson view of ecclesiology.[60] The discussion of a Knox-Robinson view of ecclesiology began to be circulated during the mid-1980s (although the final term *Knox-Robinson view* took time to become widely used).[61] Robinson did not agree with using such a term, as he believed he and Knox sometimes varied concerning their theological conclusions and approaches to ecclesiology.[62] Kuhn summarized and tested the validity

---

60. Kuhn summarized a Knox-Robinson view of ecclesiology in *Ecclesiology of Donald Robinson*, 207–13, by first discussing the similarities. "The fundamental proposition in both ecclesiologies is that the church is a gathering; all other propositions follow from this thesis. This conclusion is built upon the linguistic analysis of *ekklesia*.... Building upon the primary premise of the church as a gathering, Robinson and Knox also agreed that the church is only ever local or heavenly; there is no third category of the universal church on earth.... Both Robinson and Knox also addressed how the church occurs in heaven and on earth. Robinson focused on the categories of place, form, and time. These categories exposed the different experiences of the earthly and heavenly church more than the similarities. Knox also examined the distinctive properties of each experience, but gave particular focus to the presence of Christ in each realm.... Robinson and Knox agreed that the Word has authority over the gathering. Questions were raised (gently) about institutional authority in the form of a denomination. Both argued that there was no external authority over the local church, because the church is only a gathering." Kuhn next discussed their differences: "Of the minor differences, the most obvious are their style and approach. Robinson was an exegete who paid great attention to detail, while Knox was a theologian who thought more about the big picture.... First, they emphasized different matters in the relationship between the heavenly and earthly churches. Robinson demonstrated the place, form, and time of the heavenly and earthly churches, exposing the differences between them.... Knox, on the other hand, focused less on the properties of the gathering and more on the presence of Christ within those gatherings. Knox stressed that the presence of Christ constitutes the church. Robinson would have certainly agreed. But what Knox did differently was to ask *how* Christ is present in each congregation.... The second major difference—regarding the purpose for the gathering—followed on from the first. Knox carried forward his thesis that the church is where Christ is present. He concluded from this that the church's purpose is fellowship, both with God and with other Christians. Robinson was not necessarily averse to this purpose, though he was cautious to not make this *the* purpose of the church.... The final major difference was Robinson's inquiry into the relationship of Israel to the church. His concern throughout his study in ecclesiology was to better understand salvation history. He recognized a preservation of both Jewish and gentile identities within the church, with the new redeemed community being part of a 'new man.' Knox did not include much in his study about the relationship of Israel to the church." See also Thompson, "Knox/Robinson for Today."

61. Shiner, "Reading the New Testament," 62–63.

62. Robinson attempted to distance himself from the label *Knox-Robinson view of ecclesiology*. While he agreed that he and Knox played a role in each other's understanding of ecclesiology, Robinson believed that both he and Knox were at enough theological variance concerning their ecclesiological conclusions where the label *Knox-Robinson*

of a Knox-Robinson view of ecclesiology in his work *The Ecclesiology of Donald Robinson and D. Broughton Knox*. He presented both the unity and distinctions and the forming of a synthesis, between both scholars.[63] Shiner also argued for the existence of a Knox-Robinson view of ecclesiology while pointing out their distinctions and the fact that the two scholars did not attempt to create such a view.[64]

Robinson varied with much of traditional Anglicanism concerning the concept of the universal church and national church. He considered the earthly church as restricted to the assembly of each local congregation. Any concept of a universal church is only in the heavenly realm when all believers are gathered in Christ's presence in heaven: "The church is not ecumenical, as is commonly supposed, but supernal."[65] Robinson contrasted the local church with the universal church as "on earth, that [the church] is where two or three are gathered together in His name . . . in heaven, it is where He is seated at the right hand of the throne of God."[66]

Robinson's Efforts in Establishing Moore's Biblical Theology Program

As Robinson continued to develop his understanding of ecclesiology, his efforts in establishing Moore's biblical theology program began to take shape. The goal of Moore College was to train students on what Donald Cameron

---

view of ecclesiology was not a fitting label concerning their ecclesiological positions. See Kuhn, *Ecclesiology of Donald Robinson*, 61–62.

63. Kuhn, *Ecclesiology of Donald Robinson*, xiii–xvii.

64. Shiner, "Reading the New Testament," 98.

65. Robinson, "Church in the New Testament," 212–13.

66. Robinson, "Church in the New Testament," 213 (bracketed text added). Kuhn observed that "Robinson concluded that the church on earth does not exist in traditional institutional forms such as a denomination. While a denomination may be helpful for the church, that is the local gatherings, it is not itself a church and has no authority over the local church. In fact, there is no ecclesial authority beyond the local church as there is no church on earth apart from the local church. . . . It seems that Robinson disagreed with the institutional language of the church, but not necessarily the purpose of the institution. He believed titles like the Anglican Church of Australia were misnomers. Such institutions are service structures representative of networks of churches, but should not be called a church or the church. However, Robinson did not reject his tradition or even its notion of what/where the church is, rather he preferred to think about it under different terms. For instance, denominations need not be dismissed; they simply should not be considered 'the church.'" See Kuhn, *Ecclesiology of Donald Robinson*, 95, 118–19.

referred to in his contribution to *In the Fullness of Time* as the "clear and full knowledge of divine revelation."[67] However, while Moore taught classes on the Old and New Testaments, the college needed to train students on the relationship between both testaments as a unified Scripture to fulfill its goal of teaching Scripture's full knowledge. Additionally, the college offered no courses on the doctrines of the Old Testament or how biblical doctrine laid the foundation for a student's future ministry service. These needs resulted in Moore College offering a course in biblical theology which later developed into a robust biblical theology program.[68] The biblical theology course was born when Loane wished for Robinson to take over teaching Moore's special doctrine course in 1954. Prior to Robinson, the course initially taught the doctrine of the atonement. However, because Robinson attended a special doctrine course on ecclesiology during his studies with C. H. Dodd at Cambridge and was involved in studying ecclesiology, he requested that ecclesiology be the topic he would cover in the course.[69] Robinson stated that the church (precisely the concept of the people of God) is what (in his view) gave the Bible's story coherence. This understanding also contributed to Robinson choosing ecclesiology as the topic for the special doctrine course. He considered the concept of God's covenant with Israel as a "crucial key to the structure of the biblical story," and he was impressed by an article Packer wrote on the "pervasive presence of the covenant idea in Scripture."[70] Kuhn observed that the link between Robinson's understanding of ecclesiology and biblical theology was to examine "the movements of God to gather a particular people to himself... a coherent movement of God amongst his people."[71] God's interaction with human beings throughout

---

67. Peterson and Pryor, *Fullness of Time*, xii. Robinson worked on his significant contributions to biblical theology while serving at Moore (most of this doctrinal development occurred during the 1950s and 1960s). See Loane, "Richard Johnson Faithful Minister," 11; and "Richard Johnson: An Unlikely Hero," 24.

68. Peterson and Pryor, *Fullness of Time*, xii.

69. Shiner, "Reading the New Testament," 56–57.

70. Robinson, "Biblical Theology in Sydney," 204. Robinson's supervisor at Cambridge, C. F. D. Moule, recommended that Robinson read H. F. Hamilton's *The People of God*. Robinson read it when he began teaching the special doctrine course at Moore. He alluded to it (as well as the other writers he interacted with) in his discussion on "The significance of the covenant God made with his people Israel" as a "crucial key to the structure of the biblical story." While Robinson did not cite the title of the Packer article, he stated that Packer's article "reinforced" his view on the "significance of the covenant God made with his people Israel" and used Packer's article early on in his course.

71. Kuhn, *Ecclesiology of Donald Robinson*, 62.

Scripture, from his promises to Abraham through their ultimate fulfillment in Christ, brought structure to his understanding of biblical theology and the importance of ecclesiology in Scripture's narrative. God not only saved human beings, but, as Kuhn noted of Robinson, God saved human beings "in order to gather them to himself."[72]

Robinson's development of Moore's biblical theology program occurred through various scholars he interacted with, three of them being Dodd, Oscar Cullmann (1902–1999), and Anglican monk Gabriel Hebert (1886–1963).[73] Robinson studied under Dodd and Cullmann during his time at Cambridge (as mentioned earlier). While he did not elaborate on the specifics of their influence upon his understanding of what gave the Bible coherence, Robinson noted that he was impressed with Dodd's *The Parables of the Kingdoms*, *The Apostolic Preaching and its Developments*, and *According to the Scriptures*, and Cullmann's *Christ and Time* as he developed the biblical theology course at Moore.[74] Shiner noted that Robinson was similar to Dodd in that both scholars were open to considering all possible positions when interpreting the biblical text, and that Dodd's seminars (and Robinson's classes) allowed for the academic freedom to pursue various theological loose ends.[75] Shiner also noted that Robinson's early writings were on the parables, and that Robinson continued to be interested in New Testament eschatology, both which possibly developed through his reading of Dodd's *The Parables of the Kingdom*.[76] Gabriel Hebert respected Hammond as a theologian, and due to Robinson's interactions with Hammond, Hebert chose to dialogue theologically with Robinson from 1952 to 1960. Robinson's dialogues with Hebert helped to shape both the theology of Moore College and the theology of Australian Anglicanism.[77] Robinson

72. Kuhn, *Ecclesiology of Donald Robinson*, 63.

73. Loane, "Richard Johnson Faithful Minister," 11; and Robinson, "Biblical Theology in Sydney," 202.

74. Robinson, "Biblical Theology in Sydney," 204. See also Cullmann, *Christ and Time*. While Robinson did not elaborate on how Cullmann affected his understanding of what gave the Bible coherence, Cullmann's position of Christ being the central point in redemptive history (81–94) and his discussion of various stages of redemptive history (Part II) could have contributed to such an understanding.

75. Shiner, "Reading the New Testament," 41.

76. Shiner, "Reading the New Testament," 41. Dodd examined the eschatology of the parables, placing the kingdom of God as occurring during the time of Christ, not a future apocalyptic kingdom. See Dodd, *Parables of the Kingdom*, 157–69.

77. Anglicans in the UK primarily responded to Hebert's criticisms of fundamentalism within the Anglican Church instead of dialoguing with Hebert constructively. See

admitted that he developed the biblical theology course at Moore through ongoing dialogue and debate with Hebert.[78] Robinson's biblical theology traced redemptive history through a typological series of three stages in the fulfillment of God's promises to Abraham.[79] Robinson's three-stages concept was similar to the structure and concept developed by Hebert in his work *Christ the Fulfiller*.[80] The work resulted from Hebert's 1957 lectures at Brisbane Clergy School. His goal was to outline the Bible to "show its unity as the Book of Israel's faith." He considered the Bible to be one book that belonged to Israel, the people of God, although he considered gentile Christians (*we*) as belonging to Israel.[81] It is possible that Robinson's three stages of redemptive history were developed as a result of his dialogues with Hebert (although the extent of any direct influence upon Robinson's development of the three stages from Hebert is unclear).[82]

Robinson outlined his three stages of redemptive history as the "outworking of God's promises to Abraham."[83] The first stage was the fulfillment of God's promises to Abraham through the exodus event to its climax during the kingdom of Solomon. The exodus event is God's redemption for his people. After he redeemed his people out of bondage in Egypt, God lead them to inherit the land of Israel promised to Abraham during the conquest of Canaan under Joshua. Robinson's reading of salvation history built upon the concepts of an Old Testament promise and New Testament fulfillment to also include a partial fulfillment of Old Testament promises within the

---

Shiner, "Reading the New Testament," 56–59.

78. Robinson, "Biblical Theology in Sydney," 206.

79. See next paragraph for a discussion on the "three stages."

80. Hebert, *Christ the Fulfiller*, 10–12.

81. Hebert, *Christ the Fulfiller*, 7–9. Hebert labeled the three stages as three confessions of faith throughout the history of Israel's religion. In Campbell, "Biblical Theology at Moore," Goldsworthy stated that Robinson differed from Hebert by considering the three stages not as confessions of faith throughout the history of Old and New Testament religion but as deriving directly from the biblical text. One likely reason is that Hebert was not a fundamentalist, and he embraced biblical criticism, even critiquing fundamentalism throughout his writings. His critiques on fundamentalism resulted in a response from J. I. Packer in *"Fundamentalism" and the Word of God*. Robinson was also not a fundamentalist and was familiar with biblical criticism, but he was more cautious of biblical criticism and still drew his biblical theology from the text of Scripture rather than utilizing biblical criticism to undermine Scripture's inspiration. Robinson found it helpful to dialogue with Hebert instead of merely responding to his critiques.

82. Shiner, "Appreciation of D. W. B. Robinson," 29.

83. Robinson, "Biblical Theology in Sydney," 209.

Old Testament. The Davidic kingdom was a limited and partial fulfillment of God's promises in the Abrahamic covenant to make Abraham's seed a great nation, but the kingdom under Solomon eventually failed. The second stage was the "projection of this fulfillment in a future day of the Lord" by the prophets during Israel's exile and return.[84] The prophets looked forward to a future restoration of Israel that would be fulfilled in Robinson's third stage. The final stage was the "true fulfillment in Christ" during his birth, death, resurrection, ascension, and return to rule over a new heaven and earth.[85] Christ as the ultimate fulfillment brings about a restoration of Israel through a remnant of Jewish believers greater than that of the Old Testament Davidic kingdom, in which "Jewish Christianity fulfilled the Old Testament promise of God to restore the tabernacle of David and use the restored remnant of Israel as an instrument to save Gentiles."[86]

Robinson acknowledged that dispensationalists also traced redemptive history through a series of stages. However, some dispensationalists (such as Craig Blaising) define a dispensation as "a particular arrangement by which God regulates the way human beings relate to Him," and dispensationalists believe that "God has planned a succession of different dispensations throughout history, both past, present, and future." Robinson instead considered his three stages of redemptive history as a typology of the "outworking of God's promises to Abraham" in which the first two stages were types with a partial Old Testament fulfillment but ultimately fulfilled in the final stage with Christ.[87]

As Robinson continued to work through the doctrine of the church and his understanding of the people of God as giving the biblical

---

84. Robinson, "Biblical Theology in Sydney," 209.

85. Robinson, "Biblical Theology in Sydney," 209.

86. Robinson, "Jew and Greek," 82, 109. While Robinson laid a foundation concerning his three stages of redemptive history, Graeme Goldsworthy (see chapter 4) further developed and elaborated Robinson's three stages into three epochs.

87. Robinson, "Biblical Theology in Sydney," 209–10; and Blaising and Bock, *Progressive Dispensationalism*, 11. Robinson's position also differed from that of dispensationalists in both the number of stages as well as in how a future fulfillment fits within Robinson's stages. Robinson used three stages in contrast to some dispensationalists, such as C. I. Scofield's seven dispensations in the Scofield Reference Bible. Other dispensationalists also vary in the number of dispensations. W. H. Griffith Thomas affirmed a dispensational structure consisting of three dispensations. See Hannah, "'Thomas' in the Memorial Lectureship," 12–13. See also Kuhn, *Ecclesiology of Donald Robinson*, 56–58. The chapter will later elaborate on the "future fulfillment" aspect of where Robinson was at variance with dispensationalism.

story coherence, he would later expand his special doctrine course on the church into a broader course on biblical theology, An Introduction to the Study of the Bible. This course was to orient new students at Moore who were considering Anglican ministry service to understand the difference between the "study of Christian religion" (systematic and historical theology) and the "study of the Bible on its own terms" (biblical theology), particularly emphasizing biblical theology and teaching an introductory biblical theology course to Moore's students.[88] Robinson stated that the special doctrine course on the church "quickly developed into an introduction to the theology of the Bible as a whole . . . 'the church' as such was subsumed under the wider theme of God's creative purpose for Adam, his promise to Abraham and his seed, the elect people of Israel and the promise to the nations beyond and through Israel."[89] The course structure comprised seven lessons. The first lesson was what Robinson termed the *scope and spread* of the Bible's character.[90] This lesson was an outline of the Bible's history. While the lesson did not delve into the doctrine of the canonicity of Scripture, Robinson used broad canonical terms such as *law and prophets* and *gospel* to structure the major divisions of Scripture. The lesson also surveyed various literary genres in order for students to better understand the intentions of the biblical writers. The second lesson was on Scripture's use of the phrase *people of God*. Robinson considered the theme of the people of God to be "prominent and pervasive" and "central to God's response to the human condition."[91] The lesson also surveyed the general concept of covenant and examined particular covenants such as the Noahic, Abrahamic, and Mosaic covenants and how the theme of the people of God could be traced across the major covenants. The third lesson was on Abraham, his seed, and its significance. Robinson considered "God's promise to 'bless' Abraham" as the "hope of 'salvation'" and the "whole biblical story as the outworking of that promise."[92] Robinson would begin elaborating on the first stage of his three stages of redemptive history by discussing God's covenant with Abraham in this course. The

---

88. Robinson, "Biblical Theology in Sydney," 206–7.

89. Robinson, "'Church' Revisited," 262–63.

90. Robinson, "Biblical Theology in Sydney," 208–9; and Campbell, "Biblical Theology at Moore."

91. Robinson, "Biblical Theology in Sydney," 208.

92. Robinson, "Biblical Theology in Sydney," 208.

fourth lesson concerned the concepts of exodus/redemption and land/inheritance. This is the lesson where Robinson would continue to elaborate on the first stage of his three stages of redemptive history by leading students through the book of Exodus, then through a brief tour of the conquest of the land of Israel in Joshua to the reign of Solomon.[93] The fifth lesson covered the exilic prophets' view of promise and fulfillment of a coming day of the Lord. Robinson would elaborate on the second stage of his three stages of redemptive history by linking the prophets' view of promise and fulfillment back to the themes of exodus and land, in that the prophets would project a new redemption and "new inheritance, David, Jerusalem, and temple."[94] The sixth lesson was the lesson where Robinson would elaborate on the third stage of his three stages of redemptive history concerning the New Testament's claim that Christ is the fulfillment of everything Robinson covered in lessons one through five.[95] The final lesson was on the principles of biblical interpretation, where Robinson reviewed and summarized his three stages of redemptive history.[96] This introductory course in biblical theology led to the establishment of a robust biblical theology program at Moore as Robinson further developed Moore's biblical theology curriculum, adding additional courses on biblical theology that built upon An Introduction to the Study of the Bible, and as Moore College began requiring biblical theology courses to its students. However, Robinson published few writings concerning biblical theology. His contributions came primarily through instruction in the classroom.[97] Shiner considered the few publications Robinson contributed to biblical theology an artifact of biblical theology in Australian Anglicanism.[98] While Robinson began to think through the relationship between Jew and gentile as he further developed his understanding of ecclesiology, Robinson would further develop his distinction theology concerning Jew and gentile while developing his course on biblical theology. He felt that an examination of the relationship between Jew and gentile in redemptive

---

93. Robinson, "Biblical Theology in Sydney," 208–9; and Campbell, "Biblical Theology at Moore."

94. Robinson, "Biblical Theology in Sydney," 209.

95. Robinson, "Biblical Theology in Sydney," 208–9; and Campbell, "Biblical Theology at Moore."

96. Robinson, "Biblical Theology in Sydney," 208–9; and Campbell, "Biblical Theology at Moore."

97. Shiner, "Reading the New Testament," 56–57.

98. Shiner, "Appreciation of D. W. B. Robinson," 24.

history was an area within biblical theology that needed a theological contribution. He also wanted to reject a supersessionist covenantalism that equated the church with Israel and develop an alternative position while still avoiding an acceptance of dispensationalism.[99]

Donald Robinson's Distinction Theology

Donald Robinson's distinction theology concerning the role of Israel in redemptive history was his attempt at a mediating position between a supersessionist view (such as covenant theology) and a positive theological interest in Israel (such as dispensationalism). Robinson wrestled with how to deal with passages such as Col 3:10 and 1 Cor 12:27 which seemed to affirm Jew and gentile as one new mankind and body while retaining the New Testament's teachings concerning an ethnic distinction between Jews and gentiles. He thought about how he would define *Jew* and *gentile* as groups of ethnically distinct individuals and their relationship with each other throughout redemptive history. He also discerned how he would define the terms *church* and *Israel* in contrast to the other existing theological positions. He began his critique of both a supersessionist view and a dispensationalist view in his essay "Jew and Greek" by writing: "Modern evangelical Christians tend to adopt one or other of two opposite positions, both of which, in my opinion, are mistaken, though not equally mistaken."[100]

Robinson's interaction with dispensationalism provided one of the pillars of his distinction theology. Robinson primarily interacted with Scofield as a representative of dispensationalism in his writings on the relationship between Jew and gentile, sometimes labeling dispensationalism the Scofield or Schofield position. He did not fully accept the theological conclusions taught by dispensationalists, such as their belief in a future fulfillment of Israel's Old Testament land promises. He believed that dispensationalists taught no significance for Jewish believers in the New Testament church. He critiqued dispensationalists in his essay "Jew and Greek" by writing: "On the one hand there is the position of dispensationalism . . . which accords little or no significance to the presence of believing Jews in the New Testament churches and relegates all the Old Testament promises about the restoration of Israel to a period which is still future."[101] However, he wished to sort

99. Robinson, "Biblical Theology in Sydney," 213–14.
100. Robinson, "Jew and Greek," 81.
101. Robinson, "Jew and Greek," 81.

through and answer the theological questions concerning the relationship between Jew and gentile in redemptive history asked by dispensationalists. What is the church's relationship to Israel? How does one define the ethnic distinction between Jew and gentile? He would agree with dispensationalists that the church is not a new Israel.[102]

Robinson's understanding of supersessionist positions (such as covenant theology) provided the other pillar of his distinction theology. He was in Dodd's seminar when R. Newton Flew presented his exegesis on ἐκκλησία (see chapter 2) that linked the use of the term קָהָל about Old Testament Israel and ἐκκλησία as referring to the New Testament church as the same reality. He also interacted with scholars who were covenant theologians or held general supersessionist views, such as Earle Ellis. Ellis viewed Christians as the true Jews and "Israel after the Spirit," and the New Testament church as the new Israel, while nonbelieving Jews were the old "Israel after the flesh."[103] In his essay "Jew and Greek," Robinson critiqued scholars who accepted such positions: "On the other hand is the more usual view which regards all Christians as constituting the new Israel in this present age, and which therefore refers the promises made concerning Israel in the Old Testament to the Christian church."[104] He further elaborated his argument against scholars who accepted supersessionist positions in the chapter "Jew and Gentile in the New Testament," originally in his work *Faith's Framework*: "The popular view that God rejected the Jews and that the gospel became a wholly Gentile matter is so far at variance with the New Testament as well as with the expectation of the Old Testament that a complete reappraisal of the New Testament is called for."[105]

---

102. Robinson, "Jew and Greek," 81–85.

103. Robinson, "Jew and Gentile," 412. Robinson countered by citing Burton's position that *Israel* in the New Testament referred to the nation of Israel.

104. Robinson, "Jew and Greek," 81.

105. Robinson, "Jew and Gentile," 409–12. Robinson worked through a brief historical survey on supersessionism. He included the Epistle of Barnabas as an example of a work that transferred the promises of Old Testament Israel to the New Testament church. He also stated the position of Melito (?–ca. 180) as another example of supersessionism when Melito stated that there is "no place for continuing Israel as an example of judgment." He also referred to the Anglican Church's use of the term *true Israelites* about the church in the Book of Common Prayer, as well as the discussion that the church must convert Jews in order for them to become the true Israel as further examples of teaching supersessionism. See Robinson, "Biblical Understanding of Israel," 180–81. See also Shiner, "Reading the New Testament," 56–57, 84–89, 145.

Robinson believed that both positions inadequately represented the New Testament's teaching concerning the role of Israel in redemptive history and the relationship between Jew and gentile in the New Testament. He critiqued both positions in his essay "Jew and Greek": "In my judgement, neither of these views represents the position of St. Paul and the other New Testament writers."[106] His distinction theology as his attempt at creating a mediating position can be summarized by saying that Robinson agreed with what both positions denied but rejected what both positions affirmed. Robinson summarized his position in his essay "Jew and Greek":

> The exponents of these two positions are wrong in what they affirm, but right in what they deny . . . [dispensationalism] rightly denies that the distinctive Jewish promises—apart that is from the spiritual promises of the Abrahamic covenant—are inherited by Christians generally. The other view [a supersessionist view], however, rightly denies that God's promises to Israel have to wait for the millennium or later to be fulfilled.[107]

He agreed with dispensationalists in that they rightly deny transferring the promises of Old Testament Israel to the New Testament church. However, he also agreed that those who held a supersessionist view rightly deny a future fulfillment of such promises. Robinson further elaborates upon his mediating position in "Jew and Greek":

> What neither position allows for, but what I believe to be the teaching of the New Testament is that God's distinctive promises to Israel are in the New Testament fulfilled, not to all believers, but to Jewish believers who constitute the restored remnant of Israel; and that Gentile believers are the inheritors of other promises altogether, that is, the promises made in the Old Testament to the nations who should come to Israel's light. These two sets of promises, though distinct, are closely related, and are both finally transfigured by a new disclosure of God's purposes, namely that both Israel and the Gentiles should lose all their distinctiveness in the one new man which will be the end-product of the salvation of God in Christ.[108]

In his essay "Biblical Understanding of Israel," Robinson built upon a modified supersessionist position that the New Testament church was

---

106. Robinson, "Jew and Greek," 85.
107. Robinson, "Jew and Greek," 81 (bracketed text added).
108. Donald Robinson, "Jew and Greek," 81.

comprised of a Jewish nucleus, but that all Christians are a new Israel. After their conversion, this Jewish nucleus was absorbed into the New Testament church. This New Testament church, comprised of both Jews and gentiles, is what constituted a new Israel. Robinson modified this position in his distinction theology by retaining an ethnic distinction between Jew and gentile believers in the New Testament church. He proposed that it is the Jewish nucleus (that did not lose its Jewish ethnicity in the New Testament church), not all Christians in the church, that comprises a true Israel.[109] He believed that God's promises to Israel are to be fulfilled not to all believers in the church but to Jewish believers who comprise Israel's restored remnant. Gentile believers do not inherit God's promises to Israel but the promises that were given to the other nations. His position rejected one aspect of a supersessionist view (the church is the new Israel and inheritor of Israel's Old Testament promises in the present dispensation). While gentile believers could be considered a spiritual seed of Abraham, they are not to be equated with Israel. In the present dispensation, the terms *Jew* and *Christian* are not mutually exclusive terms. The New Testament church (unlike the modern church) was aware of an ethnic distinction between Jews and gentiles and a Jewish nucleus of believers at the core of the New Testament church. The missions to both Jew and gentile, while sharing a common gospel, are two ethnically distinct missions. Jews had a priority over the gentiles. They were presented with the gospel before the gentiles. Jews also had a priority over the gentiles concerning their divine privileges as God's chosen nation. God first made himself known to a believing remnant of Jews. It is this believing remnant of Jews who comprise the Israel of God and presented the gospel to the gentiles. Gentiles share in the spiritual inheritance of the blessings of the Abrahamic covenant (salvation in Christ) and come alongside Israel (the believing Jewish remnant) but are not Israel.[110]

Robinson retained a modified supersessionist view in his eschatological elimination of a distinction between Jew and gentile believers when both believers become one new man through their salvation in Christ. Jew and gentile believers do not become a new Israel but a new humanity (or new mankind). Robinson considered this new mankind as a new creation or spiritual, heavenly reality inaugurated at Christ's resurrection. Jew and

109. Robinson, "Biblical Understanding of Israel," 184–85.
110. Robinson, "Jew and Greek," 79, 81–85; "Adventures in Jewish-Christian Relations," 192–93; and "Jew and Gentile," 409. See also Shiner, "Reading the New Testament," 84–89.

gentile share a common salvation in Christ that transcends ethnic distinctions. Faith in Christ alone saves Jew and gentile. Jew and gentile comprise the one body of believers. Eschatologically, the new man eliminates ethnic distinctions between Jew and gentile. While he taught an ecclesiological ethnic distinction between Jew and gentile in the New Testament church in the present dispensation, and while he emphasized the language of a new man that is not a new Israel to refer to the eschatological group of believers, his teaching that both Jew and gentile lose their ethnic distinctions in an eschatological new man retained another form of supersessionism.

Robinson's position also rejected a dispensationalist view that awaits a future, literal restoration concerning the nation of Israel at what Robinson believed to be the expense of Jewish believers during the New Testament age. In his concept of the three stages of redemptive history, he considered the reign of David and Solomon in the Old Testament as a partial fulfillment of God's promises to Israel in the Abrahamic covenant. This kingdom in the Old Testament failed, requiring a new, ultimate fulfillment. Robinson believed this fulfillment occurred through Christ in the New Testament, who brought about a restored Israel (the Jewish nucleus of believers) that blessed the gentiles with the gift of salvation. There is a twofold mission in the New Testament in which Israel is restored through a Jewish remnant who believes in Christ, then brings salvation to the gentile nations. The restoring of Israel through a believing remnant of Jews in the New Testament is how Robinson viewed the restoration of Israel's kingdom and fulfillment of God's Old Testament promises. He (unfortunately) did not view this restoration as a future, literal kingdom. The extension of salvation to the gentile nations is how Robinson viewed the fulfillment of the blessing of the nations in the Abrahamic covenant.[111]

Robinson published numerous writings on the relationship between Jew and gentile in redemptive history, with seven of the pieces published in 1961 while he was at Tyndale House, Cambridge.[112] Robinson's position concerning Israel's role in redemptive history went through a series

---

111. Robinson, "Israel and the Gentiles," 16, 22–23; "Jew and Greek," 81; and "Jew and Gentile," 409. Robinson critiqued Scofield's dispensational interpretation of James's speech in Acts 15 as a theological tour de force in "Jew and Greek" by discussing that Scofield reverses the missions of restoring Israel through a Jewish remnant and offering the gospel to the gentiles, plus Scofield places the rebuilding of the temple in a future millennial kingdom. See Robinson, "Jew and Greek," 88.

112. Shiner, "Reading the New Testament," 84–89.

of doctrinal developments.[113] His contributions on the subject also varied from exegetical works on key biblical texts to biblical-theological works and practical, application-level theological works (such as his critique concerning restoring a Jewish nation in the land of Israel in response to Christian restorationism).

Robinson differed from covenant theologians who emphasized covenant as the unifying theme of Scripture. Covenant was helpful in order to appropriate a promise, but promise and fulfillment was central to Robinson's understanding of the biblical-theological grand narrative of Scripture.[114] While Robinson rejected the centrality of covenant as a unifying theme in Scripture, he found Packer's emphasis on covenant as a unifying theme of Scripture useful for his sorting through where to place covenant and promise and fulfillment within his understanding of the biblical-theological grand narrative of Scripture. While the concept of covenant was not central to his contribution to biblical theology, Robinson believed that covenantal themes could be applied to the church (such as the expansion of the gospel given to the gentiles as the fulfillment of the blessing-of-the-nations promise of the Abrahamic covenant), and that the church does have a place in redemptive history (to bring salvation to the nations, beginning with the Jewish nucleus at the center of the New Testament church).[115] Robinson's concept of promise and fulfillment as the central theme of his biblical theology would build upon the concepts of Old Testament promise and New Testament fulfillment to include a partial fulfillment of the Old Testament promises within the Old Testament itself (such as during the reign of David and Solomon). However, even such a partial fulfillment failed and required an ultimate fulfillment in the New Testament (in Christ and a restored remnant of Jewish believers).

In the theological debate between Flew and Campbell, Robinson agreed with Campbell that the use of the term ἐκκλησία concerning Old Testament Israel in the Septuagint did not equate with the use of the term ἐκκλησία to refer to the New Testament church (or the New Testament church replacing Old Testament Israel by being in continuity with Israel). Robinson traced the same exegetical data as Campbell and arrived at a

---

113. Discussed throughout the chapter.

114. He also emphasized other concepts, such as the kingdom of God above covenant, derived from his studying under Dodd. See Shiner, "Reading the New Testament," 56–57.

115. Kuhn, *Ecclesiology of Donald Robinson*, 50–52.

similar conclusion. Robinson's exegetical conclusion concerning the term ἐκκλησία was that it is biblically inaccurate to state that the church is Israel in a redemptive-historical biblical theology framework.[116] Robinson began with a church comprised of a Jewish nucleus as the original ἐκκλησία (in contrast to applying the term to the gentile churches or gentile believers). Christ's mission was first to restore Israel through a believing remnant of Jews who would comprise the true Israel of God. Christ's restoring Israel was not to transfer the promises of Israel to the church but to include Israel (the restored remnant of believers) in bringing salvation to the gentiles (as the apostles and New Testament missionaries were Jewish). Shiner referred to Robinson's position on the New Testament church as including a "Jewish nucleus whose identity was not entirely lost."[117]

In addition to Robinson's distinction theology between Jew and gentile, his contribution to biblical theology was Christocentric.[118] Christ is the representative true Israel who is the ultimate fulfillment of the Old Testament promises, and the believing Jewish remnant in Christ comprises the true Israel. Through Old Testament Israel's failing in its covenantal relationship with God, Christ, through his believing Jewish remnant, ushers into effect the blessing of the nations. Christ (summarized by Kuhn) is the "true Jew and true Israel" that brought salvation to the gentiles.[119] To Robinson, salvation comes to the gentiles through the Jews (through Israel), "but especially through the person Jesus, Israel *par excellence*."[120]

One area where Robinson transformed his theology concerned the application of the term *people of God*. Initially, he believed the term *people of God* should apply equally to Old Testament Israel and the New Testament church. His early position is that while different terms were given for the people of God in the Old and New Testament (such as *congregation* in the Old Testament and *church* in the New Testament), the "concept is one and the same," which are the people joined to Christ by faith.[121]

---

116. Robinson, "Israel and the Gentiles," 7.

117. Shiner, "Reading the New Testament," 68–70, 84–89. See also Robinson, "Salvation of Israel," 53. Robinson elaborated on the distinction between Jew and gentile throughout the New Testament by Peter's role as an apostle to the Jews alongside Paul's role as an apostle to the gentiles. See Kuhn, *Ecclesiology of Donald Robinson*, 78–83.

118. Graeme Goldsworthy further developed the Christocentrality of Robinson's contribution to biblical theology, see chapter 4.

119. Kuhn, *Ecclesiology of Donald Robinson*, 83.

120. Kuhn, *Ecclesiology of Donald Robinson*, 121.

121. Kuhn, *Ecclesiology of Donald Robinson*, 80.

He later adjusted his position by not directly applying the term *people of God* to the church itself but instead viewed the church as an activity or gathering of the people of God. Kuhn summarized Robinson's later development: "'Church' is not a synonym for 'people of God'; it is rather an *activity* of the 'people of God.' Images such as 'aliens and exiles' . . . apply to the people of God in the world, but do not describe the church, i.e. the people assembled with Christ in the midst."[122]

Robinson elaborated on his later position concerning *people of God* by responding to Alan Richardson (1905–1975). Richardson claimed that λαος θεου in the Septuagint and New Testament referred to a *continuity* between Old Testament Israel and the New Testament church to refer to the people of God. His position was similar to Flew's claim that ἐκκλησία in the Septuagint and New Testament refers to a continuity between Old Testament Israel and the New Testament church. Richardson believed that the new Testament church had taken over *people of God*, a term once reserved for Israel. Robinson began his argument against Richardson with a background examination of the term λαος by stating that λαος refers to people "bound together by certain ties and responsibilities," not ethnic origin (ἔθνος would be the word used to refer to ethnic origin).[123] One example he cited was the use of the term *my people* about Egypt in Isa 19:25. Egypt, in this context, would not become Israel, nor would Egypt replace Israel as God's people. Robinson proceeded through a brief exegetical tour on the term *people of God* in the New Testament. He referenced Acts 7:34 and Heb 11:25, which referred to Old Testament Israel. He also referenced the New Testament's quoting the Old Testament concerning the nation of Israel as the people of God in Matt 2:6 (quoting Mic 5:1), Rom 11:12 (quoting Ps 94:14), and Rom 15:10 (quoting Deut 32:43). In Acts 15:14 and 18:10, the gentiles are a people of God through their common salvation with Jewish believers in Christ. However, they are not a new Israel.[124] While the term *people of God* should not be transferred from Old Testament Israel to apply to the New Testament church, Robinson was comfortable with using the phrase *peoples*

---

122. Kuhn, *Ecclesiology of Donald Robinson*, 80–81.

123. Robinson, "Israel and the Gentiles," 8; and "Jew and Gentile," 412–15. Furthermore, the term *the people*, when referring to Israel in either the Old or New Testament, is not always qualified with the modifier *of God*.

124. Robinson, "Israel and the Gentiles," 12. Robinson also commented that Old Testament prophecies always distinguished between prophecies given to Israel and those given to the gentile nations.

of God to apply to various redeemed peoples, each comprised of their distinct ethnicity, but not the phrase *people of God*.[125]

As Robinson began to develop the relationship between the universal church and the local church, Robinson shifted the location of the church from solely being comprised of Jewish believers to include various congregations of believers who are saved through Christ, drawing from an Acts 1:8 model that began in Jerusalem and branched out "to the ends of the earth."[126] Within his position, Robinson still retained a distinction between Jew and gentile believers in the New Testament church: "Though salvation spreads outward from Jerusalem, Jew and Gentile remain distinct. . . . Gentiles are not represented as becoming Israelites or a new Israel."[127] Robinson's interpretation of Acts 1:8 began with a restored remnant of Israel that brought salvation "to the ends of the earth." Acts 1:8 presented a situation in which Jews and gentiles are equal in their salvation in Christ but distinct in their ethnicity.[128]

The heart of Robinson's distinction theology concerning Israel's role in redemptive history is his exegesis of various biblical texts throughout Scripture. Referencing Gen 12:1–3, Robinson distinguished between Jewish and gentile believers, in which gentile believers inherit the blessing-of-the-nations promise of Gen 12 as a separate promise from the promises given to Israel (as discussed earlier in the chapter). Kuhn offered a helpful summary of Robinson's exegesis of Gen 12:3: "The fulfillment of God's promises to Israel also brought fulfillment of God's blessing to the nations."[129]

Mark's Gospel is where Robinson began to elaborate on his distinction theology in the New Testament. Robinson presented Christ as the Jewish Messiah who did not give up his role nor abandon his mission to Israel to bring salvation to the gentiles. One example he referenced was the event with the Syrophenecian woman as evidence that the primary mission to Christ was first to the house of Israel and only later included mission activity to the gentiles. While Robinson used similar language to that of Stott in that Israel was preserved in the little flock of disciples as a restored Israel in his exegesis

---

125. Robinson, "Israel and the Gentiles," 12–14. Robinson summarized his argument: "Israel remains at the center of worship to the custodian of God's law and wisdom for the nations."

126. Kuhn, *Ecclesiology of Donald Robinson*, 121.

127. Robinson, "Israel and the Gentiles," 17–18.

128. Robinson, "Israel and the Gentiles," 22, 24.

129. Kuhn, *Ecclesiology of Donald Robinson*, 83.

of Mark's Gospel, he did not label the New Testament (gentile) church *Israel*. Robinson also examined the parable of the husbandmen, in which he placed it in comparison to a theme throughout the Gospel of Mark concerning a falling Israel and rising Israel. Robinson argued that it is not the entire vineyard (representative of Israel) that the gentiles replace. However, only the unbelieving leaders of Israel who rejected Christ (which comprise a falling Israel) are replaced by a remnant of leaders (beginning with the apostles) who believed in Christ (which comprise a rising Israel).[130]

"The Salvation of Israel in Romans 9–11" (with particular emphasis on Rom 11) is one of Robinson's substantial exegetical works which presented his distinction theology. To Robinson, Rom 9:25–26 is not evidence that gentile believers become Israel, but that the passage references the nation of Israel as ethnic Jews.[131] In Rom 11, Robinson identified Israel as a nation that did not lose its national identity to the New Testament church: "He [referring to Paul] nowhere suggests that Israel has lost or changed its original character. He does not, in short, propose any new definition. Israel is the people or nation of Israel, of whose identity no one had any doubt."[132] Paul is speaking of one Israel, the nation of Israel (ethnic Jews). There is no old or new Israel in the mind of Paul. There is somewhat of a purified Israel comprised of a believing remnant of Jews, but the New Testament church itself cannot be considered a new Israel or a replacement of Old Testament Israel. Robinson elaborated on this position by writing:

> Unity in sin and salvation does not mean, however, that Christian Jews and Gentiles form a new Israel. They form on one hand a new or purified Israel—or an elect remnant—and a group of converted Gentiles on the other, conscious of their relationship to and interaction with each other . . . but this unity is plainly not something that can be called "Israel." The Gentiles remain Gentiles, even under the Gospel, and Jerusalem remains Jerusalem.[133]

Robinson viewed the root of the olive tree (Rom 11) being Abraham, or more precisely the Abrahamic blessing (salvation), with the olive tree representing "Israel's dependence upon the Abrahamic blessing. Gentiles are grafted in and partake of the blessing of Abraham but can never become

---

130. Robinson, "Israel and the Gentiles," 20–21; and "'Israel' and the 'Gentiles' in the Gospel of Mark," 32–34, 39.

131. Robinson, "Israel and the Gentiles," 12.

132. Robinson, "Salvation of Israel," 49 (bracketed text added).

133. Robinson, "Jew and Gentile," 419–20.

natural branches [Israel]."¹³⁴ He also believed that the Jewish believer in Christ completed their Jewish faith, with gentiles partnering with Israel without being Israel: "Christian confession meant the completion of Jewish faith, according to Paul.... The Gentiles were to become partners of Israel but not part of Israel."¹³⁵ To Robinson, Rom 9–11 focused on the nation of Israel, with Paul writing to Jewish believers. The passage originated with natural Israel, then expanded to include a believing remnant of Israel within natural Israel. This believing remnant of Israel is Israel's hope of their salvation. Paul brought gentiles into his presentation of the olive tree only through their relationship with the believing remnant of Israel.¹³⁶

In Rom 9–11, Robinson also believed in a reciprocal role between the Jews and gentiles concerning each other's salvation. First, God's salvation for the gentiles comes through the nation of Israel. The gentile's belief in Christ comes directly from the restored remnant of Jewish believers without the gentiles becoming Israel.¹³⁷ Kuhn offered a helpful summary of Robinson's position on salvation coming from the remnant of Jewish believers: "Robinson believed the church at Jerusalem (consisting of Israelites) was the dispenser of grace to the nations."¹³⁸ Through Christ, the Jewish Messiah representing true Israel, salvation has been made possible for the gentiles. However, the salvation of the gentiles would not be possible without the believing Jewish remnant.¹³⁹ Even "under the new covenant, Israel is still the vehicle for God's renown. First, this goal of reaching the nations is achieved in and through Christ, Israel *par excellence*. Second, the apostles were Israelites, and were the first missionaries carrying the gospel to the nations. Third, in the rejection of Israel as a nation a way was opened to the Gentiles."¹⁴⁰

Not only is salvation made possible to the gentiles through the nation of Israel, but gentile believers also play a reciprocal role in the salvation of some of the remaining unbelieving Jews: "The mystery is that the Gentiles are beneficiaries of Israel's lapse but also their means of

---

134. Robinson, "Salvation of Israel," 56; and Peterson and Pryor, *Fullness of Time*, xxii (bracketed text added).

135. Peterson and Pryor, *Fullness of Time*, xxii.

136. Robinson, "Salvation of Israel," 48–50; and "Distinction Between Jewish," 142.

137. Robinson, "Israel and the Gentiles," 19.

138. Kuhn, *Ecclesiology of Donald Robinson*, 82.

139. Kuhn, *Ecclesiology of Donald Robinson*, 83.

140. Kuhn, *Ecclesiology of Donald Robinson*, 121–22.

salvation."[141] Robinson's interpretation of Rom 11:26 that "all Israel shall be saved" does not mean that all of God's people will be saved. Instead, the believing remnant of Jews expand into a fullness of believing Jews through the witness of the gentiles. The reciprocal relationship between salvation being brought to the gentiles through the Jews and the gentiles bringing salvation to formerly unbelieving Jews constituted the salvation of all Israel in Rom 11.[142] This salvation is taking place now (and was taking place during the time of Paul), with no need to await a future fulfillment (in rejection of a position that placed a future national salvation for Israel).[143] This salvation is not a separate way of salvation that leads to a Jewish universalism (or two-covenant theology). Jews and gentiles are saved through one common way of salvation, Christ.[144]

Galatians 6:16 is another passage in which Robinson critiqued a typical supersessionist interpretation represented by Earle Ellis. Ellis believed the New Testament church, the spiritual seed of Abraham, was the new Israel. Robinson countered his view by citing Ernest Burton's (1856–1925) use of Gal 6:16 that the text refers to believing Jews, not a mixed Jew and gentile audience. The book of Galatians was written to an audience of Jewish believers to reject another gospel. While gentile Christians are included in the seed of Abraham as inheritors of the spiritual blessings of Abraham (the gospel), they are not Israel.[145]

Ephesians and Colossians are two additional books in which Robinson further developed his distinction theology by exegeting the use of the terms *saints* and *elect*. In Eph 1, he argued that the use of the term *saints* referred to the saints of Israel, Jewish believers. In Col 1, Moule applied the term *saints* as referring to the New Testament church as comprised of gentile believers. Robinson countered that the use of the term *saints* in Col 1 applied to Jewish saints (the believing remnant of Jews), not gentile believers. There is a relationship between Jews and gentiles concerning their salvation in Christ's death as something both groups have in common. While gentile believers are to be considered elect of God and holy,

---

141. Peterson and Pryor, *Fullness of Time*, xxiii.

142. Robinson, "Salvation of Israel," 49–50. Robinson stated that this restoration of Israel was fulfilled at Pentecost. This restoration of Israel included the blessing of the gentile nations through Israel. See Robinson, "Israel and the Gentiles," 16.

143. Shiner, "Reading the New Testament," 84–89.

144. Robinson, "Salvation of Israel," 54–55.

145. Robinson, "Jew and Gentile," 412–13; "Israel and the Gentiles," 7–8; "Romans 9:7," 45; and "Distinction Between Jewish," 131.

they are not, however, *the* saints or *the* elect. Robinson reserved these titles for Jewish believers in both contexts.[146]

Robinson offered a handful of brief exegetical comments throughout the New Testament concerning the relationship between Jew and gentile in redemptive history. He considered 2 Cor 6:16 as a possible interpolation in the biblical text, dismissing it as evidence that the New Testament church has replaced Israel or is a new Israel. Robinson also contributed an article on Paul's use of the term *we the circumcision* in Phil 3:2–4, which he argued referred to Jewish believers. To Robinson, the term *the circumcision* as a people (qualified by *the*) always referred to a group of people who have been physically circumcised. It did not refer to a group of people being circumcised figuratively (such as being circumcised in the heart). Robinson's exegesis of Titus 2:14 argued that it likely referred to Paul and his colleagues as Jewish believers who were witnessing to gentiles, not to a gentile church replacing Israel as those who are witnessing to other gentiles. Robinson also referenced the term *the house of Israel* in Hebrews to refer to actual Jewish believers, not as referring to a mixed Jew/gentile audience. Robinson's exegesis of 1 Pet 2:9 argued that the passage likely referred to Jewish believers, not a predominantly gentile church. It could refer to Jewish believers who lapsed away from Judaism into paganism (in a similar manner to how Old Testament Israel forsook God and lapsed into worshiping pagan deities) but who later returned to the faith through salvation in Christ.[147]

Robinson summarized his exegesis of Pauline passages by stating there are distinct but connected aspects of the gospel concerning the Jews and gentiles. This distinction does not present an entirely different way of salvation concerning the Jews and gentiles (both come to the same faith in Christ). While Robinson did not directly interact with the concept, his position would reject a two-covenant theology as taught by Hechler. However, he did assert that a different presentation of the gospel is warranted depending on a Jewish or gentile evangelistic context. Paul utilized different terminology or language in his witness to a Jew or gentile based

---

146. Robinson, "Who Were 'The Saints'?," 164–68.

147. Robinson, "Israel and the Gentiles," 10–11, 13–14; "Jew and Gentile," 415–16; and "We are the Circumcision," 171–72. Robinson also critiqued Peter Richardson's (1935–) comment that there was a shift from the Jews to a predominately gentile New Testament church in the Pauline writings. Robinson argued that this concept would not be considered in the Pauline writings, as such a division between the Jews and gentiles would not have occurred until the destruction of the Jewish temple in AD 70. See Robinson, "Jew and Gentile," 420.

upon how each understood redemptive history. Jews were in bondage to the (Mosaic) law, while gentiles were in bondage to their false (pagan) religions, but Christ rescued each group of people. Paul is united to both the Jews as a believing Jew and to gentiles he witnessed to. He is united to both through one faith in Christ.[148] While both Jew and gentile shared a common salvation, both retained their ethnic distinctions. Gentiles are not Israel: "Gentile believers are not, in fact, represented as spiritual Israelites, or as forming part of the renewed Israel of prophecy."[149] Kuhn elaborated on Robinson's position by writing:

> Robinson believed that Israel is preserved as an identity (ethnic?) in the church as a demonstration of God's wisdom in bringing together Jews and Gentiles... while the church is the *gathering* of the people of God, there is good reason why it is not called "Israel."
> ... While Israel is not superseded in the church, there remains a place of prominence for Israel in the salvific purposes of God. Robinson believed the church at Jerusalem (consisting of Israelites) was the dispenser of grace to the nations.[150]

One final application concerning Robinson's theology was how he critiqued a Christian restorationist position concerning restoring a Jewish nation in the land of Israel. Robinson aided in the forming of the Council of Christians and Jews in 1980, also serving as a representative of the Anglican Diocese of Sydney. During this time, Robinson continued to work through various positions on what role a restoration of a Jewish nation in the land of Israel played in redemptive history. In his essay "Biblical Understanding of Israel," he referenced the efforts of the LSJ and Church's Ministry Among Jewish People (CMJ) concerning Jewish evangelism, as well as the role key nineteenth-century figures in Christian restorationism (such as Lord Shaftesbury) played in advocating for restoring a Jewish nation in the land of

---

148. Robinson, "Jew and Greek," 83; "Circumcision of Titus," 111; and "Distinction Between Jewish," 134–38.

149. Robinson, "Jew and Greek," 85.

150. Kuhn, *Ecclesiology of Donald Robinson*, 82 (italics added). Kuhn also elaborated on Robinson's theology in that Robinson placed the church "within the covenantal relationship God had established with Israel, yet he did not see the new covenant abolishing the identity of the Israelites or their place within the soteriological purposes of God. He believed that preservation of the Israelite identity, in distinction from the gentile converts, was fundamental to understanding the redemptive plan of God." See Kuhn, *Ecclesiology of Donald Robinson*, 120.

Israel.¹⁵¹ He was comfortable with efforts to evangelize Jews and with the work of the LSJ and CMJ. While Robinson (rightly) did not object to Jewish evangelism, he (unfortunately) disagreed with a Christian restorationist position concerning the restoring of a modern Jewish nation in the land of Israel and a return of the Jews to their land as a fulfillment of God's land promises to Israel. He believed there was a difference between God's plan of not abandoning the Jewish people (including Jewish salvation in Rom 9–11) and a Christian restorationist position that the Jews continue to have a God-promised right to the land of Israel in the present age. He rejected this position on what he believed were four hermeneutical and theological grounds. First, he believed the land promises to Israel extended further than the boundaries of the modern nation of Israel (citing Gen 15:18–21 as evidence that the land promises to Israel included Syria, Lebanon, Jordan, and northern Sinai).¹⁵² Second, he believed that the land promises to Israel were conditional upon obeying God's laws. Due to Israel's disobedience to God in the Old Testament, the Jews forfeited their land promises, according to Robinson. Third, he did not believe the New Testament contained any explicit language concerning the carrying forward of any Old Testament land promises concerning the nation of Israel (a position similar to that of Stott). He argued that the New Testament did not give much "interest in the geographic entity of the land," nor did it provide the grounds for restoring a Jewish nation in the land of Israel. Finally, he considered the salvation of the Jews (their heavenly inheritance), not a literal land promise, as the fulfillment of God's promises to them. Robinson placed the application of the land promise of the Abrahamic covenant as a heavenly reality, citing the "inheritance of the saints" as being "in the heavenly places" (Eph 1:18–21; 1 Pet 1). He considered no need for a divinely-commissioned restoration of a Jewish nation in the land of Israel in a modern-day nation of Israel or a future fulfillment. He would agree with covenant theologians that no future return of the Jewish people to the land of Israel is biblically warranted. He would modify the position that the church, comprised of both a Jewish nucleus and gentile believers, together comprise a new Israel, instead limiting the true Israel to the Jewish nucleus and arguing that

---

151. Robinson, "Biblical Understanding of Israel," 185–86. See chapter 2 for more on the LSJ and CMJ.

152. Other passages Robinson cited for evidence include Num 13 and 34; Josh 10–19; 1 Kgs 4:21–24 and 8:65; 2 Kgs 14:25; Amos 6:13; Ps 72:8; Ezek 47; and Zech 9:10.

the church is a new Adam.[153] He referred to W. D. Davies's (1911–2001) study, *The Gospel and the Land*; Robinson summarized Davies's position that the "appearance of Christ in the flesh—in the land, in Jerusalem, in the temple, made an engagement by his followers with these realities of Judaism unavoidable, yet the witness of the New Testament to the fulfillment of God's purposes points to the transcending of all three."[154] He directly cited Davies that during the time of Christ, "there was no one doctrine of the land" but "a multiplicity of ideas" concerning the land promises: "There were currents which would temper any concentration on the land, but a belief in the promise of the land to Israel by Yahweh, to whom it belonged, also persisted."[155] Robinson understood this as "while the *image* of the land remained clear, it is not easy to see how far Jews, by the end of or after the Old Testament period, entertained hope of a *physical* reoccupation of the land promised to Abraham."[156] He was not against Zionism solely as a secular, political movement. He was comfortable with Jewish people returning to the land of Israel, provided that the Jewish people offer "due regard for the non-Jewish communities already there." He did (unfortunately) reject a Christian restorationist or Christian Zionist position that a restoration of a Jewish nation in the land of Israel could be made on theological grounds or through an exegesis of the biblical text.[157]

Robinson's ecclesiological distinction theology concerning Jew and gentile affected the overall construal of biblical theology he taught in his Introduction to the Study of the Bible course. In lesson two of the course, Robinson taught that the *people of God* (which he considered Israel in the Old Testament and a restored remnant of Jewish believers in the New Testament) was that which gave coherence to Scripture's storyline. In lesson three of the course, Robinson taught on "Abraham, his seed, and its significance" where he examined God's promises to Abraham and how the biblical story unfolded as the "outworking of that promise." Robinson taught in the sixth lesson that Christ fulfilled God's promises to Abraham where Old Testament Israel partially fulfilled but failed to fully fulfill God's promises. Through Christ, the representative of true Israel, salvation was first brought to a restored remnant of Jewish believers who Robinson considered the

---

153. Robinson, "Biblical Understanding of Israel," 182–91.
154. Robinson, "Biblical Understanding of Israel," 185.
155. Davies, *Gospel and Land*, 157.
156. Robinson, "Biblical Understanding of Israel," 187.
157. Shiner, "Reading the New Testament," 187–89.

true Israel. This restored, true Israel then fulfilled the blessings to the nations by bringing salvation to the gentiles.[158]

Robinson's distinction theology can be commended for preserving an ethnic distinction between Jew and gentile in the New Testament church in his ecclesiology. Contrary to one form of supersessionism (such as covenantalism), Robinson did not consider the New Testament church as replacing Israel, nor are Jews and gentiles absorbed into a New Testament church that eliminates their ethnic distinctions. He also corrected one form of dispensationalism that placed Jewish Christians as belonging to either Israel or the church, but that a Jewish Christian cannot belong to both groups simultaneously. He also corrected a modified form of supersessionism that considered all Christians to be a new Israel, but that the New Testament church contained a Jewish nucleus. Instead, he limited the true Israel to the Jewish nucleus of believers, not to all Christians.

However, Robinson's distinction theology is not truly an alternative to supersessionism (as proposed by Robinson) but still retains a modified form of supersessionism in its eschatology. While Robinson stated that Jew and gentile do not become a new Israel but a new man, this eschatological new man still eliminates the distinction between Jew and gentile. It still replaces Israel and the Jews by absorbing their ethnic distinctions into this eschatological new man. Additionally, Robinson's critiques of dispensationalism and Christian restorationism reinterpret God's literal land promises to Abraham solely in terms of Jewish salvation and a heavenly, spiritual inheritance. While Jewish salvation (and bringing salvation to the nations) is a part of the Abrahamic promises in order to fulfill the Rom 11:26 promise "so all Israel shall be saved," God also promised Abraham that he would make of him a great nation (Gen 12:1–3) and give him a literal promised land (the nation of Israel). Robinson rejected dispensationalism's awaiting a future fulfillment of God's land promises to Abraham and Christian restorationism's view on a future restoration of a Jewish nation in the land of Israel. Instead, he reinterpreted the concept of restoration in terms of a believing remnant of Jews within the New Testament church. His position weakened the totality of God's promises to the nation of Israel by limiting some of God's promises to Jewish believers in the New Testament church.

---

158. Robinson, "Biblical Theology in Sydney," 208–9.

Conclusion

Donald Robinson established the biblical theology program at Moore College while further developing his understanding of ecclesiology. His education allowed him to question established viewpoints within biblical scholarship, including how supersessionist views (such as covenantalism) and views that held a positive theological value for Israel (such as dispensationalism and Christian restorationism) considered Israel's role in redemptive history. Robinson attempted to propose an alternative, mediating distinction theology concerning the relationship between Jew and gentile in God's salvation program. While Robinson did not adhere to all of dispensationalism's future-fulfillment conclusions nor affirm a future restoration of a Jewish nation in the land of Israel as believed by Christian restorationism, he did believe in a distinction between Jew and gentile in that the church does not replace Israel nor inherit its promises. Israel's promises belong to a believing remnant of Jews, and salvation is spread worldwide by a reciprocal role between Jews and gentiles. Jewish believers bring salvation to the gentiles, and gentile believers bring salvation back to unbelieving Jews. This mission of restoring a remnant of believing Israel as a true Israel, coupled with expanding the gospel to the gentiles, fulfills the blessing-of-the-nations promise of the Abrahamic covenant. The reciprocal role in which gentiles bring salvation back to unbelieving Jews fulfills the Rom 11:26 promise that "all Israel shall be saved" without awaiting a future fulfillment. While the church is not a new Israel, it is a new humanity as Shiner summarized: "The New Testament church does not become 'the new Israel,' but rather a unity of the sons of Abraham who are both Jews and Gentiles (Gal. 3:7), and who together become 'one man in Christ Jesus.'"[159]

Robinson's distinction theology affected the construal of biblical theology taught in his Introduction to the Study of the Bible course, especially through how he handled Christ as the representative of true Israel who is the fulfillment of God's promises to Abraham, and that a restored remnant of believing Jews comprise the true Israel who inherited the promises of Abraham. Robinson corrected some forms of supersessionism in his ethnic distinction between Jews and gentiles within the New Testament church in his ecclesiology. However, contrary to his claim, he did not propose an alternative to supersessionism. His elimination of both ethnic distinctions in an eschatological new man, as well as his

---

159. Shiner, "Reading the New Testament," 69–70.

reinterpretation of a restored Israel not in a future literal restoration of a Jewish nation in the land of Israel, but to a heavenly, spiritual inheritance of salvation to Jews within the New Testament church, still retained a modified form of supersessionism.

4

Departing from Robinson

Graeme Goldsworthy's Christocentric Biblical Theology and Goldsworthy's Successors

Introduction

GRAEME GOLDSWORTHY, ONE OF Robinson's students, contributed to the biblical theology program at Moore that further developed (while departing from) some of Robinson's teachings, also bringing them to nonacademic audiences. Goldsworthy originally departed from Robinson's distinction theology, bringing a Reformed redemptive-historical biblical theology (typical of the biblical theology of the Westminster tradition that follows Geerhardus Vos) to Moore's biblical theology program.[1] He later began to appreciate some aspects of Robinson's distinction theology without fully incorporating it into his contributions at Moore. Four of Goldsworthy's successors (Vaughan Roberts, Richard Gibson, Brian Rosner, Peter O'Brien, and Paul Williamson) carried forward at least some (or all) of Goldsworthy's Christocentric biblical theology in their contributions to Moore's biblical theology program.

---

1. The author is grateful for the work of fellow student Joel Wright who produced a paper on the place of national Israel in the theology of Graeme Goldsworthy during a PhD research seminar. His paper provided a valuable road map in navigating through the corpus of Goldsworthy literature. For additional information on a Reformed redemptive-historical biblical theology of the Westminster tradition that follows Geerhardus Vos, see Vos, *Biblical Theology*; Beale, *New Testament Biblical Theology*; and Krabbendam, "Hermeneutics in Preaching." For a critique, see Horner, *Eternal Israel*, 211–25; and Feinberg, *Continuity and Discontinuity Perspectives*.

Biographical Sketch of Graeme Goldsworthy

Graeme Goldsworthy (1934–) is an Australian Anglican Old Testament scholar and former lecturer at Moore College.[2] He attended Moore in 1956, beginning as a student of Robinson's Old Testament class from 1956 to 1957. In this class setting, he learned Robinson's three stages typology. According to Rory Shiner, Goldsworthy did not attend Robinson's special doctrine class (where Robinson taught an extensive treatment of biblical theology).[3] In addition to studying under Robinson, Goldsworthy read Geerhardus Vos's (1862–1949) *Biblical Theology*, John Bright's (1811–1889) *Kingdom of God*, Edmund Clowney's (1917–2005) *Preaching and Biblical Theology*, and G. Ernest Wright's (1909–1974) *God Who Acts*.[4] He also attended schools in the US and UK including (as did Robinson), Cambridge University, where he had the privilege of studying with some of Robinson's professors (including C. F. D. Moule).[5]

Goldsworthy began teaching biblical theology at Moore during the 1973–1974 course year and authored numerous works on biblical theology. His first, *Gospel and Kingdom*, was published in 1981. He further developed his biblical theology in *According to Plan*, published in 1991. After a brief respite from teaching, he returned to Moore in 1995 to resume teaching biblical theology, using *Gospel and Kingdom* and *According to Plan* as the structure for the course.[6] Goldsworthy and Robinson contributed to the 1996 School of Theology conference at Moore, which became published in the work *Interpreting God's Plan*.[7] He retired from Moore in 2001. He occasionally teaches as a visiting lecturer there.[8]

---

2. For additional biographical information on Goldsworthy, see "Finding the Gospel in the Whole Bible."

3. Shiner, "Reading the New Testament," 200–202.

4. Campbell, "Biblical Theology at Moore"; Gibson, *Interpreting God's Plan*, 29, 32; and Goldsworthy, *Christ-Centered Biblical Theology*, 79–82.

5. Shiner, "Reading the New Testament," 200–202.

6. In most instances, 90 percent of the class had already read *Gospel and Kingdom* before taking his class.

7. Goldsworthy, "Lecture 2," 21.

8. Campbell, "Biblical Theology at Moore."

Graeme Goldsworthy's Contribution to the Biblical Theology Program at Moore

Goldsworthy popularized some of Robinson's teachings (such as Robinson's three stages) while also making a contribution complementary to Robinson. While Robinson primarily developed his contribution to the biblical theology program at Moore within the context of classroom instruction (his written contributions were primarily articles of an academic nature and only one major written work, *Faith's Framework*, see chapter 3), Goldsworthy's contribution to Moore's biblical theology program comprised numerous major written works, including *Gospel and Kingdom*, *According to Plan*, *Gospel-Centered Hermeneutics*, *Christ-Centered Biblical Theology*, and *Preaching the Whole Bible as Christian Scripture*. Whereas Robinson's audience was primarily academic, Goldsworthy's audience was primarily preachers, although numerous nonacademic lay Christians have benefitted from reading Goldsworthy's contributions to biblical theology. Moore eventually required all students to attend biblical theology courses at the college (alluding to the lasting legacy of Robinson and Goldsworthy).[9]

Goldsworthy summarized his appreciation of Robinson's biblical theology in *Christ-Centered Biblical Theology*: "This phrase 'the study of the Bible in its own terms' is, I believe, the key to Robinson's approach to biblical theology."[10] Goldsworthy further outlined Robinson's legacy and reflected upon nine lessons he learned from Robinson: "A sense of the unity of the Bible without discounting its diversity,"[11] opening "up the Old Testament . . . in a new and exciting way,"[12] understanding "the whole Bible as Christian Scripture,"[13] "understanding . . . the structure of revelation that is broad enough to embrace typology and all the other dimensions that make up the multifaceted relationship of the two Testaments,"[14] developing "the exegetical and hermeneutical tools for dealing with biblical texts so that the practical issues of preaching and teaching can be addressed,"[15]

9. Goldsworthy, "Lecture 2," 23–24.
10. Goldsworthy, *Christ-Centered Biblical Theology*, 20–23.
11. For a discussion on the unity and diversity of the Bible, see Baker, *Two Testaments, One Bible*.
12. See also Goldsworthy, *Jesus Through the Old Testament*.
13. See also Goldsworthy, *Preaching the Whole Bible*.
14. See also Goldsworthy, *Gospel-Centered Hermeneutics*.
15. See also Goldsworthy, *Gospel-Centered Hermeneutics*; and *Preaching the Whole Bible*.

"that thematic studies are much broader than word studies and are capable of being approached with the method of biblical theology,"[16] demonstrating "that evangelicals need to be in touch with non-evangelicals and their thinking," and instilling "the importance of biblical theology in the academy and in the ministry of the local church."[17] Goldsworthy also referred to Robinson as "a 'churchman.' He clearly loves Anglicanism, its traditions and its formularies. He is in many respects very conservative in these matters."[18] Goldsworthy attempted to wade through two challenges to biblical theology, noting that some evangelicals reject or neglect to perform biblical theology, and that some nonevangelical biblical theologians (such as Gabriel Hebert, see chapter 3) fail to uphold the Bible as the inspired Word of God. It is within the tension of these two challenges that Goldsworthy attempted to offer an evangelical biblical theology that is faithful to the inspired Word of God, but in a way that an evangelical will engage in biblical theology instead of neglecting it.[19] While he popularized and built upon some of Robinson's biblical theology, he was silent in his early writings concerning Robinson's Jew and gentile distinction theology as being central to the legacy Robinson taught him.

One of Goldsworthy's main works that outlined his biblical theology is *Gospel and Kingdom*, his thesis being "God's people in God's place under God's rule."[20] He produced a biblical theology in which the Old Testament Abrahamic covenant was fulfilled in Christ, where "God promises the patriarchs that their descendants (God's people) will possess the promised land (God's place) and be the people of God, underneath his authority (God's rule)."[21] He examined the importance of grace, election, and faith. Each was an essential aspect of the promises of the Abrahamic covenant (tracing salvation history from Old Testament Israel to its fulfillment in the gospel of Christ in the New Testament).[22] While he used the term *God's people* to refer to the descendants of the patriarchs, unlike Robinson, he did not specify that these descendants are a restored

16. See also Goldsworthy, *Christ-Centered Biblical Theology*.
17. See also Goldsworthy, *Preaching the Whole Bible*.
18. Goldsworthy, *Christ-Centered Biblical Theology*, 196–98.
19. Goldsworthy, "Lecture 1," 13–14.
20. Campbell, "Biblical Theology at Moore."
21. Goldsworthy, *Gospel and Kingdom*, 54, 67–70.
22. Goldsworthy, *Gospel and Kingdom*, 17–18. See also Goldsworthy, *According to Plan*, 122–23.

remnant of Jewish believers. To Goldsworthy, God's people are believers without ethnic distinctions. Goldsworthy's other major work on biblical theology that expanded his contribution to *Gospel and Kingdom* was *According to Plan*. He defined biblical theology as that which "examines the development of the biblical story from the Old Testament to the New, and seeks to uncover the interrelationships between the two parts."[23] After surveying the place of textual criticism, biblical criticism, exegesis, and canon, Goldsworthy defined biblical theology as Christocentric: "Biblical theology thus centers on Jesus Christ as the revealer and savior. To understand the Bible, we begin at the point where we first came to know God. We begin with Jesus Christ, and we see every part of the Bible in relationship to him and his saving work. This is as true of the Old Testament as it is of the New."[24] Goldsworthy's Christocentric biblical theology united both the Old and New Testament, viewing the Old Testament through the hermeneutical lens of the gospel of Christ. Christ is the beginning reference point when examining Scripture. Goldsworthy added three ingredients to biblical theology: the literature of the Bible, the specific succession of events in the Bible, and the Bible's revelation.[25]

To Goldsworthy, Christ (as presented in the gospel) is the center of his hermeneutical approach and approach to biblical theology.[26] He believed an evangelical biblical theology should "begin with Jesus Christ and the Gospel," further elaborating: "Biblical Theology is Christological, for its subject matter is the whole Bible as God's testimony to Christ. It is therefore, from start to finish, a study of Christ."[27] The centrality of the gospel is what unites and relates the Old and New Testaments in Goldsworthy's biblical theology: "What went before Christ in the Old Testament, as well as what comes after him, finds its meaning in him. So the Old Testament must be understood in

---

23. Goldsworthy, *According to Plan*, 23. See also Baker, *Two Testaments, One Bible*.

24. Goldsworthy, *According to Plan*, 33–35. For a discussion on textual criticism, see Wegner, *Student's Guide to Textual Criticism*. For a discussion on various forms of biblical criticism, see Mangum and Estes, *Literary Approaches to the Bible*. For a discussion on exegesis, see Mangum and Westbury, *Linguistics and Biblical Exegesis*. For a canonical biblical theology, see Childs, *Biblical Theology*.

25. Goldsworthy, *According to Plan*, 52, 55, 71, 73–76. *According to Plan* also surveyed the succession of biblical events. For a discussion on the literature of the Bible, see Mangum and Estes, *Literary Approaches to the Bible*. For a helpful evangelical treatment of the doctrine of revelation, see Dockery, *Doctrine of the Bible*.

26. Goldsworthy, *Preaching the Whole Bible*, 86.

27. Gibson, *Interpreting God's Plan*, 34, 38; and Goldsworthy, *Christ-Centered Biblical Theology*, 40.

its relationship to the gospel event."[28] The centrality of the gospel of Christ is also the key to his hermeneutical approach to Scripture: "By referring to the gospel as the hermeneutical key I mean that proper interpretation of any part of the Bible requires us to relate it to the person and work of Jesus."[29] He utilized a Christological reading of the Old Testament in light of the New Testament. In one example, he believed Christ transforms the Old Testament concept of the kingdom of God into a gospel reality.[30] He attempted to distinguish between Christ and the gospel as a fulfillment instead of a replacement: "A key point in this is that Jesus did not see himself as coming to eradicate the old and to establish something totally new. The gospel event is not de novo but is seen as the completion and fulfillment of all God's saving acts and promises in the Old Testament. Jesus again and again speaks of his role as fulfilling Scripture."[31] However, Goldsworthy's use of the term *fulfillment* in his Christocentric biblical theology did not avoid all forms of a supersessionist view, as he still considered God's people to be those in Christ without ethnic distinctions.

Goldsworthy agreed with Robinson's position concerning the kingdom of God as an important theme in biblical theology. However, unlike Robinson (who considered promise and fulfillment as the central theme of biblical theology) Goldsworthy considered the kingdom of God as the

---

28. Goldsworthy, *According to Plan*, 50.

29. Goldsworthy, *Preaching the Whole Bible*, 88.

30. Goldsworthy, *Gospel and Kingdom*, 108–10. Goldsworthy summarized his position on the transforming of the kingdom of God as a gospel reality: The New Testament "repeatedly maintains that Christ is the fulfilment of these terms, images, promises and foreshadowings in the Old Testament which were presented in a way that is different from the fulfilment. For the New Testament the interpretation of the Old Testament is not 'literal' but 'Christological.'" He elaborated on his position as follows: "Jesus Christ . . . contains in himself the Kingdom of God. The gospel is a gospel of man restored to proper relationships in Christ. Now, these relationships involve the whole of reality: God, man, and the created order. As Eden and Canaan are in Christ, so God's perfect world is in Christ. This truth has one vital implication often forgotten by evangelicals, but which the Old Testament reinforces by its historicity. The gospel is not simply 'forgiveness of sins' and 'going to heaven when you die'. The gospel is a restoration of relationships between God, man and the world. The typology of the Bible and the transformation of Old Testament imagery by the gospel should not be misused to lift us completely outside the created world. The gospel involves us not only with God, but with our fellow men and with the world. How this fact should affect the Christian's view of the world, politics, culture, the arts, ecology and science, should be our continuing concern." See Goldsworthy, *Gospel and Kingdom*, 108, 122.

31. Goldsworthy, *Preaching the Whole Bible*, 47–48.

central theme of biblical theology: "Jesus tells us that its central theme is the coming of the kingdom of God."[32] He further elaborated on the concept of the kingdom of God as biblical theology's central theme: "I would even suggest that this goal, *the Kingdom of God*, is a more central issue in the Old Testament than is the redemptive process of bringing people into that Kingdom."[33] He did have a place for the concepts of covenant and promise and fulfillment, although he did not consider either central themes of Scripture within his biblical theology. He placed covenant as an important theme without it being the central theme: "The covenant provides a unifying thread running the length of biblical revelation in salvation history. The covenant expressed the gracious commitment of God to his creation, a creation at the head of which he established mankind as the ruler in space and time."[34] He considered the Noahic covenant the first direct mention of a covenant in Scripture, although he believed it pointed back to an existing covenant at creation. In agreement with a typical viewpoint of covenant theology, he considered each of the covenants is a different expression of a single covenant: "Thus there is one covenant which has a number of different expressions in the course of redemptive history. The first of these is the initial commitment of God to the creation."[35] He linked the concept of promise and fulfillment to his concept of salvation history: "Salvation history and typology are also connected with the thematic polarity of promise and fulfilment. . . . One implication of this is that the Old Testament is incomplete as to the working out of God's purposes and thus cannot be

---

32. Goldsworthy, *According to Plan*, 72–73.

33. Goldsworthy, *Gospel and Kingdom*, 46–47. Goldsworthy elaborated on his position of the kingdom of God as biblical theology's central theme: "How can we characterize this history so that we are able to see the real unity within it? I suggest we look at the Old Testament as a *history of redemption*. In other words, the key to the Old Testament is not the part Israel plays—as important as that is—but the part God plays in redeeming a people from slavery and making them his own. The first approach would be to reduce the Old Testament to an example of ancient national history; the second interprets Israel's history as a part of God's redeeming activity to man. Nor is redemption the only theological idea which provides structure to the Old Testament, for redemption is a process which leads to a goal. Has not the Old Testament something to say about that goal? Indeed it has—the redeemed people of God are the people of God's kingdom. I would even suggest that this goal, the *Kingdom of God*, is a more central issue in the Old Testament than is the redemptive process of bringing people into that Kingdom. Of course we cannot really separate the two so strictly. The process needs a goal; the goal has to have a process or method of attainment."

34. Goldsworthy, *Gospel-Centered Hermeneutics*, 227.

35. Goldsworthy, *According to Plan*, 114, 192.

fully understood apart from the fulfilment in the New Testament."³⁶ Goldsworthy further defined salvation history as follows:

> Some may question the joining of the words salvation (used adjectivally) or redemptive to history because of the problem of the relationship of theology to history. I can see no real difficulty in doing so. I understand these terms to mean that God's work of salvation or redemption is done within human history, and that the biblical account of salvation is given within the framework of historical narrative . . . The incarnation of God the Son is the ultimate declaration that God works among us in space and time. Jesus of Nazareth as a historical figure establishes the validity of the story that leads to him and that flows from him. Not only does salvation take place within our history, but the purposes of God are what constitute human history in the first place.³⁷

Goldsworthy traced salvation history throughout the Old Testament toward its ultimate fulfillment in Christ as the figure who entered human history in order to bring salvation to humanity, shifting the focus on the role Old Testament Israel plays within salvation history to the role God plays in redeeming Israel, and eventually, redeeming all of humanity: "The key to the Old Testament is not the part Israel plays—as important as that is—but the part God plays in redeeming a people from slavery and making them his own."³⁸

Within his discussion of the kingdom of God, Goldsworthy further developed Robinson's three stages typology of biblical theology (see chapter 3), which he referred to as the Robinson-Hebert schema or approach to biblical theology.³⁹ In his ETS lecture (presented by Constantine Campbell), Goldsworthy wrote that while the Robinson-Hebert approach can be labeled a Moore College approach to biblical theology, he was reluctant to apply such a label to the position. He added other distinctives to what he considered comprise a Moore College approach to biblical

---

36. Goldsworthy, *Gospel-Centered Hermeneutics*, 243. In the next sentence, Goldsworthy noted: "The two Testaments are interdependent, in that the New must complete the Old, but the New also needs the Old to show what it is that is being fulfilled." Lacking from his discussion is how one should interpret Old Testament promises within their Old Testament context.

37. Goldsworthy, *Christ-Centered Biblical Theology*, 60–65.

38. Goldsworthy, *Gospel and Kingdom*, 46–47.

39. Campbell, "Biblical Theology at Moore." W. J. Phythian-Adams also developed the three stage approach. See Goldsworthy, *Christ-Centered Biblical Theology*, 25–27.

theology (discussed later). However, he placed the Robinson-Hebert approach at the center of his understanding of biblical theology: "It is this understanding of the 'big picture' and the role of typology that captured my imagination over fifty years ago, and that has been at the centre of my preoccupation with biblical theology ever since."[40] While he elaborated upon the Robinson-Hebert approach of the three stages as being central to his understanding of biblical theology, he did not include Robinson's distinction theology concerning Jew and gentile in the centrality of Robinson's biblical theological legacy left upon him.

Goldsworthy modified the Robinson-Hebert approach to refer to what he termed are three epochs of the kingdom of God.[41] His three epochs used a similar structure to that of Robinson: "The proposal is that the kingdom of God is revealed in three stages: in Israel's history from Abraham to Solomon's building of the temple, in prophetic eschatology, and in its fulfilment in Christ."[42] His three epochs traced the same reality of the kingdom of God through three different stages.[43] He formed each of the three epochs into an A-B-C structure that further developed Robinson's structure:

> In A (the kingdom revealed in Israel's history) we include the whole history of God's activity outside of Eden up to and including David and the first part of Solomon's reign. The key figures are Abraham as recipient of the promises of God, and David as the one to whom a certain measure of the fulfillment of these promises comes. This epoch becomes the first anchorage for the doing of biblical theology. The second epoch, B, takes in the historic decline of Israel, including the exile and beyond, but the major impetus in revelation is the prophetic promise of a future perfect salvation. The third epoch, C, is the fulfillment of the

---

40. Goldsworthy, *Christ-Centered Biblical Theology*, 20–23. Goldsworthy's reference to the role of typology is referring to Robinson's three stages of redemptive history.

41. Goldsworthy, *Christ-Centered Biblical Theology*, 45, 175–79, 190. At times, Goldsworthy used the terms *three stages* and *three epochs* interchangeably. On pages 175–79, he clarified his use of the term *epoch*: "It is clear that Robinson uses the word 'typology' in his own way by defining it in terms of the 'three stages' of revelation that he discerns in the Bible. These are not so much epochs as modes of revelation. Epoch, however, is not an entirely inappropriate term in that these stages are sequential though with some overlap of the first two."

42. Goldsworthy, "Kingdom of God as Hermeneutic Grid," 11.

43. Goldsworthy, *Gospel and Kingdom*, 108–10.

historic promises to Abraham and his descendants, and of the prophetic hope, in Jesus Christ.[44]

Goldsworthy further developed two of Robinson's stages. He further developed the second stage (or second epoch) of Israel's monarchy's (what Robinson considered a partial fulfillment of the Abrahamic covenant) by considering the second epoch as an early form of the kingdom of God. He also traced how the second epoch (Israel's monarchy) gave way to the third epoch (Christological fulfillment):

> When this historical experience of Israel, which patterned salvation, reached its climax in the kingdom of David and Solomon, the rot set in. As the strength and faithfulness of Israel declined and the whole fabric which pre-figured the kingdom of God crumbled and fell apart, the truth of the kingdom was given to the prophetic word of revelation.[45]

Goldsworthy also developed Robinson's third stage (or third epoch), adding that Christ's first advent, not a future consummation, brings about the ultimate fulfillment of the kingdom of God. This Christological fulfillment serves as the antitype to Old Testament Israel's salvation history as the type: "The kingdom of God is indeed being restored to Israel, but it will come about through the preaching of the gospel in all the world."[46] While Goldsworthy viewed a restored kingdom of God through the preaching of the gospel, lacking in the discussion is a restoration of a literal kingdom of God in order to fulfill God's promises to Israel. In *Christ-Centered Biblical Theology*, he further related each of the three epochs to the themes of creation, the fall, the flood, Abraham, Moses and the exodus, David, Zion, Solomon and the temple, the Old Testament wisdom literature, and the New Testament mission to the gentiles.[47]

---

44. Goldsworthy, *Preaching the Whole Bible*, 245–47. Goldsworthy's A-B-C structure is nearly identical to the structure seen in Hebert, *Christ the Fulfiller*, 9–12.

45. Goldsworthy, *Gospel and Kingdom*, 54–55; and Goldsworthy, *Gospel and Revelation*, 216.

46. Goldsworthy, *Jesus Through the Old Testament*, 44–46; and Goldsworthy, *Preaching the Whole Bible*, 238.

47. Goldsworthy, *Christ-Centered Biblical Theology*, 159–63.

Graeme Goldsworthy's Christocentric Biblical Theology

In Goldsworthy's earlier writings, Robinson's distinction theology played less of an essential role in his overall contribution to biblical theology. He instead emphasized a Christocentric biblical theology with Christ as the ultimate fulfiller of the Old Testament promises: "The New Testament constantly refers, either explicitly or implicitly, to Christ as the fulfiller of the promises, prophecies and expectations of the Old Testament."[48] This appeared to some as deemphasizing the role of Israel in biblical theology.[49]

Goldsworthy traced his Christocentric biblical theology across various exegetical writings, expanding Robinson's use of the term *Israel*. He applied the term *true Israel* directly to Christ (as did Robinson) but also considered Christ as the representative of the kingdom of God, linking his Christocentric biblical theology to its unifying theme of the kingdom of God: "Jesus is the kingdom of God that has already come in a representative though potent way."[50] Instead of the kingdom of God being fulfilled in a future, literal kingdom, Goldsworthy viewed the kingdom of God as being fulfilled in Christ's first coming through the preaching of the gospel to the nations.

Goldsworthy defined the people of God as a remnant of Israel restored in Christ. He applied the phrase *people of God* directly to Christ as the representative of the true people of God.[51] He traced the concept of the people of God from Israel to a faithful remnant of Israel to its ultimate fulfillment in Christ and those who are in Christ: "The people of God are defined by their union with Christ, a union that in turn is defined by who and what Christ is."[52] One important note is that Goldsworthy's description of those who are in Christ is silent on an ethnic distinction between Jew and gentile, an area Robinson specifically elaborated upon in his distinction theology.

Goldsworthy traced the concept of sonship (Son of God) throughout redemptive history to show how Christ ultimately fulfilled the role as the Son of God. He considered Adam to be the first son of God, viewing multiple representatives of the nation of Israel as various sons of God throughout redemptive history, with Christ being the ultimate Son of God and fulfiller

---

48. Goldsworthy, *Jesus Through the Old Testament*, 51.

49. Barry Horner's critique will be discussed later in the chapter.

50. Goldsworthy, *According to Plan*, 204–6; and "Kingdom of God as Hermeneutic Grid," 14.

51. Goldsworthy, *According to Plan*, 67–68, 204.

52. Goldsworthy, *Gospel and Kingdom*, 110–12: and "Lecture 3," 46.

of God's sonship role in redemptive history: "The son of God, therefore, is first of all Adam, then the nation of Israel, and then this nation's royal representative who is the son of David."[53] The "son of David" in this instance refers to Christ: "Jesus, as God's Son, fulfills the offices of prophet (speaking God's word), priest (making purification for sins), and king (creating, and ruling at the right hand of the Majesty on high). But the Son is not only the mediator of God's act of creation; he is also the upholder of the universe."[54] Believers who are in Christ become sons of God and sons of the resurrection by being in relationship to the resurrected Son of God: "Jesus is declared to be Son of God through his resurrection; we are united to Jesus; our resurrection is established by the resurrection of Jesus. We are thus sons of God because we are sons of the resurrection."[55] He further linked the concept of the Son of God to his definition of the people of God: "Matthew, Mark, and Luke demonstrate that Jesus fulfilled the calling and requirements of the people of God presented in the Old Testament—from Adam to Israel to David. 'Son of God' is the title that belongs to God's people of whom the final and true Son is Jesus."[56]

Goldsworthy's Christocentric biblical theology was his attempt to form a mediating position between covenant theology and dispensationalism (similar to how Robinson made an attempt with his distinction theology). Goldsworthy rejected the view that the church itself becomes the new Israel:

> It has been one of the mistakes of some Reformed theologians to emphasize the role of the church as the new Israel and the new people of God without first highlighting Jesus as the new Israel . . . Yet Jesus indicated that the Old Testament was about him, and thus it is not first and foremost about us.[57]

While Goldsworthy agreed that dispensationalists have a valid point concerning the church as not a new Israel, he did not agree with the theological system of dispensationalism. In its place, he offered a fulfillment theology in Christ: "The term replacement is somewhat pejorative and clouds the issue. I would rather see the emphasis on 'fulfilment theology,'

---

53. Goldsworthy, *Son of God*, 60–70, 84.
54. Goldsworthy, *Son of God*, 52–54.
55. Goldsworthy, *Son of God*, 94–105.
56. Goldsworthy, *Son of God*, 54–56.
57. Goldsworthy, *Christ-Centered Biblical Theology*, 30–33.

with Christ at the centre as the true Israel."[58] However, in Goldsworthy's explanation of fulfillment, it appears that Israel is replaced in the history of redemption by Christ himself and those in Christ. Goldsworthy's position was not a mediating position between covenant theology and dispensationalism but still retained a form of supersessionism, and it was still within a Reformed redemptive-historical biblical theology. He also attempted to use similar language to Robinson concerning the gospel creating one new man in Christ that brings together Jew and gentile: "The story of God's people begins with Adam, and it is to be expected that it will conclude in some way with a new Adam."[59] However, Goldsworthy considered the new Adam to be both Christ and believers in Christ. Robinson limited it to an eschatological new Adam (or new man) of believing Jews and gentiles who are ethnically distinct.

Goldsworthy believed that Christ saved Jews and gentiles: "Evangelicals are committed to the uniqueness of Christ. We reject the notion that all roads lead to God, for the simple reason that the Bible expressly rejects it."[60] While, like Robinson, he did not directly use the term, he did reject a two-covenant theology. He asserted that salvation is found only in Christ: "Christ alone means that salvation is found nowhere else but in the person and work of Jesus Christ."[61] He also stated that he did not consider the Old Testament's program as salvation by works, but that the Messiah (Christ) saves Old Testament and New Testament saints.

> We should be careful to understand election in its Old Testament form. If Israel was elect, does that mean that every Israelite will be in the eternal kingdom? No, it does not.... If a whole generation of Israelites perished in the wilderness, does this mean that they are all excluded from the eternal kingdom? Again, the answer is no.[62]

58. Goldsworthy, *Christ-Centered Biblical Theology*, 30–33.
59. Goldsworthy, *Christ-Centered Biblical Theology*, 60–65, 207–13.
60. Goldsworthy, *Preaching the Whole Bible*, 16–18.
61. Goldsworthy, *Gospel-Centered Hermeneutics*, 47–48.
62. Goldsworthy, *Jesus Through the Old Testament*, 16; and *According to Plan*, 181. Goldsworthy elaborated on the Old Testament form of election as follows: "Undoubtedly the grace of God is the most remarkable feature of his covenant and saving acts. God chooses absolutely without condition a people who deserve nothing. In the course of their history he unfolds to them a way of salvation that not only applies to them, but that will one day in its fullness have significance for all the nations of the earth. From the beginning there can be no dispute that the grace of God means that election is unconditioned by any virtue in those who are chosen, and that salvation is a free gift received by faith alone. But free grace and unconditional election must not be allowed to obscure

Goldsworthy's Christocentric biblical theology caused some critics (such as Barry Horner) to consider it a supersessionist form of biblical theology. In his work *Eternal Israel*, Horner considered Goldsworthy's Christocentric biblical theology to be a Reformed redemptive-historical biblical theology (typical of the biblical theology of the Westminster tradition that follows Vos) that replaced the role of Israel in redemptive history not with the church, but with Christ.[63] He considered Goldsworthy's Christocentric biblical theology as hyper-Christocentric in that Goldsworthy attempted to fit a Christocentric hermeneutic upon the biblical text, even if such biblical passages did not refer to Christ. In his discussion on Goldsworthy, Horner stated that Goldsworthy's biblical theology "is overwhelmed with the centrality of Jesus Christ, and him as the embodiment of the gospel. Doctrinally speaking, this controls everything."[64] He further elaborated on the "hyper-Christocentric" position of Goldsworthy:

> There is such a thing as hyper-Christocentricity, and it is most spiritual to admit it. There is very definitely biblical Christocentricity, yet it is not for us to go to extremes in extending this emphasis, especially in terms of our hermeneutic. Adjusting to this truth requires thinking outside the box, so to speak, so as to return to what exclusively is inside the Book of God.[65]

In the place of a hyper-Christocentric biblical theology that attempted to externally force a Christocentric interpretation and fulfillment

---

the place of God's judgment. We have already seen how judgment was revealed against all wickedness in the days of Noah, against Babel and the sinful city of Sodom, against a hard-hearted Egyptian king and his nation and against the pagan Canaanites. According to the Bible no such judgment ever falls that is not deserved. Such judgments, especially when their execution appears to us to be especially barbaric, must be understood in the light of the complete biblical picture of human rebellion against God. What, then, shall we say about judgment on the elect? Once the saving grace of God is effectively displayed in the exodus from Egypt, the prophetic word concentrates on the nature of the covenant relationship. In the book of Deuteronomy particularly there are stern warnings against turning away from the covenant. Israel is saved by grace alone, but to be saved is not merely to be acquitted of guilt. It is a positive restoration to fellowship with the living God. There is always a real choice in front of the people of God: the way of life or the way of death, covenant blessings or covenant curses." See Goldsworthy, *According to Plan*, 180–81.

63. Horner, *Eternal Israel*, 219–25. Horner labeled Goldsworthy's biblical theology a form of Process Biblical Theology.

64. Horner, *Eternal Israel*, 221.

65. Horner, *Eternal Israel*, 222.

upon biblical texts, Horner argued that it is better to interpret Scripture through a literal hermeneutic that does not weaken nor replace Israel's importance in redemptive history. Unlike Robinson's distinction theology that retained an ethnic distinction between Jew and gentile in the New Testament church, Goldsworthy's biblical theology (in which Christ in his person and in his personal ministry is the fulfillment of the promises to Israel, and those in Christ inherit Israel's promises) weakened the importance of Israel's role in redemptive history and retained a form of supersessionism. Those in Christ, without any form of ethnic distinction between Jew and gentile, are the replacement of Israel.[66]

Goldsworthy later began to appreciate Robinson's distinction theology concerning Israel's role in redemptive history adopting some of its associated interpretations of texts without fully incorporating it into his biblical theology. In one example, he changed his position concerning Rev 7 (he came closer to Robinson's position). He originally placed both groups together as representing the same individuals:

> We notice also in this chapter of Revelation that John uses two distinct word pictures to express his meaning. In the first he portrays the sealing of a perfect number of the people of Israel. It is not his intention to refer to the literal nation of Israel. He has too frequently followed the other writers of the New Testament in applying the old Israelite terminology to the true people of God, the new Israel in Christ, to slip back into Jewish particularism.[67]

He later rejected transferring the title *Israel* concerning the 144,000 to gentiles, instead interpreting the 144,000 in Rev 7 as Jewish believers.[68] His revision also incorporated a distinction between the 144,000 Jewish believers and the great multitude in Revelation as gentile believers. He cited Robinson's distinction theology as helping to revise his position concerning the 144,000 of Rev 7:

---

66. Horner also labeled Moore's biblical theology program as a supersessionist, Reformed biblical theology with a similar theological position to Vos. He also critiqued Jensen's history of the biblical theology program at Moore and his history of Australian Anglican evangelicalism, stating that Jensen "suggests no present distinctive interest by Sydney Anglicanism in Israel and the Jew, especially their remarkable ongoing presence in modern history, albeit in unbelief." See Horner, *Eternal Israel*, 217–18.

67. Goldsworthy, *Gospel and Revelation*, 192. See also Goldsworthy, *Christ-Centered Biblical Theology*, 168–70.

68. Shiner, "Reading the New Testament," 203–4.

I have been spurred on by the writings of Donald Robinson who has written a number of articles in which he cogently argues that the distinction between Jew and Gentile is not lost in the New Testament. That is, although Jew and Gentile believers are made into one new man in Christ (Eph. 2:15), this unity does not remove all distinctions until its final eschatological fulfilment. Paul still maintains that the gospel is "to the Jew first" (Rom. 1:16; 2:9–10). His whole argument regarding his hope for the salvation of the Jew in Romans 9–11 hinges on this distinction. Galatians 3:28 does not remove this distinction any more than it removes the ongoing distinctions between male and female. Oneness in Christ does not mean that all differences are removed. A consequence of this is that I now favour a different interpretation of Revelation 7, namely that the 144,000 symbolizes the perfect number of the saved of Israel, and the great multitude represents the Gentiles saved as a result of Israel's servant status to be a light to the Gentiles.[69]

In *Gospel-Centered Hermeneutics*, Goldsworthy alluded to a third view between dispensationalism and supersessionism in which the church consists of a restored Israel of believing Jews plus gentiles who share in Israel's blessings. He incorporated some of Robinson's position into this view, without emphasizing Robinson's distinction theology:

> A third view takes the Old Testament ideas of the ingathering of the Gentiles to the restored Israel as worked out in that the gospel is to the Jew first. The church then consists of the restored or spiritual Israel (Christian Jews) plus the converted Gentiles who are privileged to share in Israel's blessings. This preserves the structure of the covenant promises to Abraham.[70]

In his *Christ-Centered Biblical Theology*, Goldsworthy provided his clearest elaboration on Robinson's legacy concerning Israel and the church. While the people of God include a few gentiles, their inclusion came about through an acceptance of the God of Israel. During the exile, the prophets spoke of the day of the Lord in which Israel will bless the gentiles and become the focus of the people of God: "The Gentiles are not seen as replacing Israel or, it would seem, as ceasing to be Gentiles. Israel will be a light to lighten the Gentiles. Israel, the priestly nation, becomes the means through which Gentiles can become God's people

---

69. Goldsworthy, *Christ-Centered Biblical Theology*, 169.
70. Goldsworthy, *Gospel-Centered Hermeneutics*, 245.

along with Israel."[71] Goldsworthy also elaborated on Robinson's concept that while the same gospel of Christ saves Jewish and gentile believers, Jews retain their ethnic distinctions within the New Testament church. Their salvation in Christ brings about the fullness of their Jewishness: "It is all the more understandable that the Jewishness of Jesus is emphasized. By embracing Jesus, Jewish Christians have not forsaken their Jewishness but rather have entered into its fullness."[72]

Goldsworthy also considered Robinson's distinction theology as not a form of dispensationalism but a mediating position. Christianity was the "beginning of the fulfilment of the covenant promises to Abraham as these are developed in Old Testament prophetic eschatology . . . salvation comes to Israel first, and only then are the Gentiles included."[73] He further elaborated on Robinson's mediating position by not equating it with dispensationalism:

> It would be wrong to suppose that Robinson has simply capitulated to the Dispensationalists' view, which keeps Israel and the church separate—for distinction is not the same as separation. . . . Only by maintaining the distinction can we accommodate Jesus' claim that "salvation is from the Jews" (John 4:22), or Paul's insistence that the gospel brings salvation "to the Jew first and also to the Greek." (Rom. 1:16; 2:10)[74]

Goldsworthy also agreed with Robinson's rejection of Christian restorationism's advocating for restoring a Jewish nation in the land of Israel on what he claimed where biblical and hermeneutical grounds. While Goldsworthy used the terms *renewed Canaan* and *new earth* to refer to the eschatological fulfillment of the promised land, like Robinson, he considered the discussion of the land of Israel to have subsided in the New Testament after Christ's fulfillment.[75] Unlike Robinson, he did not directly cite W. D. Davies's *Gospel and the Land* in his rejection of Christian restorationism. However, Davies's position on the land of Israel seemed to shape Goldsworthy's view in a similar manner to that of Robinson. Goldsworthy rejected the movement of Christian restorationism (he referred to it as Christian Zionism), stating that the New Testament does not support such a "literal

---

71. Goldsworthy, *Christ-Centered Biblical Theology*, 207–13.
72. Goldsworthy, *Son of God*, 52–54.
73. Goldsworthy, *Christ-Centered Biblical Theology*, 170–72.
74. Goldsworthy, *Christ-Centered Biblical Theology*, 207–13.
75. Goldsworthy, *According to Plan*, 192–93; and *Jesus Through the Old Testament*, 68.

fulfillment of prophecy": "Christian Zionism not only reshapes the New Testament's view of the future, but also affects the present period in which such a future is anticipated."[76] He considered eschatological Zion (Israel) to be "where Jesus reigns now at the right hand of God and this is where we come by faith in the gospel," applying this concept to his unifying theme of the kingdom of God: "For the New Testament the locality of the Kingdom is Jesus Christ himself. And, lest we be misled by a misplaced and unbiblical emphasis, Jesus Christ is shown as risen and seated on the right hand of God in the heavenly places."[77] Both Robinson and Goldsworthy rejected premillennialism because, in their view, there is no distinct future fulfillment in Christ's fulfillment of all Old Testament prophecies:

> It seems that Robinson does not subscribe to the distinction that some make between prophecies of the first coming and those of the second coming of Christ. The distinction is rather between the fulfilment of all prophecy in Christ's first coming, and the consummation of all prophecy that is yet to come at his *parousia*.[78]

Goldsworthy and Robinson interpreted Rev 20 through the lens of amillennialism, referencing the Old Testament prophets as the theological grounding for such an interpretation: "That is, literalism cannot survive because the prophets did not promise a future involving both the literal restoration of Israel *and* the gospel."[79] While he rejected the movement of Christian restorationism, he did consider Jewish salvation to be important: "One does not have to be a Zionist to appreciate Paul's emphasis on God's method of salvation, in that the gospel is 'to the Jew first.'"[80] In contrast to Christian restorationism, Goldsworthy did not believe in a future national salvation of Israel but did agree with offering salvation to both Jews and gentiles in the present:

---

76. Goldsworthy, *Gospel-Centered Hermeneutics*, 170–71.

77. Goldsworthy, *Gospel and Kingdom*, 112–15. In addition to his rejection of a future restoration of a Jewish nation in the land of Israel, Goldsworthy's Christocentric fulfillment of the kingdom of God also considered Christ to be the new temple, eliminating the need of a future millennial temple. See Goldsworthy, "Lecture 3," 39–40.

78. Goldsworthy, *Christ-Centered Biblical Theology*, 213–15. Goldsworthy did not directly defend nor argue against Robinson's position concerning Christ's kingdom. He merely mentioned it. However, he seemed to be in silent agreement with Robinson's position.

79. Goldsworthy, *Gospel and the Revelation*, 292–96.

80. Goldsworthy, *Gospel-Centered Hermeneutics*, 171.

> Some have used this statement to reinforce a view that Jesus was indicating that there are two different events to come: one is the restoration of the kingdom to Israel as a specifically Jewish salvation; the other is the world mission to the gentiles through the gospel. . . . This, I suggest, does not fit the biblical facts, and we should understand Jesus to be saying that the kingdom is indeed being restored, but it will come to Jew and gentile alike through the preaching of the gospel.[81]

Goldsworthy popularized a Christocentric biblical theology (that shared a Reformed redemptive-historical biblical theology similar in teaching with covenant theologians such as Vos) that incorporated some of Robinson's teachings (such as developing Robinson's three stages into his three epochs) but lacked any discussion of Robinson's distinction theology concerning Jew and gentile in his early writings. Goldsworthy's popularizing of Moore's biblical theology program occurred in tandem with the eclipsing of Robinson's distinction theology by Goldsworthy's Reformed, redemptive-historical, Christocentric biblical theology. His biblical theology in which the promises of the Abrahamic covenant are fulfilled ultimately in Christ and in those who are in Christ retained a form of supersessionism (as rightly noted by Horner) and were not a mediating position between dispensationalism and supersessionism. Like Robinson, he also (unfortunately) retained a rejection of Christian restorationism (Christian Zionism) or any literal future fulfillment of Israel's land promises. Unlike Robinson, he also rejected a future national salvation of Israel, but he did agree with Robinson that Jewish evangelism should be practiced. He later appreciated some of Robinson's distinction theology, using Robinson's position as a lens to modify some aspects of his interpretations (such as how he interpreted the 144,000 in Rev 7). However, he never fully incorporated Robinson's

---

81. Goldsworthy, *Preaching the Whole Bible*, 238. Goldsworthy referred to Acts 1 concerning "this statement": "The disciples had accepted the generally held Jewish idea that the coming of the Messiah would mean the unambiguously final advent of the kingdom of God. Jesus' death disappointed them, but their hope was revived by the resurrection. Surely the kingdom would now appear, and hence the question to that effect in Acts 1:6, 'Will you now restore the kingdom to Israel?' The answer that Jesus gives indicates that this question is misplaced. We must assume that his answer is not a put-down but a genuine answer to the question. He tells them, 'You will receive power when the Holy Spirit comes upon you; and you will be my witnesses in Jerusalem, in all Judea and Samaria, and to the ends of the earth' (Acts 1:8)." Goldsworthy also dismissed that Acts 1:6 referred to a literal restoration of the kingdom, instead that the restoration of the kingdom comes about through the preaching of the gospel equally to both Jew and gentile.

distinction theology into his biblical theology. Due to Goldsworthy's biblical theology becoming popular among pastors and nonacademic audiences, he attracted an interest in Moore's biblical theology program. His contribution to Moore's biblical theology program through his numerous published works drew the attention of the masses to Moore College, even though Robinson's distinction theology cannot clearly be seen in Goldsworthy's writings (except in minor areas where Goldsworthy "appreciated" Robinson's legacy). Some of Goldsworthy's successors (such as Vaughan Roberts, Richard Gibson, Brian Rosner, Peter O'Brien, and Paul Williamson) carried forward at least some (at times all) of Goldsworthy's Christocentric biblical theology while also being silent concerning Robinson's distinction theology. Goldsworthy's later appreciation of some aspects of Robinson's distinction theology were more fully appreciated by future Moore scholars, including Lionel Windsor and additional scholars (see chapter 6).

Vaughan Roberts

Vaughan Roberts (1965–) studied Goldsworthy's biblical theology (particularly Goldsworthy's *Gospel and Kingdom*) and brought Goldsworthy's biblical theology to the average lay Christian in his work *God's Big Picture*. Roberts agreed with Goldsworthy's Christocentric biblical theology and Robinson's concept of promise and fulfillment by tracing promise throughout the Old Testament and fulfillment throughout the New Testament. Roberts agreed with Goldsworthy's concept that the kingdom of God is the central unifying theme of Scripture, also including the importance of the idea of covenant in Scripture without making it his main unifying theme of Scripture. Roberts modified Goldsworthy's thesis from *Gospel and Kingdom* in *God's Big Picture* as "God's people in God's place under God's rule and blessing."[82]

Roberts traced Goldsworthy's concept of three epochs through an eightfold grand narrative of Scripture. In the Old Testament, Roberts surveyed the pattern of the kingdom in the garden of Eden and the perished kingdom in the fall, the promised kingdom in the Abrahamic covenant, the partial kingdom in Israel's history leading up to the monarchy, and the prophesied kingdom during Israel's exile and the Old Testament prophets. In the New Testament, Roberts surveyed the present kingdom inaugurated by Christ, the proclaimed kingdom after the death and resurrection

---

82. Roberts, *God's Big Picture*, 9, 17, 21–22, 50.

of Christ, and the perfected kingdom in the eschaton.[83] He believed that a common salvation for Jews and gentiles could be traced back to the Abrahamic covenant: "Right from the very start God's plan of salvation was universal; it encompassed all nations." He further elaborated on the salvation covenant's Christological fulfillment in the New Testament: "He [Abraham] was accepted by God, not on the basis of his own goodness, but by faith in the promises of God. That has always been the way of salvation for sinful human beings . . . that same gospel has now been finally fulfilled in Jesus Christ."[84]

Like Robinson, Roberts stressed the significance of believers in Christ forming a new humanity with Christ as the new Adam: "As a result, if we trust in him, we enter into a new humanity, headed not by Adam, the sinner, but by Jesus, the righteous new Adam."[85] Unlike Robinson, he did not make any distinction between Jew and gentile concerning the people of God: "He, and those from all nations who trust in him, are God's people; and we can look forward to enjoying the fullness of God's blessing, not on earth, but in heaven, the new Jerusalem."[86] Like Goldsworthy, he viewed Christ as the new Israel although he modified Goldsworthy's position by directly applying the language of the new Israel to the church in a supersessionist fashion:

> He is calling together a new Israel, with twelve disciples as the foundation, rather than twelve tribes. . . . The old Israel rejects Jesus and will, in turn, be rejected by God. . . . From now on the true Israel is not focused on the land of Palestine and does not consist of those who are physically descended from Abraham. It rather consists of his spiritual descendants: those, both Jew and Gentile, who follow his example and place their trust in God's promise fulfilled in Jesus. . . . The new Israel is the church, all those who trust in Christ. Peter writes to a Christian audience, consisting primarily of Gentiles, and boldly applies to them some of the titles that had previously been the property of the Israelites alone. . . . The true Israelite, or member of the people of God, is not simply someone who is physically descended from Abraham and outwardly obeys the Jewish law, but rather the converted believer in Christ.[87]

83. Roberts, *God's Big Picture*, 24–26.
84. Roberts, *God's Big Picture*, 53–55 (bracketed text added).
85. Roberts, *God's Big Picture*, 117–18.
86. Roberts, *God's Big Picture*, 55.
87. Roberts, *God's Big Picture*, 117–18, 138–39.

Roberts further developed Robinson's position of rejecting Christian restorationism by placing Christ as the fulfillment of the promises of the Abrahamic covenant while rejecting a future restoration of a Jewish nation of Israel:

> The New Testament never leads us to expect that there will be any fulfilment of the Old Testament promises other than their fulfilment in Christ.... We are not encouraged, for example, to look for their fulfilment in the State of Israel.... That is to expect a renewal of the model that has now been dismantled. The permanent reality is found in Christ.[88]

The language of *nation*, *temple*, and *land* are, according to Roberts, to be considered symbolic language that is not to be literally fulfilled but to be Christologically fulfilled: "In a similar way, God made his promises to Israel in ways they could understand. He used categories they were familiar with, such as the nation, the temple and material prosperity in the land. But the fulfilment breaks the boundaries of those categories. To expect a literal fulfilment is to miss the point."[89]

Richard Gibson

Richard Gibson (1960–), who has lectured at Moore College, contributed to the session on "Biblical Theology at Moore" at the 2011 ETS National Meeting. He stated that biblical theology is deeply embedded in him due to his time serving at Moore. His paper surveyed the descriptive task and provided an informative snapshot of the biblical theology program at Moore. The program aims to give students a deeper understanding of "God's message to us in the form it actually takes."[90]

Gibson's paper primarily focused on the Introduction to the Bible course originally developed by Robinson (which is now part of Moore's External Studies Department to train church members or ministry leaders in theological studies). The course has also been used as a predecessor and gateway toward formal education in biblical theology at Moore College. Introduction to the Bible is one of five required courses at Moore,

---

88. Roberts, *God's Big Picture*, 114–15.

89. Roberts, *God's Big Picture*, 115.

90. Gibson, "Biblical Theology at Moore." "God's message to us in the form it actually takes" is a definition of biblical theology Gibson gives in his lecture.

covering the message of the Bible as a whole and how the message of the Bible unfolds from beginning to end. The course also teaches how each biblical book relates to the Bible historically and theologically while also teaching the task of biblical theology. While Robinson originally taught the course, the course now surveys a Christocentric biblical theology based on Goldsworthy's *Gospel and Kingdom*. In 2007, a course on Promise to Fulfillment was added to the program, which builds upon Introduction to the Bible and teaches an inductive approach to Bible study while providing a primer on biblical interpretation. One cannot complete a BD or a BTh at Moore without completing the core biblical theology courses (BD students can complete a course in hermeneutics further in the program).[91]

Gibson's paper possibly alluded to Robinson's legacy at Moore through the structure of Moore's biblical theology courses but not the content of such courses. Moore continues to offer the Introduction to the Bible course, and the college added a course on Promise to Fulfillment (Robinson considered promise and fulfillment as central to his understanding of biblical theology). However, in terms of the course content in Moore's biblical theology program, the primary position that Gibson attempted to equate with Moore is Goldsworthy's Christocentric biblical theology (as seen in his early work *Gospel and Kingdom*). Notably absent from Gibson's paper is any reference to Robinson's distinction theology or a significant contribution concerning Israel's role in redemptive history. While Gibson served as the editor for the 1996 Moore School of Theology's publication of its papers in *Interpreting God's Plan: Biblical Theology and the Pastor*, a contribution from Gibson concerning Robinson's distinction theology concerning Jew and gentile and how he would incorporate it into Moore's curriculum would be valuable for the future development of Moore's biblical theology program.[92]

Brian Rosner

Brian Rosner (1959–) is a scholar at Moore College who also studied at Dallas Theological Seminary. Two of his main contributions to the biblical theology program at Moore include his work as one of the editors and

---

91. Gibson, "Biblical Theology at Moore."

92. It is possible that Gibson did not consider Robinson's distinction theology as a significant issue since he primarily followed Goldsworthy as the primary contributor to Moore's biblical theology program.

contributors to the *New Dictionary of Biblical Theology* and his 2011 ETS paper titled "Biblical Theology at Moore: Reflections on One Scholar's Research." In his article in the *New Dictionary of Biblical Theology* on biblical theology, Rosner asserted that "the task of biblical theology is to present the teaching of the Bible about God and his relations to the world in a way that lets the biblical texts set the agenda," in contrast to systematic theology, which includes extra-biblical discussion of the Christian faith.[93] He further defined biblical theology as that which "explores the Bible's rich and many-sided presentation of its unified message. It is committed to declaring 'the whole counsel of God . . . [in order] to feed the church of God.'"[94] Rosner agreed with Goldsworthy's Christocentric biblical theology in that Christ united both testaments: "Indeed, the Messiah is the theme which unites the Old and New Testaments. . . . If biblical theology seeks to connect text and truth . . . it never forgets that Jesus is the truth."[95]

In his ETS paper, Rosner considered biblical theology to be more of a bridge than a destination, a process more than a product. To Rosner, biblical theology is not the end goal of biblical studies, but it is a tool in aiding readers to understand the whole counsel of God. Biblical theology provides a bridge between biblical exegesis and systematic theology. Additionally, he considered the method and approach to biblical theology of more importance than attempting to define biblical theology. While Rosner still defined biblical theology (in his *New Dictionary of Biblical Theology* article), he preferred that scholars spend less time attempting elaborate definitions of biblical theology and simply go about the task of doing biblical theology. His goal in his contribution to biblical theology is to answer the following questions: First, does the Bible itself provide a central theme? Second, is there a place for Jewish intertestamental literature in biblical theology?[96] Finally, should readers of the Bible always expect continuity between the testaments?[97] To answer his first question, he discussed biblical theology's versatility by attempting to uncover a central unifying theme in how biblical theology examines the relationship between both testaments, elaborating on his article in the *New Dictionary of Biblical Theology*. His paper first examined the classic concepts that theologians have presented for a unifying

---

93. Rosner, "Biblical Theology," 5–6.
94. Rosner, "Biblical Theology," 9–10 (bracketed text added).
95. Rosner, "Biblical Theology," 10.
96. See Chapman and Köstenberger, "Jewish Intertestamental Literature."
97. See Baker, *Two Testaments, One Bible*.

theme of Scripture (including covenant, kingdom of God, and promise and fulfillment), explaining that biblical theology is versatile in that there are other major unifying themes of biblical theology. Two examples Rosner provided include clothes (from the clothing of Adam and Eve in the garden of Eden to the clothing of the resurrected bodies in the eschaton) and violence (how biblical theology begins with a fallen world in the garden of Eden that moves toward redemption in Christ).[98] He observed that there are multiple avenues in which one can express a central theme of biblical theology. Biblical theologians can choose one of the classic concepts or innovate a biblical theology around additional concepts (such as the two examples Rosner provided). Unlike Robinson and Goldsworthy, Rosner did not settle on one particular central or unifying theme of Scripture. To answer his second question, he asserted that Jewish intertestamental literature does provide a helpful background study for biblical theology, as Jewish intertestamental literature can shed some valuable light on the historical and ethical context of the New Testament (as New Testament ethics is Rosner's other major field of study). To answer his last question, Rosner stated that one cannot always trace a continuity between both testaments. This is possibly due to Rosner's decision not to settle on one unifying theme of Scripture. If there are multiple avenues in which scholars can present a central or unifying theme of Scripture, then the continuity between both testaments may not always be clearly traced.[99]

While Rosner briefly mentioned the relationship between Jew and gentile as a significant theme within biblical theology, he did not directly address his position on Israel's role in redemptive history in his paper.[100] Many of his other writings primarily focus on Paul's moral and ethical writings without directly addressing Israel's role in redemptive history or the relationship between Jew and gentile in the church. As one who has been involved with both Moore College and Dallas Theological Seminary, this contribution from Rosner would benefit the future development of the biblical theology discussion at Moore. It would be helpful to determine how much of Dallas Theological Seminary's position on dispensationalism

---

98. For examples of theologians who have presented classic concepts of a unifying theme of Scripture: J. I. Packer (chapter 2) is an example of covenant, Goldsworthy is an example of kingdom of God, and Robinson (chapter 3) is an example of promise and fulfillment.

99. Rosner, "Biblical Theology at Moore."

100. Rosner, "Biblical Theology at Moore."

affected Rosner's understanding of biblical theology and where Rosner aligns with or departs from Robinson's distinction theology.

Peter O'Brien

Peter O'Brien (1935–) is a scholar at Moore College who reached an exegetical conclusion concerning the term ἐκκλησία similar to Robinson in which ἐκκλησία is viewed as ultimately a heavenly reality. He also agreed with Robinson's position on ἐκκλησία as applying to local gatherings of believers, not a national church or earthly universal church since an earthly universal church cannot gather all at once. The goal of the Christian is to gather in a heavenly, eschatological assembly, with the local church being "earthly manifestations of that heavenly assembly gathered around God and Christ."[101] He considered Jew and gentile as becoming a new man in Christ:

> A particularly important motif in Ephesians is the reconciliation of Jew and Gentile to God "in one body" (*en heni somati*, 2:16) through the cross. In a passage which shows how Gentiles have been made heirs of God's promises (2:11–22), the apostle focuses attention upon Christ's peacemaking work upon the cross. God's purpose was to create out of the two great divisions of mankind "a single new humanity" in Christ (2:15 NEB). This has been effected by reconciling Jew and Gentile to God in the body of Christ (cf. 3:3–6): the expression "one body" refers, not to the physical body of Christ on the cross (spoken of as "his flesh" in v. 15), but to the church of which Jewish and Gentile believers are alike members, and it is equivalent to "the one new man" of v. 15.[102]

However, unlike Robinson, his concept of a new man eliminated the distinction between Jew and gentile while they were still in the New Testament church ("the church of which Jewish and Gentile believers are alike members"), not in an eschatological new man. He retained a form of ecclesiological supersessionism while Robinson's retaining of a form of supersessionism occurred eschatologically.

---

101. O'Brien, "Church as a Heavenly," 90–93, 97.
102. O'Brien, "Church as a Heavenly," 110–11.

Paul Williamson

Paul Williamson is another scholar at Moore who defined biblical theology as "a holistic enterprise tracing unfolding theological trajectories throughout Scripture and exploring no biblical concept, theme or book in isolation from the whole."[103] Williamson carried forward a Christocentric biblical theology similar to that of Goldsworthy: "Each concept, theme or book is considered ultimately in terms of how it contributes to and advances the Bible's metanarrative, typically understood in terms of a salvation history that progresses towards and culminates in Jesus Christ."[104] Williamson placed covenant as his major unifying theme of biblical theology and the theological center of Scripture.[105] His significant contribution to the biblical theology program at Moore is how he defined the concept of covenant as that which "ratifies an already forged or existing elective relationship" and "involves the making of solemn promises by means of a verbal and/or enacted oath."[106]

Williamson disagreed with Robinson's position concerning the use of the term *people of God*, applying it not only to Israel in the Old Testament but to the church in the New Testament without any ethnic distinctions, not just to a Jewish nucleus of believers: "One of the obvious contrasts between the Old and New Testaments is that in each the people of God are different. In one God's saving activity focuses primarily on a national entity (i.e. ethnic Israel); in the other such focus centres on an international community (i.e. the global Church)."[107] Paul served as an example of one who thought the New Testament church fulfilled the promises of the Abrahamic covenant. Not only is Abraham a father of a great nation, but a father of many nations, in which the seed of Abraham is more than a single nation. Williamson alluded to this concept of many nations in his explanation of the Abrahamic covenant: "No longer is the emphasis on a national entity that will stem from Abraham. Instead, the primary focus is transferred to an international community to whom Abraham will mediate blessing."[108] The fulfillment of Abraham's offspring are the spiritual offspring of faith in

---

103. Williamson, *Sealed with an Oath*, 17. See also "Covenant," in *New Dictionary of Biblical Theology*; and "Covenant," in *Dictionary of the Old Testament*.

104. Williamson, *Sealed with an Oath*, 17.

105. Williamson, *Sealed with an Oath*, 19–20, 29, 30–34.

106. Williamson, *Sealed with an Oath*, 42.

107. Williamson, "Abraham, Israel, and the Church," 99.

108. Williamson, *Sealed with an Oath*, 82–84.

Christ, with their complete fulfillment occurring in a new eschatological community as prophesied in the book of Revelation: "While certainly including biological descendants of Abraham, this new covenant community is not defined by biological ancestry but rather by spiritual descent."[109] Williamson used the language of an ideal Israel as the fulfillment of the new covenant in Isaiah, Jeremiah, and Ezekiel: "Thus the new covenant projects the ultimate fulfilment of the divine promises on to an ideal Israel (i.e. a community of faith) located in a rejuvenated universe (Isa. 65:17; 66:22)." He carried forward the concept of an ideal Israel fulfilled in Christ and the church into the book of Acts: "Jesus as the fulfilment of the Old Testament's messianic hope and the church as the people of God, the genuine heirs of the covenant promises in the Old Testament."[110] In agreement with Goldsworthy, Christ is the ultimate fulfillment of the promises to Abraham and the representative true Israel that brings salvation to the nations. Williamson also believed that ethnic identity was never the sole requirement for salvation or to inherit the promises made to Abraham, not even to Old Testament Israel. In Rom 9–11, salvation is solely in Christ. The branches of unbelieving Israel have been broken off, and they do not inherit the promises of the Abrahamic covenant. He retained a form of supersessionism by applying the promises of the Abrahamic covenant to include the spiritual descendants of Abraham, the New Testament church, both Jews and gentiles without ethnic distinctions.[111] He also (unfortunately) rejected Christian restorationism's importance concerning the land of Israel (especially a literal fulfillment of Israel's land promises) in a similar manner to that of Robinson by stating the New Testament considered the physical (land) promises of the Abrahamic covenant to be subservient to the spiritual (salvation) promises.[112]

Conclusion

Goldsworthy popularized a Christocentric biblical theology through his various published works (especially *Gospel and Kingdom* and *According to Plan*) which helped in turn to popularize Moore's biblical theology program. While he incorporated some of Robinson's teachings into his

---

109. Williamson, *Sealed with an Oath*, 146.
110. Williamson, *Sealed with an Oath*, 179–81, 185–86.
111. Williamson, *Sealed with an Oath*, 183–85, 188–92.
112. Williamson, "Abraham, Israel and the Church," 99, 101, 115–17.

biblical theology (such as developing Robinson's three stages into the three epochs of redemptive history), his early writings lacked Robinson's distinction theology concerning Jew and gentile in his position and instead incorporated a Reformed, redemptive-historical, Christocentric biblical theology. While he attempted to articulate a mediating position between dispensationalism and supersessionism in that Christ is the fulfillment (not the replacement) of Israel's promises, his position retained another form of supersessionism (that Israel was replaced by Christ and believers in Christ). As critics (such as Barry Horner) began to point out that Goldsworthy did not eliminate supersessionism in his position, he appeared to rediscover and appreciate some of Robinson's distinction theology concerning Jew and gentile. He used it as a lens to adjust some of his theological positions (such as the 144,000 in Revelation) while not fully incorporating it into his biblical theology.

Goldsworthy's paper, "Biblical Theology at Moore: Origins and Guiding Principles," presented by Constantine Campbell at the 2011 ETS conference outlined what he (Goldsworthy) referred to as the "commonality of a Moore College approach to biblical theology."[113] He offered the following theological distinctives of a Moore College approach to biblical theology: First, the "authority, reliability, and unity of Scripture," second, the "centrality of Jesus," third, a "redemptive-historical structure of biblical revelation," and finally, "typology in relationship of the Old and New Testament."[114] Notably absent from Goldsworthy's four distinctives is Robinson's distinction theology or any reference to the role of Jew and gentile or Israel and the church in redemptive history. While Goldsworthy appreciated Robinson's distinction theology in his later writings, he never fully incorporated it into his understanding of a Moore College approach to biblical theology.[115]

---

113. Campbell, "Biblical Theology at Moore."

114. Campbell, "Biblical Theology at Moore." Goldsworthy's definition of an evangelical biblical theology, his discussion of a Christocentric biblical theology, and his concept of the three epochs elaborate on each of these four theological distinctives. Robinson's concept of the three stages in chapter 3 also elaborate on the third and fourth distinctives.

115. Moore College has now made biblical theology a required subject of all its degree and certificate programs, testifying to the importance of biblical theology at the college. The college has also applied the distinctives of a Moore College approach to biblical theology, such as its annual Moore College School of Biblical Theology conference at the college. The conference has allowed scholars at Moore College to continue further contributing to the biblical theology program at Moore. One significant application was the 1997 work produced due to the conference lectures of the Moore College School of Biblical Theology, *Interpreting God's Plan*. See Campbell, "Biblical Theology at Moore."

All of the scholars at Moore College who were successors to Goldsworthy would agree with his four distinctives of a Moore College approach to biblical theology. Each would affirm the "authority, reliability, and unity of Scripture," the "centrality of Jesus," a "redemptive-historical structure of biblical revelation," and "typology in relationship of the Old and New Testament."[116] Vaughan Roberts, Richard Gibson, Brian Rosner, Peter O'Brien, and Paul Williamson were in agreement with at least some (or all) of Goldsworthy's Christocentric biblical theology, but like Goldsworthy, were silent concerning Robinson's distinction theology. Roberts popularized Goldsworthy's Christocentric biblical theology in a structure that could be understood by the lay Christian while ignoring any concept of Robinson's distinction theology. Gibson primarily considered Moore's biblical theology program as teaching Goldsworthy's Christocentric biblical theology and was absent on a discussion concerning Israel's role in redemptive history. Rosner agreed with at least some aspects of Goldsworthy's Christocentric biblical theology while being silent concerning Israel's role in redemptive history. O'Brien agreed that Christ is the fulfillment of the true Israel, but, unlike Robinson, his concept of a new man eliminated the ethnic distinction between Jew and gentile while part of the New Testament church. Williamson agreed with much of Goldsworthy's Christocentric biblical theology but also considered the New Testament church as the true Israel.

---

116. Campbell, "Biblical Theology at Moore."

5

Fully Departed from Robinson

D. Broughton Knox, William Dumbrell, and Their Successors' Reformed Redemptive History Approaches to Biblical Theology

Introduction

LIKE GOLDSWORTHY, THE CONTRIBUTIONS of D. Broughton Knox and William Dumbrell to Moore's biblical theology program also departed from Robinson's distinction theology and are two additional examples of typical Reformed redemptive history approaches to biblical theology. Unlike Goldsworthy, neither scholar showed a later appreciation of Robinson's distinction theology in their contributions to Moore's biblical theology program. Four of their successors (Peter Bolt, Barry Webb, Kevin Giles, and Malcolm Richards) also departed from Robinson's distinction theology and, like Knox and Dumbrell, never showed a later appreciation of Robinson's distinction theology in their writings.

Biographical Sketch of D. Broughton Knox

D. Broughton Knox (1916–1994) studied classics and Greek at the University of Sydney. He completed his bachelor of divinity at St. John's College, Highbury (University of London, later the London College of Divinity), under T. W. Gilbert. He completed his master of theology in biblical and historical theology from London University.[1] He completed his DPhil in Reformation studies at Oxford in 1953 with his thesis "The

1. Kuhn, *Ecclesiology of Donald Robinson*, 132–35.

Doctrine of Faith in the Reign of Henry VIII."[2] He contributed to the *New Bible Handbook* and *New Bible Dictionary* and contributed his first journal article to the *EvQ* in 1941.[3] He was also a consulting editor of the *RTR* beginning in 1947.[4] He contributed some articles for the *RTR* but wrote little for an academic audience. He delivered most of his contributions outside of *RTR* in chapel or conference messages (except his contributions to the *Australian Church Record*).[5]

Knox first served as curate at St. Andrew the Less in Cambridge, also spending four years as a chaplain in the Royal Navy. He first taught at Cambridge, where he interacted with members of the InterVarsity Fellowship (IVF, including Stuart Barton Babbage). The IVF led to the formation of Tyndale House, Cambridge.[6] He was also a tutor and New Testament lecturer at Wycliffe Hall and an assistant curate at St. Aldate's. Most of his ministry work occurred during his service at Moore College. He began his career at Moore as a residential tutor under T. C. Hammond (later appointed vice principal under Marcus Loane in 1954), and he became involved in Moore's student ministry. He was later appointed principal under Archbishop Mowll. He grew the college to include degree programs in theology, working with London University on offering a BD and the Australian College of Theology offering a BTh. He expanded the library at Moore, moving the campus near the University of Sydney. His approach to education at Moore focused on biblical scholarship instead of practical theological education. However, his emphasis on biblical scholarship was to train pastors, focusing his education for the church, not merely the academy.[7] He retired as Moore's principal in 1985, serving the longest term as principal of the college.[8] He continued lecturing at Moore until

---

2. See Knox, *Doctrine of Faith*.
3. His first journal article was "The Date of the Epistle to the Galatians."
4. O'Brien, *God Who Is Rich in Mercy*, xiv.
5. Kuhn, *Ecclesiology of Donald Robinson*, 132–35. See also Knox, "D. B. Knox: The Authority of the Bible"; and *D. Broughton Knox: Selected Works*.
6. IVF is a member of the International Fellowship of Evangelical Students (IFES). For a history of the IVF and IFES, see Hunt and Hunt, *For Christ and the University*; and Johnson, *Brief History*. For more on Stuart Babbage, see New College, "Rev. Dr. Stuart Barton Babbage AM." For a history of Tyndale House, see Noble, *Tyndale House and Fellowship*.
7. Kuhn, *Ecclesiology of Donald Robinson*, 132–35.
8. O'Brien, *God Who Is Rich in Mercy*, xi–xv.

1988 when he founded George Whitefield College in Cape Town, South Africa. He retired from George Whitefield College in 1992.[9]

Knox was a member of the Faith and Order Commission in the World Council of Churches and participated in the 1952 Commission at Lund, attending as a representative for the Australian Church of England at the World Council of Churches Assembly at Evanston and the 1954 Anglican Congress at Minneapolis.[10] He became a canon of St. Andrew's Cathedral in 1959, serving on the Prayer Book Commission and the church's Doctrine Commission. He served on the board of the Australian College of Theology, the Board of Studies in Divinity at the University of Sydney, and participated in the Fellowship for Biblical Studies.[11] He was a general synod, synod, and standing committee member in the Sydney Diocese.[12]

D. Broughton Knox's Understanding of Ecclesiology

Knox primarily focused on the doctrine of God in his theological contributions, but like Robinson, his most well-known theological legacy was his contributions to ecclesiology. Kuhn noted that Knox considered ecclesiology an area within Anglican evangelicalism that needed further doctrinal development.[13] Robinson and Knox taught ecclesiology and developed most of their ecclesiology during their careers at Moore. Their positions on ecclesiology have been collectively considered the Knox-Robinson view of ecclesiology by numerous scholars, although neither Robinson nor Knox used the label to refer to their understandings of ecclesiology.[14] Knox

---

9. Kuhn, *Ecclesiology of Donald Robinson*, 132–35.

10. For more on the World Council of Churches, see "World Council of Churches," in *Oxford Dictionary of the Christian Church*.

11. O'Brien, *God Who Is Rich in Mercy*, xiv–xvi. For more on the Australian College of Theology see "About—History." For a history of the Fellowship for Biblical Studies see "History."

12. Kuhn, *Ecclesiology of Donald Robinson*, 132–35.

13. Kuhn, *Ecclesiology of Donald Robinson*, 134–35.

14. Kuhn summarized a Knox-Robinson view of ecclesiology in *Ecclesiology of Donald Robinson*, 207–13. See also Thompson, "Knox/Robinson for Today." Shiner also referred to the Knox-Robinson view of ecclesiology in "Reading the New Testament," 98. Robinson (see chapter 3) attempted to distance himself from the label Knox-Robinson view of ecclesiology. While he agreed that he and Knox played a role in each other's understanding of ecclesiology, Robinson believed that both he and Knox were at enough theological variance concerning their ecclesiological conclusions where the label Knox-Robinson view of ecclesiology was not a fitting label concerning their ecclesiological

contributed a handful of articles concerning ecclesiology to the *Australian Church Record*. However, he never wrote a substantial work on ecclesiology (his contributions concerning ecclesiology have been pieced together through his writings and notes).[15] Kuhn produced the first synthesis of Knox's understanding of ecclesiology and evaluated the Knox-Robinson view of ecclesiology in his work *The Ecclesiology of Donald Robinson and D. Broughton Knox*. He surveyed areas where Knox and Robinson were in agreement and where both scholars varied from each other.[16]

Knox linked his understanding of ecclesiology with his understanding of the doctrine of God since he considered the church is where believers are in fellowship with each other and God. He considered the Word of God the "distinguishing mark of Christian fellowship" and a parallel between the concept of fellowship within the Trinity and human fellowship within the church.[17] Knox, like Robinson, defined ἐκκλησία as a gathering, further nuancing a Christian ἐκκλησία as a "gathering of believers around Christ" and that the church is an "activity of the people of God."[18] Knox also agreed with Robinson that the ἐκκλησία is found within the local assembly of believers (by stating the "local church is essential to the nature of the church"), as well as any concept of a universal church is solely a spiritual heavenly reality, rejecting the universal church as an earthly reality.[19] Unlike Robinson, Knox sided with R. H. Newton Flew by connecting the use of ἐκκλησία about Old Testament Israel in the Septuagint to the New Testament church's use of the term ἐκκλησία as a single entity.[20]

---

positions. See Kuhn, *Ecclesiology of Donald Robinson*, 61–62.

15. See Knox, *D. Broughton Knox: Selected Works*.

16. Kuhn, *Ecclesiology of Donald Robinson*, 207–13. One area both Knox and Robinson were in agreement was that "the church is only ever local or heavenly; there is no third category of the universal church on earth," 208. One area in which both scholars were at variance was "Robinson's inquiry into the relationship of Israel to the church. His concern throughout his study in ecclesiology was to better understand salvation history. He recognized a preservation of both Jewish and gentile identities within the church, with the new redeemed community being part of a 'new man.' Knox did not include much in his study about the relationship of Israel to the church," 210.

17. Kuhn, *Ecclesiology of Donald Robinson*, 140.

18. Kuhn, *Ecclesiology of Donald Robinson*, 140, 210.

19. Kuhn, *Ecclesiology of Donald Robinson*, 149, 208.

20. Kuhn, *Ecclesiology of Donald Robinson*, 179.

D. Broughton Knox's Contribution to the Biblical Theology Program at Moore College

Both Robinson and Knox helped to shape the theological trajectory at Moore College. While Knox was a systematic theologian focusing on Reformation theology, he read broadly both in and outside his field of study. He believed in the sufficiency of Scripture and shifted his systematic theology from a traditional position that focused on the theological thought of scholars throughout church history to focusing primarily on the biblical text itself. When he taught systematic theology at Moore, he used Hammond's *In Understanding Be Men* as only a supplemental textbook. Scripture was his primary textbook, as he wanted to demonstrate to his students how his theological conclusions came directly from the biblical text.[21]

While a systematic theologian (who studied under Hammond), Knox's theological conclusions (like Robinson's) were grounded in biblical theology. Kuhn considered Knox a type of biblical theologian due to his emphasis on Scripture as his primary focus for drawing his systematic theological conclusions.[22] He contributed to Moore's biblical theology program by lecturing on the New Testament. In his systematic theological contributions, he filtered all biblical doctrines through the lens of Scripture, which he considered the chief way of knowing God. Robinson and Knox played a reciprocal, complementary role to each other's contributions in which Knox drew from Robinson's biblical theological and linguistic contributions. In return, Robinson drew from the systematic theological studies of Knox.[23]

Knox's View of Israel and the Church in Redemptive History

While Knox made numerous contributions to ecclesiology, the role of Israel in redemptive history and its relationship to the church was not a major issue discussed in what little comprised Knox's academic contributions. He contributed to the subject in his *RTR* article "The Church and the People of God in the Old Testament." He began by surveying the nation of Israel's role in redemptive history in the New Testament, noting that early Christians in Acts were loyal Jews, and those who kept the law in James and the Pauline

---

21. Kuhn, *Ecclesiology of Donald Robinson*, 136–37.
22. Kuhn, *Ecclesiology of Donald Robinson*, 137.
23. Kuhn, *Ecclesiology of Donald Robinson*, 139.

epistles, similar to Robinson's understanding of a New Testament church that comprised a Jewish nucleus.[24] This was the only area of minor possible agreement with Robinson. Reflecting on the Old Testament, Knox stated that "the initiative of God in redeeming His people is the keynote of the Old Testament," in which he considered the Old Testament people of God (the nation of Israel) to be the Old Testament church, drawing a connection between the Old Testament church with the New Testament church.[25] Knox did believe that Old Testament Israel was the people of God due to God's call upon them in the Abrahamic covenant of Gen 12, summarizing as follows: "We conclude then that Israel was the people of God because God called them and that the ground of this call is to be found solely in God's character of love, justice, and mercy."[26] However, he also considered the New Testament church as a continuance of an Old Testament church typical of a Reformed covenant theology view: "The glory of God was the purpose of the calling of the Old Testament church. It is the purpose of the church's existence today."[27] Knox also differed from Robinson and asserted a typical Reformed covenant theology view of redemptive history since he considered the relationship of covenant to be the central relationship by which God operated with his people and the unifying theme of Scripture (instead of the concepts of promise and fulfillment), tracing various covenants throughout the Old Testament to the new covenant in which the church is the recipient of God's new covenant.

Knox affirmed a Christocentric biblical theology in which the Old Testament prophecies are fulfilled in Christ. He also asserted that the New Testament church, not only Christ, fulfilled the promises of the Abrahamic covenant to bless the nations.[28] Goldsworthy also held to each of these positions. Knox considered the New Testament church as both the continuance of and the replacement of the Old Testament nation of Israel: "The early Christians were certain that the Jewish nation, by rejecting and crucifying its Messiah, had ceased to be God's instrument."[29] He used the language of remnant in Rom 9–11 to refer to the true Old Testament church consisting of saved Israelites, while transferring this

24. Knox, "Church and the People," 12.
25. Knox, "Church and the People," 13.
26. Knox, "Church and the People," 14.
27. Knox, "Church and the People," 15.
28. Knox, "Church and the People," 16, 18.
29. Knox, "Church and the People," 12.

remnant concept to the New Testament church, even to regenerate church members in contrast to unregenerate church members. He disagreed with Robinson's use of the concept of the people of God in Rom 9–11 by including gentile believers in a way that blurred their ethnic distinctions: "In a truer sense, the people of God, once identified with the Hebrews, was now no longer confined by this natural restriction. The wild olive branch had been grafted in on to the old root."[30]

Knox disagreed with Robinson by considering the entire New Testament church, both Jews and gentiles without ethnic distinctions, the new Israel. He considered Old Testament Israel as a saved nation and saving nation. Unlike Robinson, he also applied the similar terms saved community and saving community to the totality of the New Testament church.[31] Knox also considered Israel as no longer the people of God: "There is no doubt that Israel was God's chosen instrument. But for two thousand years they have been laid aside, rejected. They were His people, His church. This is no longer true."[32] While Robinson retained an ethnic distinction between Jew and gentile in the New Testament church, Knox would not.

While Knox had some minor possible agreements with Robinson's concept of a the New Testament church beginning with Jewish believers, he differed from Robinson's teaching to uphold a typical Reformed covenantal redemptive-historical biblical theology concerning the relationship of Israel and the church in his contribution. He also blurred any distinction between Jew and gentile by including gentile believers in his view of the people of God and Israel.

Biographical Sketch of William Dumbrell

William Dumbrell (1926–2016) was an Australian Anglican priest and biblical scholar. He studied at Moore College beginning in 1955. He completed his MA at the University of Sydney in 1958, his BD and MTh in 1966 at the University of London in 1961, and his ThD at Harvard University in 1970. He was ordained in February 1956, serving in the Anglican Church and teaching at various academic institutions throughout his career, including Regent College (1984–1988), Macquarie University, Moore Theological College (1988–1994), University of Sydney, Trinity Theological College

---

30. Knox, "Church and the People," 13.
31. Knox, "Church and the People," 16–17.
32. Knox, "Church and the People," 18.

(Singapore), and Emmaus Bible College. He also served as the first academic dean at Regent College.[33]

Dumbrell wrote numerous significant contributions to biblical theology, including *Covenant and Creation*, *The Faith of Israel*, *The End of the Beginning*, and *The Search for Order*. He also wrote commentaries on various New Testament books, including Romans, Galatians, Hebrews, the Gospel of John, and Revelation.[34]

William Dumbrell's Contribution to the Biblical Theology Program at Moore

Dumbrell (like Goldsworthy) was a student of Robinson who also contributed to the biblical theology program at Moore and (like Robinson and Knox) contributed to the doctrine of ecclesiology in his academic writings. Michael Jensen considered Dumbrell's contributions "crucial for shaping how Sydney Anglicans think about and preach from the Bible."[35] In his article "Paul and Salvation History in Romans 9:30—10:4" (in *Out of Egypt: Biblical Theology and Biblical Interpretation*), Dumbrell offered a fivefold approach to biblical theology. First, he considered biblical theology to present a "macro view of revelation in history."[36] Second, one cannot construct an independent Old Testament or New Testament theology, only a biblical theology in which both testaments are interdependent.[37] Third, there is no center to organizing biblical theology since biblical theology traces a divine movement from Gen 1–3 to Rev 21–22.[38] Fourth, biblical theology is a unified theology without competing threads.[39] Finally, while

---

33. Davies, "William John Dumbrell." See also Powell, "Moore Veteran Called Home."

34. Regent College, "Remembering Dr. William J. Dumbrell." See also Dumbrell, *Galatians*; *Hebrews*; *John*; *Revelation*; *Romans*; and Davies and Harman, *Everlasting Covenant*.

35. Jensen, *Sydney Anglicanism*, 30.

36. Dumbrell, "Paul and Salvation History," 287–88. Dumbrell clarified his approach in *End of the Beginning*.

37. See Baker, *Two Testaments, One Bible*.

38. See Eichrodt, *Theology of the Old Testament*. Dumbrell viewed covenant as a central unifying theme of Scripture, but unlike Eichrodt, he does not consider it a center.

39. In "Paul and Salvation History," 287–88, Dumbrell wrote: "My belief in a unitary thread of purpose connecting the whole Bible, which the biblical narratives themselves reveal, means that there cannot be within the one canon competing or differing theologies though there may be different emphases within a unitary theology." Dumbrell also

the final form of the text is an ongoing scholarly discussion, an evangelical biblical theology must be a canonical biblical theology that accepts the canonical text as the study of biblical theology.[40]

Dumbrell, like Knox, placed the concept of covenant as a unifying theme. Dumbrell's arrangement of the biblical covenants started with what he defined as the covenant with creation at the Noahic covenant in Gen 6:18 as one of the foundational biblical covenants. The Noahic covenant is the first time in Scripture where the term *covenant* is used. However, he viewed the Noahic covenant as building upon an existing covenant-with-creation model in the garden of Eden. Dumbrell considered all successive covenants (including the Abrahamic covenant) "movements forward from this creation base of Genesis 6:18."[41] He placed the covenant with creation at Gen 6:18 instead of Gen 1–2 since, while Gen 1–2 was a model to the Gen 6:18 covenant, the fall brought about the need to purge the original evil before the inauguration of a fully developed covenant with creation that occurred in the Noahic covenant: "Such a covenant would likely contain the purpose of divine engagement with the world and humanity in Gen 1–2, particularly in regard to humanity's benefit from, and stewardship of, creation (Gen. 1:28). Moreover, the Eden account (Gen. 2:4–17), by the presence of evil in Eden, cannot reflect God's final purpose but seems to model what is to come."[42] His analysis of the Abrahamic covenant in Gen 12:1–3 reflected on its context in Gen 11, contrasting God's movement of grace toward Abraham to make of him a great nation and great name versus humanity's attempt to make for themselves a great name.[43] While the explicit term *covenant* is not used until Gen 15:18, like the relationship between the covenant with creation in Gen 6:18 and Gen 1–2, Dumbrell considered Gen 12:1–3 as a model of the Abrahamic covenant in Gen 15:18. Dumbrell considered Gen 15 a passage that "clearly confirms an already existing [covenantal] relationship."[44] His categorization of Gen 12:1–3 vis à

---

clarified his approach in *End of the Beginning*.

40. Dumbrell, "Paul and Salvation History," 287–88. For more on a canonical biblical theology, see Childs, *Biblical Theology*.

41. Dumbrell, *Covenant and Creation*, 4–5.

42. Dumbrell, *Covenant and Creation*, 4–5.

43. Dumbrell, *Faith of Israel*, 27.

44. Dumbrell, *Faith of Israel*, 27 (bracketed text added).

vis Gen 15:18 is a "summary of relationships begun by God with Abram, to which the title 'covenant' is later given in Genesis 15."[45]

Dumbrell's View of Israel and the Church in Redemptive History

Dumbrell, like Robinson, used the term ἐκκλησία in the New Testament to refer to local churches with an ultimate fulfillment in a heavenly reality.[46] However, he sided with Flew on the use of ἐκκλησία to refer to a continuity between Old Testament Israel and the New Testament church, stating that ἐκκλησία in Matt 16:18 refers to "the renewed Israel, the gathered people of God."[47] Unlike Robinson's position on the use of the term λαός as referring to the people of God, he used the term λαός to refer to a continuity between Old Testament Israel and the New Testament church: "From the Gentiles who now belong to him as does Israel.... By using λαός, a word customarily used for Israel, James links the new people, the Gentiles, to Israel."[48]

In his writings on Gen 12:1–3, Dumbrell defined the great nation as ultimately a redeemed or worshiping community, and the story of the great nation vis à vis Israel is that the redeemed or worshiping community of ethnic Israel of the Old Testament is always and simply a type or representative of the great nation promised in Gen 12:1–3:

> True, the call of Israel is the initial fulfillment of divine redemptive purposes, but Israel was ever meant to be only a living example of what the Kingdom of God in political reality could mean. In her own way, Israel as a nation ... was to be a symbol of the final society which we meet in Rev 21–22.[49]

He made a similar argument in *The Faith of Israel*: "Perhaps the 'great nation' of this passage is to be taken eschatologically, to mean the company of the redeemed who will fulfill the call to Abram (cf. Rev. 5:11). We may therefore look to the New Testament to fulfill the concept of Israel, which failed to be realized in the OT."[50] Dumbrell further elaborated on Old Testa-

---

45. Dumbrell, *Covenant and Creation*, 73.
46. Dumbrell, *Search for Order*, 266–68.
47. Dumbrell, *Search for Order*, 172–73.
48. Dumbrell, *Search for Order*, 230.
49. Dumbrell, "Covenant with Abraham," 46.
50. Dumbrell, *Faith of Israel*, 28.

ment Israel as a type or representative when he referred to Old Testament Israel as a mere anticipation or image of the great nation of Gen 12:2:

> For though Israel is certainly the nation which the Abrahamic promises have immediately in view, Israel as a nation, as a symbol of divine rule manifested within a political framework, was intended itself to be an image of the shape of final world government, a symbol pointing beyond itself to the reality yet to be . . . a final world system will emerge; a "great nation" will come into being of which the nation of Israel was but a mere anticipation.[51]

Because of national Israel's continuing failure to obey God's commandments and ultimately reject Christ as its Messiah, Israel was only an ideal or model of a future community, according to Dumbrell: "The OT presentation is idealistic; a model is presented in the book of Exodus to which historical Israel never conformed. This inevitably translated the ideal into an eschatological hope carried by believing communities."[52] Israel's history was "a series of disappointing pilgrimages towards goals never achieved," in which the nation of Israel in the Old Testament would not "enter the blessing of 'rest' attached to these promises" (referring to the promises of the Abrahamic covenant).[53]

Who are the individuals that comprise Dumbrell's concept of a redeemed or worshiping community? Dumbrell began his discussion in slight possible agreement with Robinson in that the individuals of a redeemed or worshiping community comprise a believing remnant of Jews plus gentiles, which "share in the rights which were once exclusively those of national Israel."[54] Dumbrell also considered Israel as the one who brings salvation to the world: "The Abrahamic covenant will (Gen. 12:3) lead to world evangelization through a chosen descendant of Abraham: Israel."[55] He considered the Abrahamic covenant as the introduction to "the course of development for all future redemptive eschatology."[56] Dumbrell's position concerning the believing remnant of Jews plus gentiles who comprise the redeemed or worshiping community also slightly agreed with Robinson in that both groups are united together in an eschatological heavenly

---

51. Dumbrell, *Covenant and Creation*, 75–76.
52. Dumbrell, *End of the Beginning*, 150, 191.
53. Dumbrell, *End of the Beginning*, 128; and *Covenant and Creation*, 73.
54. Dumbrell, *End of the Beginning*, 158.
55. Dumbrell, *Covenant and Creation*, 62.
56. Dumbrell, *End of the Beginning*, 131.

reality of a new man. However, Dumbrell (unlike Robinson) equated this new man with a new people of God that comprise the ἐκκλησία, the New Testament church, whereas Robinson was hesitant to apply the phrase *people of God* to the New Testament church.[57] Dumbrell held a Christocentric biblical theology similar to Goldsworthy that placed the fulfillment of God's promises to Israel in Christ as the fulfillment of Israel: "Through the narrative of the life of Jesus, Matthew demonstrates that Israel's vocation finds its fulfilment in Jesus. . . . And demonstration was necessary, for the fulfilment signifies rejection of national Israel and the realization of various prophecies in quite unexpected ways."[58] However, he went further than Goldsworthy's position by considering the death of Christ as the inauguration of a new redeemed community or worshiping community, with its final eschatological fulfillment occurring in the book of Revelation: "Both Rev 1:6 and 5:9–10 assume that a new worshiping community (i.e., and 'Israel') has arisen through the death of Christ. . . . A new community united by common worship has arisen in whom is realized the consummation of every eschatological hope to which humanity has been related throughout the Bible."[59] Dumbrell also went further than Knox's position of the New Testament church becoming a new Israel to instead consider Old Testament Israel as merely a type or representative ultimately fulfilled in an eschatological redeemed or worshiping community by stating: "Genesis 12:2 may initially have had Israel in view, but Israel as representative of the wider saved community to stem from her witness."[60]

Dumbrell observed the use of the term *nation* (גוי) in Gen 12:2 is generally used for other world nations instead of Israel, continuing his exegesis by stating that the term גוי is typically used in a negative context when referring to Israel.[61] Dumbrell made a somewhat valid argument concerning the distribution of the use of the term גוי referring to Israel in contrast to when it is used to describe other nations. However, in contrast to Dumbrell, there is an even distribution of positive and negative uses of גוי when referring to Israel. Dumbrell correctly noted that the Hebrew term for *people* (עַם) is the term most frequently used for Israel in the OT.[62]

57. Dumbrell, *Search for Order*, 12.
58. Dumbrell, *Search for Order*, 178–79.
59. Dumbrell, *End of the Beginning*, 159–60.
60. Dumbrell, *Faith of Israel*, 28.
61. Dumbrell, *Covenant and Creation*, 75. See also *Faith of Israel*, 28.
62. Dumbrell, *Covenant and Creation*, 75.

He understood גוי as "an ethnic unity that is geographically delineated and bound by society, land, and culture." He also observed that גוי could refer to Israel as a great nation later on in its history when Israel as a nation was contrasted with other gentile nations (an "emergence of Israel as a political unit at a later stage and that the qualifier 'great' in Genesis 12:2 sets Israel off from its world").[63] However, Dumbrell grouped the גוים (the nations, plural) with the גוי (the nation, singular), considering the nations as a collective unity of the redeemed forming a great nation.[64] This grouping together of the nations with the nation without a distinction between the גוי as it refers to the physical seed of Abraham (the Jews) versus the גוים of the other redeemed (gentile) nations is an area where Dumbrell differed from Robinson's position, as Robinson made a distinction between the promises made to the Jews and the nation of Israel and the promises made to the other redeemed gentile nations.

Dumbrell interpreted the fulfillment of גוי in the Gen 12:1–3 Abrahamic covenant to refer not to the physical offspring of Abraham but instead to what he referred to as a redeemed society consisting of a final political unity fulfilled in Rev 21–22.[65] His interpretation of Gen 12:1–3 had a redemptive societal fulfillment in which an eschatological community of redeemed individuals forms a new political entity from a God-initiated and God-established government (using the terminology *worshiping* or *redeemed community* or *new Israel*) that "must therefore be a worshiping community called into being by a great reception, whose ideal role will be to reflect through worship the nature of God, the Redeemer."[66] He placed a wedge between the ethnic nation of Israel and a future redeemed community that began to occur in Isa 6: "By the content of Isaiah 6, for the first time in the Old Testament, a clear wedge had been driven between the nation and a community of faith to emerge from it."[67] This wedge became a separation at Christ's "separation from national Israel" in Matthew: "While recognizing the ministry of Jesus as originally directed to national Israel (Matt. 10:5–6; 15:24), Matthew views the ties with Judaism

---

63. Dumbrell, *Faith of Israel*, 28. Dumbrell also observed that the use of גוי in Gen 12:2 "could broadly have Israel's later political constitution in mind" as referring to Israel in contrast with other gentile nations. See Dumbrell, *Covenant and Creation*, 75.

64. Dumbrell, *Covenant and Creation*, 74–75. See also "Covenant with Abraham," 50.

65. See Dumbrell, *End of the Beginning*, for his treatment on Rev 21–22.

66. Dumbrell, *Covenant and Creation*, 75–76; and *End of the Beginning*, 122.

67. Dumbrell, *Covenant and Creation*, 236–39.

as having been cut. Thus, the mantle is understood as having been taken from Israel (21:43) and given to a new people of God."[68] Christ rejected the nation of Israel and created "a New Community. . . . In Christ the new community fulfills the Exod 19:3b–6 role of Israel."[69] Not only did Dumbrell understand this new community as a fulfillment of the Abrahamic covenant, but he also placed the concept of a new community as the fulfillment of the new covenant of Jeremiah:

> The term "Israel" will not be able to be used again to refer solely to the nation. Although the postexilic writings witness disappointing attempts by the returned community to set back the historical clock, the course of the future people of God has been determined. Jeremiah prepares us for Israel's final punishment, then for a new exodus to be accomplished by the death of Christ, followed by the divine imposition of a new covenant. In effect, the proclamation of a new Israel—Jeremiah uses "Israel" predominantly as a theological term—a new covenant, and thus a new age for the people of God is the book's message.[70]

For Dumbrell, there is no physical seed of Abraham or an ethnic Israel as the fulfillment of the eschatological promises given in the Abrahamic covenant. Israel is always and simply a type of a future eschatological redeemed community:

> Certainly, the call of Israel and her constitution may be immediately in mind, but only as a pledge of what is still to come beyond that call; namely, the final political reality—the kingdom of God. . . . Israel as a nation may later exhibit features of this since her constitution is God-given, but the true political structure aimed at in Gen 12:1–3 will not come into being until the whole company of the redeemed are gathered together in a New Heaven and a New Earth.[71]

Dumbrell also utilized similar sonship language to that of Goldsworthy but went further than Goldsworthy's position by applying it to his concept of the redeemed community: The "children of God" is now a "new community as a replacement for Israel" and the "concept of sonship claimed by Israel had now been given by John to Christians."[72]

---

68. Dumbrell, *End of the Beginning*, 152; and *Search for Order*, 155.
69. Dumbrell, *End of the Beginning*, 120.
70. Dumbrell, *Faith of Israel*, 150.
71. Dumbrell, *End of the Beginning*, 131.
72. Peterson and Pryor, *Fullness of Time*, 91.

Dumbrell also departed from Robinson in his exegesis on Rom 9:30—10:4, concerning what he labeled a post-cross view on Israel's role in redemptive history: "Paul is speaking not about Israel historically (the traditional view) but about post-cross Israel still offering obedience to the Jewish law under a Mosaic covenant whose validity and institutions ceased with the death of Christ."[73] He believed that the post-cross position of Old Testament Israel and the New Testament church shifted Israel's standing as the people of God to the New Testament church: "In Romans 9:30—10:4, Paul is talking about Israel in a post-cross situation, and thus about the change in Israel's national standing brought about by the death of Christ."[74] In Rom 9–11, he did not believe that Paul still considered unbelieving Jews as people of God: "Paul's attitude to non-Christian Israel in his day. Were they, for him, still the people of God? . . . My short answer, to stem from this chapter, is no."[75] Unlike Windsor (see chapter 6), Dumbrell defined Paul's vocation as a missionary to a new people of God that included gentiles: "Paul's vocational understanding, a major tenet of his theology, appeared in the form of a commitment to missionary activity that included the Gentiles in a new people of God. . . . Paul henceforth saw that Jew and Gentile are related as one people of God under the primacy of the Abrahamic covenant."[76] Robinson and Windsor restricted the people of God throughout the Pauline corpus to ethnic Jews. In contrast, Dumbrell included gentiles in his interpretation of the people of God without any clear ethnic distinction between the two people groups.

In Rom 9, Dumbrell examined the role of believing gentiles in redemptive history, stating that such gentiles would always be incorporated into Israel. He agreed with Robinson's believing remnant of Jews along with gentiles, but he disagreed with Robinson's retention of their ethnical differences:

> God always had in mind their incorporation into Israel, while, by the same purpose, Israel would be constituted by a believing remnant comprised of Jews and Gentiles, since salvation was always by grace and never by race, a point that Paul made clear in Romans 9:6–13. . . . The fulfilment of divine purposes, which the death of

---

73. Dumbrell, "Paul and Salvation History," 286.
74. Dumbrell, "Paul and Salvation History," 289.
75. Dumbrell, "Paul and Salvation History," 287.
76. Dumbrell, *Search for Order*, 263.

Christ achieved, brought several new facts into this beginning of the kingdom of Christ.[77]

Believing gentiles were now brought into a right relationship with God through the death of Christ in fulfillment of the new covenant in Jeremiah: "There was the fact that the death of Jesus had introduced Jeremiah's renewed covenant. . . . Paul's statement in 9:30 then signifies that some Gentiles . . . were now in a right relationship with God through faith as members of the new covenant."[78] While Robinson believed the salvation mission came from Israel to the gentiles, Dumbrell transferred the salvation mission to a restored Israel, the church:

> The death of Christ introduced a totally new factor into the history of Israel and of the world. . . . With the rending of the veil of the temple immediately consequent upon the death of Jesus (Mk. 15:38), Israel and her institutions had been dismissed, and access to God was now available independently of the temple. . . . Israel's commission to be a light to the nations, the world's evangelist, was to be transferred to the new body to emerge at Pentecost, the church or the restored or remnant Israel.[79]

A new, Spirit-filled Israel at Pentecost constitutes the fulfillment of the Abrahamic covenant. Dumbrell elaborated, "The purpose of the Sinai covenant, to enable the fulfillment of the Abrahamic covenant through Israel, could now be put into commission in the new Spirit-filled Israel of Pentecost."[80] He equated this fulfillment with the ἐκκλησία, the New Testament church: "The ἐκκλησία that Jesus will build will in fact be this alternate profile of Israel."[81]

Dumbrell elaborated on his position of Old Testament Israel as a failed entity in his discussion of Rom 9:30—10:4:

> In the Old Testament the emphasis is almost exclusively upon nationalistic Israel as a failed entity, which never responded to its national commission to be a light to the nations (Ex. 19:5–6; Is. 49:6). But within Israel there was undoubtedly a core of faithful dedicated to obedience to the covenant. . . . The fact remains that the church begins on the day of Pentecost with a believing Israel

---

77. Dumbrell, "Paul and Salvation History," 288.
78. Dumbrell, "Paul and Salvation History," 288.
79. Dumbrell, "Paul and Salvation History," 288–89.
80. Dumbrell, "Paul and Salvation History," 291.
81. Dumbrell, "Paul and Salvation History," 297.

called in response to national Israel's failure. In short, the new covenant with Israel never involved national Israel but was a reality only for the new or restored Israel.[82]

This believing-Israel language used by Dumbrell was similar to that used by Robinson. However, he considered the new covenant with Israel to be only for a new or restored Israel that included gentiles: "The new covenant will facilitate a restored, obedient Israel to fulfil the commission imposed by virtue of its election as the people of God (Ex. 19:5–6). That commission was, for Israel, a charge to be a light to the world." He summarized his position as follows:

> Israel will no longer be called upon to attract the nations to Jerusalem and her temple by her difference as a kingdom of God nation. The mission of restored Israel will now be in the wider world since, with the death of Jesus, the notion of a literal, this-world promised land had disappeared. In its place the world itself emerges as the new promised land, a type of the final antitype of the new creation.[83]

In his exegesis of Rom 9:30—10:4, Dumbrell also utilized the language of sonship in a similar manner to how he utilized such sonship language in his exegesis of the Abrahamic covenant. He considered both Jew and gentile to be considered the true sons of God: "All the Galatian believers, from both Jewish and Gentile backgrounds, have been brought to new experience as the true sons of God by their faith (or by this faith ... not by ethnic connection). They have inherited adoption as sons, formerly Israel's position."[84] He also referred to those in Christ as the seed of Abraham: "If the category of belonging to Christ applies, then distinctions vanish.... As Abraham's seed, believers share in the promises to Abraham. Thus those in Christ are the true 'sons of Abraham,' not Jews as such ... the full identification of believers with the faith of Abraham."[85] For Dumbrell,

> Romans 9:30—10:4 is a post-cross situation in which ethnic Israel stands rejected and has been replaced.... At the death of Jesus, the Jewish era had passed away and Jewish institutions had been divinely discarded. While Paul never makes this point a formal

---

82. Dumbrell, "Paul and Salvation History," 296–97.
83. Dumbrell, "Paul and Salvation History," 291–92.
84. Dumbrell, "Paul and Salvation History," 301.
85. Dumbrell, "Paul and Salvation History," 301.

conclusion, it seems clear, particularly from Galatians, that this is the understanding that guided Paul's thought.[86]

Peter Bolt

Peter Bolt (1958–) is a former lecturer at Moore College who taught in Moore's biblical theology program. Bolt has made (and is making) numerous contributions to biblical theology, including *The Cross from a Distance* and an upcoming commentary on the Gospel of Mark in the Evangelical Biblical Theology Commentary series, as well as other exegetical works.[87] He also served as one of the editors of *Donald Robinson: Selected Works*.

While Bolt appreciated the legacy of Robinson through his work in Robinson's *Selected Works*, he did not provide a substantial contribution concerning his position on Israel's role in redemptive history. He briefly summarized a few comments in his 1991 Vision Day message at St. Matthias, "God's Vision of Church." Like Robinson, he translated ἐκκλησία as simply meaning gathering or assembly, demonstrating how the term ἐκκλησία is used generically throughout the New Testament without carrying theological weight applied to the New Testament church.[88] He also agreed with Robinson's position on the 144,000 in Rev 7, viewing them as Israelites who are distinct from the gentiles.[89] Unlike Robinson, he directly labeled the New Testament church as the people of God without a clear ethnic distinction between Jews and gentiles within the church.[90]

Bolt also commented briefly on the end of religion in his 2003 Moore College Annual Lectures volume, *The Cross from a Distance*. He considered Judaism (what he labeled as God's religion) as abolished and superseded by Christ, believing that both Jew and gentile now have access to God through Christ:

> The coming of Jesus abolishes this distance, and so, in another of God's great paradoxes, the Messiah's fulfilment of the law means that Old Testament religion is superseded.... The proper response

---

86. Dumbrell, "Paul and Salvation History," 297, 310.

87. See Sydney College of Divinity, "Professor Peter Bolt."

88. One example is his reference to the mob against Paul which was referred to as an *assembly* in Acts 19.

89. Shiner noted that Paul Barnett held a similar position in *Apocalypse Now and Then*. See Shiner, "Reading the New Testament," 203.

90. Bolt, "God's Vision of Church."

to Jesus is something completely non-religious. With the coming of the bridegroom, along with the abolition of religion, comes faith.[91]

Through his sermon and writings, one can glimpse Bolt's position concerning Israel's role in redemptive history. He considered the death of Christ as the end of Judaism. Christ's death replaced the religion of the Jews with a nonreligious faith in Christ.[92] Bolt could further contribute a more comprehensive position on Israel's role in redemptive history that would be useful, especially on how he would align with or depart from Robinson's position.

Barry Webb

Barry Webb (1945–) is a lecturer at Moore College who agreed with some of Robinson's ecclesiology and Goldsworthy's biblical theology. Like Robinson, he considered the church a new society that is both a local, earthly gathering, but it is also a heavenly reality.[93] Like Goldsworthy, he placed a gospel-centered hermeneutic as his foundation in constructing an evangelical biblical theology. The majority of the New Testament is an exposition of the Gospels in a similar manner the majority of the Old Testament is an exposition of the Torah.[94] He considered Christ's fulfillment of the kingdom of God as a central element in his biblical theology, asserting that the concept of Christ ushering in the kingdom of God in Mark 1:14–15 is the hermeneutical key to his biblical theology.[95] He did not consider the concept of the kingdom of God as being restricted to the hope of Israel, but to all nations, with the new Jerusalem being the new home of believers. Christ is the fulfillment of the kingdom of God. Like Goldsworthy, he also argued that Jesus fulfilled the role that Israel failed to fulfill:

---

91. Bolt, *Cross from a Distance*, 29–30. Bolt would disagree with Robert Banks's position that Jews were able to continue to observe certain Jewish customs (such as circumcision) after their salvation. Bolt instead considered the cross as the end of practicing the Jewish religion. Faith in Christ is the replacement of Judaism.

92. Bolt, *Cross from a Distance*, 127. While he did not directly mention gentiles or the New Testament church replacing Israel in redemptive history, one can possibly infer from his writings that he retained a form of supersessionism that the Jews' (and Israel's) role in redemptive history ended with the death of Christ.

93. Webb, "Role of OT and of Biblical Israel."

94. See Goldsworthy, *Gospel-Centered Hermeneutics*; and *Preaching the Whole Bible*.

95. Gibson, *Interpreting God's Plan*, 52–53, 56–57, 62–64.

> The Israel of the Old Testament had failed to live up to its calling as the covenant people of God. But what Israel had failed to do, Jesus himself did for Israel. He loved God perfectly, with all his heart, mind, soul and strength, as Israel should have done, and then he took total responsibility for Israel's failure and gave his own perfect life as a sacrifice to atone for their sin.[96]

Like Dumbrell, Webb considered Israel a model society and a light to the nations in the Old Testament. Yet he defined this model society as simply a model or example of a future redeemed community. Old Testament Israel is merely a paradigm, type, and prototype of a future community in which Israel is replaced by the church. The land promises to the nation of Israel have given way to a new Christian fellowship. The ethical laws of Old Testament Israel remain a source of Christian ethics for the church, but that is the extent of their validity. He used similar redeemed community language to that of Dumbrell. However, unlike Dumbrell, he asserted that both Israel and the church are prototypes of a new creation (Dumbrell only considered Israel as a type of a new creation), contrasting the concepts of God, Israel, and land in the Old Testament prototypes to new concepts of God, redeemed humanity, and a new creation in the New Testament.

To Webb, the concept of the people of God can "never, in the end, be merely nationalistic or racially based," and "must ultimately be a vast, multicultural, multi-ethnic community drawn from all nations, united finally by their common acknowledgment of him as the only true God."[97] As Israel's Messiah, Christ fulfilled the promises to Israel. Israel's rejection of their Messiah led to the forming of a new, renewed Israel: "Israel in general chose to reject Jesus and fell under God's judgment . . . but it is also a matter of record that Jesus had prepared the way for the emergence of a new (renewed) Israel, by preaching the kingdom of God, calling for repentance, and preparing the twelve apostles to lead the new community he was calling together."[98] Webb retained a form of supersessionism by considering all believers (including gentiles) as forming a new Israel:

---

96. Webb, *Message of Zechariah*, 175.
97. Webb, *Message of Zechariah*, 43.
98. Webb, *Message of Zechariah*, 43, 172–75. While some scholars within traditional dispensationalism offered a similar interpretation to Webb in that the rejection of the kingdom of God by Israel led to the formation of the church, Webb's position varied with dispensationalism in that Israel's rejection of their Messiah led to a new, renewed Israel in which gentiles are the replacement of the Jews.

Israel's special relationship with God was brought to completion (fulfilment) in Jesus Christ, but participation in that fulfilment depended on acceptance of him as God's Messiah. That is the essence of the powerful gospel message Peter preached to the great gathering of Israelites in Jerusalem on the day of Pentecost. He was offering them participation in the fulfilment of God's covenant with Israel by accepting Jesus Christ as their Messiah. They would become members of the new "reborn" Israel that had emerged out of the old.[99]

Kevin Giles

Kevin Giles (1940–) is an Anglican scholar who studied at Moore College and read Robinson and D. Broughton Knox. While he disagreed with Robinson's ecclesiological conclusions, his work *What on Earth Is the Church?* helps to understand biblical theology and ecclesiology taught at Moore through Giles's dialoguing with Robinson's position. Giles disagreed with Robinson by asserting that the church is the new people of God and new Israel without any ethnic distinction. He also disagreed with Robinson's use of the term ἐκκλησία as applied to the universal church as a heavenly reality. Giles linked Robinson's interpretation to the theological thinking of J. N. Darby and dispensationalism. He considered ἐκκλησία as more than just an assembly, but a community that God has called into existence, while he also linked the Old Testament Septuagint's use of ἐκκλησία to the New Testament church's use of the term ἐκκλησία, applying it to the New Testament church being the true Israel. Like Flew, he drew a continuity between Old Testament Israel and the New Testament church and considered the New Testament church and Old Testament Israel one people of God. He also considered the term λαός concerning the people of God throughout the book of Acts as referring to Israel and the church as one people of God. Unlike Robinson, he considered the term *the saints* throughout the Pauline corpus to refer not only to Jewish believers, but to the entire New Testament church, both Jew and gentile without any ethnic distinctions. One area where he agreed with Robinson is that Jew and gentile are saved through Christ through a reciprocal role of salvation in which the gospel was given first to the Jews, then to the gentiles, then back to unbelieving Jews who became jealous of the gentiles. Giles, like Robinson, considered this trajectory the fulfillment of "all

---

99. Webb, *Message of Zechariah*, 175.

Israel shall be saved" (Rom 11:26). However, unlike Robinson who considered Jewish believers as the true Israel, Giles considered the New Testament church, both Jews and gentiles, as the true Israel. He also disagreed with Robinson's interpretation of the 144,000 in the book of Revelation. Instead of viewing the 144,000 as ethnic Jews (as Robinson did), he (unfortunately) considered the church (the Christian community) as the interpretation of the 144,000.[100] Giles ultimately disagreed with Robinson concerning Israel's role in redemptive history. However, his dialogues with Robinson allude to a developing tradition at Moore College that are useful in discussing the plausibility of a Moore School of Biblical Theology.

Malcolm Richards

Malcolm Richards preached a message at Moore Theological College, "The New Israel: Taken Over by Jesus." Richards considered the new Christians in Acts (without any ethnic distinctions) who gathered together as forming a new Israel. This new Israel was formed in a new relationship with God (by worshiping and praising God) and a new relationship with each other. This new community was a witnessing and worshiping community (Richards agreed with Dumbrell's concept of a new worshiping community as forming a new Israel). He traced a trajectory that moved from the known of Judaism in the Old Testament to the unknown of a new Israel in the New Testament. However, the new Israel in the New Testament, unlike Robinson, eliminated all ethnic distinctions within the New Testament church.

Conclusion

D. Broughton Knox and William Dumbrell are two scholars who had only minor agreements with Robinson but mostly disagreed with him concerning Israel's role in redemptive history. Like Goldsworthy, they are two additional examples of typical Reformed redemption-history approaches to biblical theology. Knox was a systematic theologian at Moore but grounded his theological conclusions in biblical theology, drawing his theological conclusions directly from Scripture. Unlike Robinson, he considered the new Israel to be the totality of the New Testament church,

---

100. Giles, *What on Earth Is the Church?*, ix–x, 11–14, 24–25, 88, 92, 106, 108, 112, 127–29, 175–76.

both Jews and gentiles without ethnic distinctions. He also asserted the New Testament church is unified with an Old Testament church. Dumbrell considered biblical theology to present a "macro view of revelation in history" that traces a "divine movement" from Gen 1–3 to Rev 21–22.[101] He asserted that the great nation of Gen 12:1–3 was only a type of an eschatological, redeemed, worshiping community fulfilled in a new Israel of believing Jews and gentiles without their ethnic differences. He also asserted that Romans 9:30—10:4 speaks of a restored Israel, but unlike Robinson, his concept of a restored Israel consists of all believers in the New Testament church without retaining their ethnic differences. Unlike Goldsworthy, neither scholar showed any later form of appreciation for any aspects of Robinson's distinction theology.

Peter Bolt, Barry Webb, Kevin Giles, and Malcolm Richards also diverge from Robinson's distinction theology concerning Israel's role in redemptive history. Bolt considered Israel's religion to be abolished with the death of Christ on the cross. Webb considered Israel to be a type or prototype of future worshiping community, the church (using similar language to that of Dumbrell). Giles rejected most of Robinson's ecclesiology and only agreed with Robinson's concept of the reciprocal role of salvation between Jews and gentiles. Richards considered the New Testament church, comprised of both Jews and gentiles, as the replacement of Israel.

---

101. Dumbrell, "Paul and Salvation History," 287–88.

6

Toward a Robinson Revival

Lionel Windsor's Evangelical Post-Supersessionist Theology and Additional Scholars

Introduction

AS DISCUSSED IN THE previous two chapters, many of Robinson's successors who popularized biblical theology at Moore College were absent in incorporating Robinson's distinction theology concerning Jew and gentile in the New Testament church into Moore's curriculum. A handful of Robinson's successors (such as Goldsworthy) eventually appreciated at least some aspects of Robinson's distinction theology without fully incorporating it into Moore's biblical theology program. In later years, there has seemed to be a revival of and interest in Robinson's distinction theology in the biblical theology contributions of Moore scholars. With Lionel Windsor's contribution, one can begin to see the return of an emphasis on Robinson's distinction theology to Moore's biblical theology program. Additional scholars (Robert Banks, George Athas, Phillip Jensen, Anthony Nichols, Martin Pakula, Ma'afu Palu, Jeff Read, and W. H. Salier) provide further examples of scholars who have expressed a revival of interest in Robinson's distinction theology.

Biographical Sketch on Lionel Windsor

Lionel Windsor (1974–) is an Anglican minister in the Diocese of Sydney and New Testament lecturer at Moore College. He began teaching at Moore in 2006 and became a full-time New Testament lecturer in 2015. He received his bachelor of divinity at Moore in 2005, also studying for his master of theology at Moore until 2009 under Brian Rosner. He received his PhD at Durham University in 2012 under Francis Watson (his PhD thesis was *Paul and the Vocation of Israel*).[1] He also taught at Durham University until 2012 and wrote numerous academic and ministry-related works, including *Reading Ephesians and Colossians After Supersessionism* in 2017.[2]

Lionel Windsor's Contribution to the Biblical Theology Program at Moore

Windsor carried forward what he referred to as "the Robinson-Goldsworthy vision for biblical theology," which he characterized as "both strongly Christological and structurally Israel-shaped."[3] Unlike Robinson or Goldsworthy, Windsor did not contribute to a phased biblical theology structure (such as Robinson's three stages or Goldsworthy's three epochs). Windsor's contribution to the biblical theology program at Moore is targeted at attempting to correct a supersessionist view through what he labeled his evangelical, post-supersessionist position.[4] Like Robinson, Windsor believed in a distinction between Jew and gentile in redemptive history, but he did not accept dispensationalism. He rejected dispensationalism's dividing of redemptive history into a series of dispensations and its separation between the church and Israel in the current age, believing that dispensationalism obscures the preaching of the gospel as coming through Israel to the gentile nations. Windsor agreed with Goldsworthy that Christ is the fulfillment of God's promises to Old Testament Israel. However, he rejected Goldsworthy's position that Christ is a replacement of Old Testament Israel.

In developing his evangelical, post-supersessionist position, Windsor particularly drew upon the work of R. Kendall Soulen. Soulen rejected a Christocentric biblical theology that placed Christ's incarnation at the center of biblical theology. He instead placed his center of biblical theology at what Windsor referred to as the "eschatological reign of the God of Israel": "The gospel is good news about the God of Israel's coming reign,

---

1. Windsor, *Reading Ephesians and Colossians*, xi.; and "About Me."
2. Windsor, "Curriculum Vitae."
3. Windsor, *Reading Ephesians and Colossians*, xi, 3, 21, 24.
4. See Windsor, *Reading Ephesians and Colossians*, 3–4, for a definition and discussion of evangelical post-supersessionism. See also Soulen, "Post-Supersessionism."

which proclaims in Jesus' life, death, and resurrection the victorious guarantee of God's fidelity to the work of consummation, that is, to fullness of mutual blessing as the outcome of God's economy with Israel, the nations, and all creation."[5] Soulen also taught there is a "distinction between Jew and Gentile . . . intrinsic to God's work as the Consummator of creation [that] is not erased but realized in a new way in the sphere of the church."[6] Windsor appreciated Soulen's emphasis on the consummation of God's eschatological reign and his distinction between Jew and gentile. However, he disagreed with Soulen's rejection of a Christocentric biblical theology, believing that it "reduced the significance of Christ" in Ephesians and Colossians. He cited Eph 1:7, 10 and Col 1:14, 20 as example passages that are emphatically Christocentric.[7]

The Messianic Judaism movement (particularly in the teachings of Mark Kinzer) also added to Windsor's theological context. In *Postmissionary Messianic Judaism*, Kinzer rejected a supersessionist view that replaces the church with Israel: "The Jewish people are still Israel, a holy people, upon whom the redemption of the world ultimately hinges."[8] He was comfortable with a form of continuity between Old Testament Israel and the New Testament church when the church was comprised of a Jewish nucleus, but as the nucleus was absorbed into a predominately gentile congregation, the church began to accept a form of supersessionism:

> When the *ekkelesia* contained a visible Jewish nucleus, its right to claim continuity with Israel was reasonable and not necessarily supersessionist. When that nucleus disappeared, the claim to direct continuity with Israel became spiritual and abstract, and easily morphed into a claim to be a replacement for Israel.[9]

Kinzer taught that Jewish believers should still participate in the Jewish community and are obligated live a Jewish lifestyle in obedience to God's Torah. As gentiles are brought into a relationship with Jews (Israel), they experience the blessings of the nations.[10] Windsor also interacted with

---

5. Windsor, *Reading Ephesians and Colossians*, 10. See also Soulen, *God of Israel*, 113, 138, 157.

6. Soulen, *God of Israel*, 169 (bracketed text added).

7. Windsor, *Reading Ephesians and Colossians*, 10.

8. Kinzer, *Postmissionary Messianic Judaism*, 142.

9. Kinzer, *Postmissionary Messianic Judaism*, 43.

10. Kinzer, *Postmissionary Messianic Judaism*, 263–302. See also Windsor, *Reading Ephesians and Colossians*, 10.

a debate between Kinzer and Craig Blomberg. Blomberg had issues with Kinzer's use of obligated concerning obedience to God's Torah.¹¹ Windsor observed that Blomberg considered Kinzer's Messianic Judaism as a form of two-covenant theology and responded by stating that Kinzer's Messianic Judaism is an ecclesiological, not soteriological, position.¹² Jews are not obligated to keep God's Torah in order to be saved, but that Jews are permitted to obey God's Torah as ecclesiologically distinct from gentile Christians practicing a gentile form of Christianity.

Lionel Windsor's Evangelical Post-Supersessionist Theology

Windsor primarily articulated his evangelical, post-supersessionist theology in his work *Reading Ephesians and Colossians After Supersessionism* (a work in a series of "after supersessionism" volumes by a range of authors). Windsor elaborated on a threefold definition of his evangelical, post-supersessionist theology. First, he rejected a supersessionist position in that he did not believe the New Testament church replaced Old Testament Israel in redemptive history. Second, he believed in a special place and calling for Israel that was distinct from the gentiles in redemptive history. Third, he assigned a "positive value to Jewish distinctiveness" in their relationship to the gentiles. He considered the New Testament mission of salvation as coming from Israel and being brought to the gentile nations.¹³

Windsor rejected a supersessionist view of Ephesians and Colossians in three areas he considered were incorrect interpretations of the biblical text. He first rejected the view that invalidates any form of physical circumcision (citing Eph 2:11–12 and Col 2:11–13). While he rejected any theological position that required circumcision as essential to salvation (he believed that physical circumcision cannot bring salvation to anyone apart from Christ), he also interpreted Eph 2:11–12 and Col 2:11–13 as not regarding circumcision in general as invalid. These passages tried to eliminate a hostility between Jews and gentiles. Some Jews pushed for the physical circumcision of gentiles or only associated with physically circumcised individuals. He also rejected the view that Christ had abolished the Jewish observance of the Mosaic law (citing Eph 2:14–15 and Col 2:13–23) by asserting that Eph 2:15 does not nullify Jewish observance of the Mosaic law. Referencing

---

11. Blomberg, "Freedom from the Law," 41–42.
12. Windsor, *Reading Ephesians and Colossians*, 10.
13. Windsor, *Reading Ephesians and Colossians*, 5–6.

Zoccali, he viewed the death of Christ in that passage as having made some of the functions of the commandments of the law according to first-century Jewish interpretation unnecessary. Christ's death atoned for the sin of both Israel and the gentile nations and made both groups of believers holy in the sight of God. Following the law's commandments is no longer viewed as a means to distance Jews from any hostility of the gentiles. It is this use of the law as a buffer between Israel and the gentiles that has been eliminated, not "necessarily . . . other uses of the law," such as in "demarcating Jewish identity as [an] integral subordinate identity in Christ, or . . . source for community praxis for Jews and gentiles alike."[14]

Windsor also rejected an interpretation of Eph 2:14–16 and Col 3:11 in which a new humanity promised in Christ eliminated all Jewish/gentile distinctions. He asserted that the new humanity of Eph 2:14–16 and Col 3:11 does not replace Israel but comprises both Jews and gentiles who retain their ethnic distinctions (Windsor goes further than Robinson's distinction theology by retaining a Jew/gentile distinction in his concept of a new humanity). The new humanity did not eliminate the distinction between Jew and gentile but their divisiveness (as some Jews considered the law as a separation between them and the gentiles). Gentiles who believe in Christ do not replace Israel but come near to Israel and are reconciled alongside Israel.[15] Christ is not a replacement for Israel but the fulfillment of God's promises to Israel and God's promises to other nations through Israel. Jews and gentiles are now in communion with each other but are not a unity that erases their ethnic distinction. The distinction of Jews has been "transformed to serve a positive purpose for the apostolic mission."[16] The gentiles' calling is also distinct from Israel:

> The gentiles' "calling" to unity with Israel in Christ does not imply that they are made the same as Israel in every respect. Their calling is a distinctly gentile calling . . . both passages occur in

---

14. Windsor, *Reading Ephesians and Colossians*, 142. Windsor cited Zoccali, "What's the Problem with the Law?," 411 (bracketed text added). Zoccali stated that Gal 3:10–12 should not be used in a sense that the Torah's significance for Jews ended with Christ's death. He asserted that Paul believed in the Torah's continuing significance as a marker of Jewish identity. However, gentile Christians do not need to undergo conversion to Judaism, as they are already righteous due to their salvation status in Christ (as are Jewish Christians). When citing Zoccali, Windsor stated, "Zoccali's comments here concern Gal 3:10–12, but are just as applicable to Eph 2:15."

15. Another essay that asserted a similar position is Hoch, "New Man of Ephesians 2."

16. Windsor, *Reading Ephesians and Colossians*, 61–62, 129–31, 203.

letters that affirm that all believers are "called" to receive eschatological blessings through Christ (1 Cor 1:9, cf. vv. 1–8; Eph 1:18, cf. 4:4). Yet 1 Cor 7:17, 20 refer to a distinct station in life, in which each believer is "called."[17]

Windsor viewed the saints of Ephesians as the Jerusalem apostolic community (while not ruling out that it could refer to Jews in general) while expanding the term to incorporate Christ's salvation of the nations through Israel. The *saints* refers to both the distinctive holiness of Israel and the remarkable holiness of the gentiles. The *we/you* passages of Eph 1:11–14; 2:11–22; and 3:1–6 refer to a distinction between Jews (the *we*) and gentiles (the *you*) without falling into a separate way of salvation for Jews in contrast to gentiles: "On the one hand, Jews stand in an equal position with the non-Jews with respect to sin, judgment, and salvation through the gospel. On the other hand, Jews have a certain privilege and pre-eminence with respect to the gospel."[18]

Windsor agreed with Robinson's position on Rom 9–11 that referred to a renewed Israel as the apostolic community of disciples.[19] Gentiles are blessed alongside Israel as the fulfillment of the Gen 12:1–3 Abrahamic covenant, but they do not replace Israel. The reason for Paul's apostolic mission is Christ's work in sharing Israel's blessings with the nations. Windsor also agreed with Robinson that Gal 6:16 referred to actual Jews who believe in Christ as the Israel of God, with Christ fulfilling of the role of being Abraham's offspring. Jews and gentiles in Christ allowed them to be in Abraham while still distinguishing Jews who believe in Christ as the Israel of God.[20]

Before writing *Reading Ephesians and Colossians After Supersessionism*, Windsor laid some of the groundwork for his evangelical, post-supersessionist theology in his dissertation *Paul and the Vocation of Israel*. In his work, not only does Israel have a role (what Windsor termed as *vocation*) in redemptive history, but Paul (as an Israelite) has a direct role (vocation) as a Jewish believer and missionary teacher to the gentiles in order to resolve the hostility between Jew and gentile in God's plan.[21] He defined the term

---

17. Windsor, *Reading Ephesians and Colossians*, 179.

18. Windsor, *Reading Ephesians and Colossians*, 18, 61–62, 85–86, 157.

19. Windsor, *Reading Ephesians and Colossians*, 51, 89, 101–3, 124, 129, 144, 157, 169–70, 195–96, 209–10.

20. Windsor, *Reading Ephesians and Colossians*, 56, 90–91, 153.

21. Windsor, *Paul and the Vocation of Israel*, 246.

vocation as applied to Israel's role in redemptive history, as well as specifically to Paul's mission as a Jewish apostle:

> Paul was convinced that Israel had received a special divine revelation which conferred on Jews a distinct divine vocation. Paul, in other words, was committed to the view that God's global purposes in Christ included a special place—and correspondingly a special role—for the Jewish people.... The term "vocation" here refers to the notion that the distinct existence and concrete practice of Jewish people stems from a special divine intention and implies a special role for Jews within God's wider purposes ... the distinct existence and concrete practice of Jewish people stems from a special divine intention, an intention which can imply a particular divine role for Jews in relation to non-Jews.[22]

Paul's apostolic vocation as a missionary to the gentiles fulfilled Israel's divine vocation.[23]

Windsor argued that Paul believed that the Jews were given a particular divine vocation by receiving God's revelation of the Mosaic law. The Jews were the recipients and teachers of God's revelation to the gentile nations. Windsor later redefined the Jews' divine vocation Christologically as a salvation message that was preached to the gentile nations from and through the nation of Israel. Just as the Jews were given God's revelation through the Mosaic law, they were given the gospel message through Christ. The Jews were to preach Christ's salvation message to the gentiles. Windsor's argument is threefold. First, there is still a distinction and positive value for Jews, even within the Christian church. Second, this positive value of Jewish distinction resulted from the Scriptures and Mosaic law being "a special gift of divine revelation to Israel," and third, Paul affirmed that "God's revelation to Israel provides Israel with a special role or task within God's wider purposes—a divine vocation."[24]

Windsor rejected a supersessionist view of Rom 9–11 that the New Testament (predominantly gentile) church becomes a new Israel: "The Scriptures themselves contain no examples of non-Israelites becoming 'Israelites' simply by worshiping the God of Israel ... the terms 'Israel' and 'Jew' are referring to ethnic Jews throughout."[25] The olive tree of Rom 11

22. Windsor, *Paul and the Vocation of Israel*, 1, 9, 248.
23. Windsor, *Paul and the Vocation of Israel*, 19.
24. Windsor, *Paul and the Vocation of Israel*, 12, 20.
25. Windsor, *Paul and the Vocation of Israel*, 49.

is not that "Gentiles are joining Israel itself, nor to eradicate [eradicating] Israel's ethnic distinctiveness," but that

> Paul is using the metaphor to describe the relationship between Israel and Christ-believing Gentiles: both share in the same root, and that "Israel" is more "naturally" related to this root than the Gentiles are, even if there has been a temporary "breaking off" because of unbelief... it is not intended to imply Gentiles are now to be regarded as members of Israel.[26]

Windsor made a handful of exegetical contributions concerning Israel's role in redemptive history throughout the New Testament. In Rom 2:28–29, Windsor believed that Paul placed Jewish identity "among those Jews who exist within the Christ-believing communities," not "every member of these Christ-believing communities."[27] In Gal 3:29, Windsor argued that Paul was not referring to the New Testament church comprised of gentile Christians as a new Israel. While Abraham should be considered the father of many nations, there is a distinction between the seed of Abraham as it applies to Israel and gentile Christians. Like Robinson, Windsor believed that gentile Christians comprise a seed of Abraham through their salvation in Christ but are not a replacement for ethnic Israel. He also believed that Gal 6:16 referred to actual Jews, not the New Testament church, stating that Gal 6:16 refers to at least one of the following possibilities: all Jews, Jews Paul wished to believe in Christ, Jewish believers in Christ, or even Paul's Jewish opponents. In Phil 3:3, Windsor argued that *we the circumcision* refers to Paul and Timothy, Jewish believers in Christ and missionary teachers to the gentiles. Windsor's distinction between Jew and gentile did not lead to a two-covenant theology: "We are contending that Paul did not conceive of a distinct value of Jewishness principally in terms of salvation, but rather in terms of a special vocation arising from their possession of a unique divine revelation (the Law, or the Scriptures more generally)."[28] The Jews' special vocation was to receive God's divine revelation in Scripture and teach it to the gentile nations.

Windsor also refuted the idea of the church as a third race. Windsor argued that the concept of a third race was a viewpoint of the Epistle of Barnabas (which he labeled as presenting a supersessionist view), which stated that Christians are the recipient of God's covenant with Israel and

---

26. Windsor, *Paul and the Vocation of Israel*, 53 (bracketed text added).
27. Windsor, *Paul and the Vocation of Israel*, 61.
28. Windsor, *Paul and the Vocation of Israel*, 14, 49, 53.

that a new humanity or third race of Christians replaced Israel. He appealed to Ephesians in his refutation that the new humanity is comprised of both Jew and gentile, with both still retaining their ethnic distinctions, not comprising a third race. The New Testament church (ἐκκλησία) does not replace Israel or become a third race but is a united gathering (assembly) of Jew and gentile believers in Christ who retain their ethnic distinctions.[29]

Windsor appreciated the biblical theologies of both Robinson and Goldsworthy but primarily appreciated Robinson's distinction theology between Jew and gentile (this was absent in Goldsworthy's earlier writings). He even went further than Robinson's position by retaining a Jew/gentile distinction in his concept of a new humanity. While Windsor did not reject a Christocentric interpretation of Ephesians and Colossians, his emphasis on the Jew/gentile dynamic of both books ensured that an appreciation of the distinction between Jew and gentile in the New Testament church was not lost (an area of weakness in Goldsworthy's writings). Windsor's contributions to biblical theology were more targeted in that he did not provide a structured biblical theology as seen in Robinson and Goldsworthy. Instead he focused on correcting specific supersessionist interpretations throughout the biblical text (such as Ephesians and Colossians) to retain the importance of Israel's role and the distinction between Jew and gentile in redemptive history. With Windsor, one can begin to see the return of an emphasis on Robinson's distinction theology in to the contributions of Moore College scholars.

Robert Banks

Robert Banks (1939–), one of Robinson's students, wrote a widely read work on the church titled *Paul's Idea of Community*.[30] He considered the church to be a new Adam and followed Robinson's concept of ἐκκλησία as referring to an assembly.[31] Shiner provided a helpful summary of Banks in comparison to Robinson:

> With Robinson he argued that Paul resolves the Jew-Gentile relationship not in the church becoming Israel, but in Israel and the Gentiles becoming "Adam at Last," the new humanity. . . . He accepted and even extended Robinson's claims that ἐκκλησία only

29. Windsor, "Formation of Gentile," 378, 380, 383, 388.
30. Shiner, "Reading the New Testament," 113.
31. Banks, *Paul's Idea of Community*, 24–25, 34–37.

refers to actual gatherings, even going so far as to argue that Paul's persecution of "the church" must have involved persecution of Christians as they were gathered.[32]

While he compared the Septuagint's use of the term ἐκκλησία concerning Old Testament Israel to that of the New Testament's use of ἐκκλησία about the church, unlike R. H. Newton Flew and like J. Y. Campbell and Robinson, he did not apply any religious connotation to the term ἐκκλησία.[33] He also asserted that the church is primarily a local gathering with any idea of a universal church as only a heavenly reality, not consisting within an earthly universal church.[34] While he believed that both Jews and gentiles receive salvation in Christ, he also agreed with Robinson's distinction theology between Jew and gentile. He provided one example in his exegesis on Rom 11: the olive tree is Jewish. Israel still has a future role in redemptive history: "Paul does not view the Christian community, with its predominantly Gentile membership, as altogether replacing Israel in God's purposes."[35] Gentiles are grafted into a Jewish olive tree. It is the Jews who first gave the gospel, both to other Jews as well as to the gentile nations. Even after they believed in Christ, Jews and gentiles continued some of their lifestyle customs. Paul did not object to this continuance of lifestyle customs as long as such customs were not imposed upon other ethnicities as a requirement for salvation (since salvation is through Christ alone).[36]

George Athas

George Athas contributed to the discussion on Jew and gentile in *Donald Robinson: Selected Works; Appreciation*. He rejected a view of the New Testament in which readers attempt to insert themselves into the biblical

32. Shiner, "Reading the New Testament," 199.
33. Banks, *Paul's Idea of Community*, 34–35.
34. Banks, *Paul's Idea of Community*, 43–48.
35. Banks, *Paul's Idea of Community*, 119. Banks noted that gentiles can only share in the spiritual blessings of Jews because they were grafted into the olive tree. He also observed that Jews played a role in the salvation to the gentiles as well as to other Jews, so that there is still a role for Israel in redemptive history.
36. Banks, *Paul's Idea of Community*, 118–20. Examples Banks provided on some of the customs Jews carried over after their salvation was observance of the Sabbath, refraining from certain foods, and practicing circumcision. He noted that their observance of such customs was not an issue for Paul except for the Jews who insisted that such observances were requirements of salvation.

text in areas that directly apply to the role of Israel in redemptive history, considering the distinction between Jew and gentile as the "exegetical key for understanding the New Testament."[37] Throughout the Gospels, Athas surveyed Christ as the Jewish Messiah and the apostles as Jewish apostles, showing how both Israel and Christ fit together in the Gospels as an extension of the faith of Israel. Considering the book of Hebrews as written to a Jewish audience, its proper interpretation is not that Christians are falling away from the faith but that some Jews are falling short of the faith by failing to accept Christ as their Messiah. When Jews rejected Christ, they were rejecting that which the nation of Israel held sacred. In his explanation of the book of Galatians, he believed that Gal 4:1–6 does not state that Jews were rescued from the law. Their slavery was not to the law but to the world (and worldliness). In contrast, gentiles were never under the Jewish law. While both Jew and gentile can call God *Father* through Christ, Gal 3:28 refers solely to salvation, not an elimination of all ethnic distinctions. His exegesis of the book of Romans cautions readers that Paul's use of *we* in Romans refers to Paul and his companions, not a passage in which current believers should import themselves into the interpretation of *we*. In Rom 9–11, Athas carried forward Robinson's reciprocal role of the gospel as going from Jews to gentiles and back to Jews, salvation first going to the gentiles through the Jewish evangelists, and salvation going back to unsaved Jews through the gentiles. He elaborated on Jewish evangelism in Rom 12:12, stating that, while the gospel is no longer restricted to the Jews, it is still "to the Jew first," citing Rom 1:16 and 2:10.[38]

Phillip Jensen

Phillip Jensen (1945–) agreed with many of Robinson's teachings, and Shiner considered Jensen to be "the most influential Sydney Anglican preacher of his generation" and stated that Jensen teaches Robinson's position "regarding the place of Israel in the NT, the identity of 'the saints' as Jewish Christians and the ongoing significance of Jewish identity today."[39] In his message on the book of Romans, "Israel's Future," Jensen stated that God's plan for salvation was always universal. Old Testament Jews and first-century New Testament Jews did not fully understand the concept of

---

37. Athas, "Reflections on Scripture," 126.
38. Athas, "Reflections on Scripture," 126, 136.
39. Shiner, "Reading the New Testament," 203–4.

bringing salvation to non-Jews, especially how to incorporate non-Jewish Christians into the early New Testament church. God was always working through the Jews to bring salvation to the gentiles and the other nations. There was a reciprocal role when God brought salvation to the gentiles. Unbelieving Israel would be made jealous in order to be brought back to God. While God judged sinful Israel, Israel's failure concerning their rejection of Christ as their Messiah did not thwart the plan of God. It brought the plan of God into effect, leading to the salvation of the gentile nations, the envy of Israel, and bringing salvation back to unbelieving Israel. The gospel went out from Israel to the gentile nations because as Jewish Christians fled Jerusalem, they preached the gospel to the gentile nations, allowing the gospel to go out to the world. While *Israel* in Romans does not necessarily always equal *national Israel* concerning unbelieving Jews, there is a remnant and a true Israel in the New Testament—Jewish Christians—similar to how there was always a remnant of true Israel in the Old Testament. The olive tree (Rom 11) began as Israel (where the branches of unbelieving Jews were broken off and gentiles grafted in) comprising an olive tree that is Israel plus the grafted in gentiles. Because the olive tree began as Old Testament Israel, the New Testament church must not remove Jewishness from Christianity. God is not finished with the Jews, as they were and still are God's chosen people and will be saved through evangelization as coming from the gentiles. Furthermore, if God judged sinful Israel, his chosen people, how much more will he judge gentiles who reject him?[40]

Anthony Nichols

Anthony Nichols (1938–2019) contributed a chapter to *In the Fullness of Time*, in which he appreciated Robinson challenging the anti-Jewish stereotype of a supersessionist view. His article contrasted how he (in agreement with Robinson) interpreted the term *Israel* (as referring to ethnic Israel) with the translators of the Good News Bible (a Bible translation heavily used throughout Australia). Nichols observed that the translators incorrectly changed the translation of or dropped the term *Israel* throughout Scripture, and such incorrect translations weakened the importance of Israel's role in redemptive history.[41] He provided numerous examples of such incorrect translations. In the Old Testament, *Israel* is replaced by *Jacob* throughout

40. Jensen, "Israel's Future."
41. Peterson and Pryor, *Fullness of Time*, 112–13, 118, 121–27.

Gen 35–50, although God has already given Jacob the name Israel in Gen 32:28. In the New Testament, the Gospel of John in the Good News Bible (GNB) reduces the terms *Jew, Jews,* and *Jewish* from seventy-one in the Greek New Testament to forty-one in the GNB. Nichols also provided a useful discussion on οἱ Ἰουδαῖοι in the Gospel of John in which he contrasted John's authorial intent with Bratcher's interpretative positions. In Rom 9:4, 6b, and 31, the GNB replaces *Israel* with *God's people*. In Gal 6:16, GNB replaces *Israel* with the general phrase *all God's people*.[42]

Martin Pakula

Martin Pakula (1969–) is an Anglican minister and a Jewish Christian, offering another contribution to the discussion on Jew and gentile in *Donald Robinson: Selected Works; Appreciation*. His chapter argued for the need to evangelize the Jewish diaspora, citing his debt to Robinson for bringing this need into the discussion within Anglican evangelicalism. In his discussion on Rom 9–11, Pakula refuted a supersessionist view by not equating the Rom 11 olive tree with the New Testament church. The olive tree is Jewish, and even the church that gentile Christians join is Jewish, not primarily gentile. He considered the Jews' initial rejection of Christ as that which opened the door to giving the gospel to the gentiles, but that Jews will turn to Christ through evangelism from the gentiles. He also considered witnessing to Jews as primary in evangelism: the gospel is to the Jew first. The natural branches of the Rom 11 olive tree are Jews. Pakula still believed in a common salvation for Jews and gentiles in Christ and did not consider both missions as separate soteriological tracks but two different evangelistic emphases in which Jewish evangelism takes priority over gentile evangelism. He argued that Gal 3:28 affirms a common salvation status in Christ but does not eliminate all ethnic or gender distinctions. In Eph 1:11–14, Pakula considered *we* as referring to Paul plus Jewish Christians and *you* as referring to gentiles; current believers should not import themselves into the interpretation of *we*. Like Robinson, Pakula interpreted the *people of God* and *the saints* as referring to Jewish believers in Ephesians, also believing that Jews and gentiles comprise a new humanity but not a new Israel.[43]

---

42. Peterson and Pryor, *Fullness of Time*, 119–20, 122–25. Nichols offered an in-depth examination on how the GNB replaces *Israel* with *God's people* on pages 122–23.

43. Pakula, "Biblical Theology of Israel," 105–10.

Ma'afu Palu

Ma'afu Palu is another contributor to the discussion on Jew and gentile in *Donald Robinson: Selected Works; Appreciation*. His chapter provided theological contextualization concerning the distinction between Jew and gentile in redemptive history in agreement with Robinson's distinction theology concerning the relationship between Jew and gentile in the New Testament and Goldsworthy's Christocentric biblical theology since he considered Christ to be the interpretive key of Scripture. To Palu, the distinction between Jew and gentile goes beyond their ethnic distinctions and includes their spiritual standing before God. Jews have been given greater spiritual understanding concerning God than gentiles. Jews are still saved through the same way of salvation as gentiles (through salvation in Christ). He also briefly exegeted Rom 11 in his chapter, agreeing with Robinson that the root of the olive tree is the Abrahamic blessings not to be equated with the New Testament church.[44]

Jeff Read

Jeff Read is another Jewish Christian who contributed a chapter on the discussion on Jew and gentile in *Donald Robinson: Selected Works; Appreciation*. He used Robinson's exegetical method to further develop his contribution concerning Israel's role in redemptive history in Rom 11. In Rom 11:11–36, Israel's rejection is not final. While the gospel has gone out to the gentiles due to the Jews' initial rejection of Jesus as their Messiah, unbelieving Jews accept the gospel because of gentiles who witnessed to them. Israel's acceptance of the gospel parallels the dry bones event of Ezek 37. He believed that both Jew and gentile are saved through God's mercy through their belief in Christ as their Messiah and that all Israel being saved in Rom 11 does not refer to every individual Israelite but a collection of Israelites who are saved through the gospel of Christ. He considered the olive tree (Rom 11) as a Jewish tree. The gospel had especially been given to the Jews. Read concluded that Christianity is not a western religion but a Jewish one, attempting to remind the modern western church not to forget its Jewish roots.[45]

---

44. Palu, "Significance of the Jew-Gentile Distinction," 141–46.
45. Read, "That You May Not Be Conceited," 114–22.

W. H. (Bill) Salier

W. H. (Bill) Salier (1959–) is another contributor to the discussion on Jew and gentile in *Donald Robinson: Selected Works; Appreciation*, building upon Robinson's teaching to examine the relationship of Jew and gentile in the Gospel of John. In his contribution, Salier began with a discussion on Robinson's distinction theology in which Robinson did not confound the role of Jew and gentile in redemptive history but considered Jew and gentile as distinct but related. He continued the discussion by surveying Jesus's ministry and signs to the Jews in the Gospel of John, later examining Jesus's ministry to the gentiles in the Gospel of John. He was able to provide a parallel contribution to Robinson's discussion of a rising and falling Israel within the Gospel of Mark (see chapter 3), outlining a similar contribution concerning a rising and falling Israel within the Gospel of John. He also compared the theme of a restored Israel in Isaiah, where the Greeks come to Israel, placing its fulfillment in John 12 with the Greeks coming to Christ. He also discussed the use of the terms λαός and ἔθνος in the Gospel of John, stating that the oscillation between the terms cannot be evidence that the New Testament church replaces Old Testament Israel. If there is any replacement of Old Testament Israel in Scripture, Christ would be the replacement (or a better term being *fulfillment*) of the promises to Israel.[46]

Conclusion

Robinson's distinction theology concerning Jew and gentile in the New Testament church began to see a revival in later contributions to Moore's biblical theology program. Lionel Windsor brought more appreciation of Robinson's distinction between Jew and gentile in his published writings (such as *Reading Ephesians and Colossians After Supersessionism*). While he did not provide a phased structure to his contributions to biblical theology (unlike Robinson and Goldsworthy), his evangelical, post-supersessionist interpretation of Ephesians and Colossians retained the importance of a distinction between Jew and gentile in the New Testament church, and even went further than Robinson by retaining the Jew/gentile distinction in his concept of a new humanity.

Additional scholars (Robert Banks, George Athas, Phillip Jensen, Anthony Nichols, Martin Pakula, Ma'afu Palu, Jeff Read, and W. H. Salier)

---

46. Salier, "Jew and Gentile in John," 95–103.

agreed with Robinson's distinction theology and utilized Robinson's theological methodology in their own writings. Banks and Jensen brought Robinson's distinction theology concerning the relationship of Jew and gentile in the New Testament church to a wider audience. Athas provided a useful application of Robinson's methodology that cautioned readers not to insert themselves into the interpretation of biblical passages that pertained to ethnic Jews. Anthony Nichols appreciated Robinson's position on the term *Israel* and contributed an article on what he deemed were incorrect translations of the term in the Good News Bible. Pakula argued for prioritizing Jewish evangelism in missions by appreciating and elaborating on Robinson's exegesis of Rom 9–11 and Eph 1:11–14. Palu elaborated on Robinson's concept of the root of the Rom 11 olive tree as the Abrahamic blessing which gentiles can share in alongside Jews, but that both groups retain their ethnic distinctions. Read reminded readers not to forget the Jewish roots of Christianity and agreed with Robinson's position concerning the reciprocal role of the gospel first to the Jews, then to the gentiles (who were witnessed to by the Jews), and back to unbelieving Jews (who were witnessed to by gentiles). Salier applied Robinson's methodology to trace a theme of a rising and falling Israel throughout the Gospel of John similar to Robinson's tracing a theme of a rising and falling Israel throughout the Gospel of Mark.[47]

---

47. Shiner mentioned a couple of additional areas in which the legacy of Robinson has continued to the modern day. He discussed the use of Robinson's legacy concerning the Katoomba Youth Leaders Convention (now NextGen), at the AFES National Training Event, and in the external studies courses at Moore College. See Shiner, "Reading the New Testament," 200–202. For more on NextGen, visit nextgen.kcc.org.au. For more on the AFES National Training Event, see Australian Fellowship of Evangelical Students, "National Training Event." For more on the external studies courses at Moore, see the section on Richard Gibson in chapter 4.

7

Summary and Conclusion

Introduction

IT HAS BEEN AN interesting journey through this historical survey of Donald Robinson and biblical theology at Moore College. This book has examined the reception of Donald Robinson's distinction theology concerning Israel's role in redemptive history in the biblical theology program at Moore Theological College. It has sought to answer the question, Is it feasible to speak of a Moore School of Biblical Theology?

Research Conclusions

After surveying some influential ways of construing the biblical, theological role of Israel in Anglican thought (which were significant in Donald Robinson's context) in chapter 2, chapter 3 discussed that the biblical theology program at Moore College can be traced back to Donald Robinson. It also examined Robinson's distinction theology concerning Jew and gentile in the New Testament church. Robinson's distinction theology was his attempt at offering a mediating position between supersessionism and dispensationalism. However, his eschatological position of a new man that eliminated ethnic distinctions between Jew and gentile in his concept of a new man retained another form of supersessionism. Contrary to his claims, his distinction theology was not a mediating position between supersessionism and dispensationalism. It was still a modified form of supersessionism that did not adequately retain an eschatological distinction between Jew and gentile in God's eschatological plan.

SUMMARY AND CONCLUSION

The scholars who popularized Moore's biblical theology program, including Graeme Goldsworthy, Vaughan Roberts, Richard Gibson, Brian Rosner, Peter O'Brien, and Paul Williamson (chapter 4), D. Broughton Knox, William Dumbrell, Peter Bolt, Barry Webb, Kevin Giles, and Malcolm Richards (chapter 5), largely ignored Robinson's distinction theology in their contributions to Moore's biblical theology program concerning Israel's role in redemptive history. Their positions have more in common with a traditional Reformed redemptive-historical biblical theology following the Westminster tradition of Geerhardus Vos. Unlike Robinson's distinction theology that at least gave prominence to an ecclesiological distinction between both Jew and gentile in the New Testament church as distinct ethnicities (even though it failed to retain such an eschatological distinction), any ethnic distinctions were lost in the contributions of many of Robinson's successors. Goldsworthy's (and Roberts's) Christocentric biblical theology viewed Christ and those in Christ as the new and true Israel, regardless if they were ethnically Jews or gentiles. Knox considered Israel as set aside and replaced by the New Testament church that had no reference to any ethnic distinctions between Jew and gentile within the church. Dumbrell (and Webb) viewed Israel as merely a type or prototype replaced by an eschatological worshiping community as the new Israel with no ethnic distinctions between Jew and gentile. Williamson agreed with much of Goldsworthy's Christocentric biblical theology but also considered the New Testament church (without any reference to a Jew or gentile distinction) as the true Israel. Gibson primarily considered Moore's biblical theology program as teaching Goldsworthy's Christocentric biblical theology and was absent on a discussion concerning Israel's role in redemptive history or even much of Robinson's contributions to Moore's biblical theology program.

However, Goldsworthy's later writings, as well as the contributions of Lionel Windsor, Robert Banks, George Athas, Phillip Jensen, Anthony Nichols, Martin Pakula, Ma'afu Palu, Jeff Read, and W. H. Salier (chapter 6) show a revival in appreciating at least some aspects of Robinson's distinction theology into the biblical-theological discussion at Moore College. While some of Robinson's successors (such as Goldsworthy) did not fully incorporate all of Robinson's theology into their contributions to biblical theology even as they began appreciating some aspects of it, others (such as Windsor, Banks, Athas, Pakula, Palu, and Read) have given Robinson's distinction theology a revival in the theological discussion at Moore. It is possible that as future scholars continue to incorporate more of Robinson's unique theological position into Moore's biblical theology program that the trajectory of a Moore School of Biblical Theology will be shaped by Robinson's distinction theology concerning Israel's role in redemptive history.

Additional Areas of Future Research

Here are additional areas in which future research and development would provide a valuable contribution building upon the research conclusions of this book. First, further research concerning the plausibility of a Moore School of Biblical Theology would add to the discussion presented in this book. There are other areas of biblical theology in the works of the scholars covered in this book that could contribute to the discussion of whether it is feasible to speak of a Moore School of Biblical Theology. This book examined the lens of Robinson's distinction theology concerning the relationship between Jew and gentile in the New Testament church and the role of Israel in redemptive history as one possibility. Another lens that could be examined is how well Robinson's three-stages typology of biblical theology was received and popularized by Robinson's successors (such as Goldsworthy).

Additionally, the distinction between Jew and gentile in the New Testament church, which Robinson postulated and defended, a distinction Robinson noted at the time was not recognized by either of the popular approaches to the question of Israel (dispensationalists or Christian restorationists on the one hand or supersessionists such as covenantalists on the other hand) is a key feature of progressive dispensationalism. Progressive dispensationalism has developed in the dispensational tradition (away from Scofield) independently from Robinson. Two scholars who popularized progressive dispensationalism were Craig Blaising and Darrell Bock. Earlier dispensationalists taught that Jewish Christians were no longer part of Israel but were grouped together with gentile believers in the New Testament church without emphasizing their ethnic distinctions as Jews. In progressive dispensationalism, while both Jew and gentile believers rightly share a common salvation in Christ, Jewish Christians are not excluded from receiving the fulfillment of Israel's future promises, including the literal fulfillment of Israel's future land promises. Progressive dispensationalism eliminated the remaining forms of supersessionism that Robinson retained in his distinction theology. Robinson considered the promises to Israel not fulfilled in a future millennial kingdom but through the preaching of the gospel from Jewish Christians (the true Israel) to gentiles, and reciprocally back to other unbelieving Jews. While Robinson was correct in that the gospel would go forth from Jewish Christians to the gentiles and reciprocally back to unbelieving Jews (in fulfillment of Rom 11:26, "so all Israel shall be saved"), he stopped short by limiting the fulfillment of Israel's promises and not incorporating a literal fulfillment of them, including God's land promises to Israel to be fulfilled in a literal nation of Israel. Additionally, Robinson's concept of an eschatological new man that eliminated the ethnic distinctions between Jew and gentile retained a modified form of supersessionism. Progressive dispensationalists instead considered a future fulfillment of Israel's promises, and unlike earlier forms of dispensationalism, this included Jewish Christians within the New Testament church, similar to Robinson's position. However, Paul's concept of one new man in Christ was a contrast between the saved and the unsaved in which both Jew and gentile share in their salvation. It did not affirm an eschatological elimination of the ethnic distinctions between Jew and gentile concerning the fulfillment of Israel's promises. Progressive dispensationalists provide a useful dialogue partner to Robinson due to progressive dispensationalism's connection between Israel's promises and Jewish believers in the church today. Since (contrary to Robinson) progressive dispensationalists maintain a future fulfillment of Israel's literal national and territorial promises, recognizing a connection between Jewish believers in the church and the promises of Israel does not necessarily require a suspension of the future fulfillment of Israel's promises. A dialogue between those who are interested in preserving Robinson's distinction theology with progressive dispensationalists on this ecclesiological and eschatological matter and its implications for biblical theology would provide a useful contribution for future research.[1]

The relationship between New Christian Zionism, as popularized by Gerald McDermott, in contrast to Robinson's distinction theology, would also provide a useful contribution for future research.[2] McDermott defined and summarized his position on the movement of New Christian Zionism as follows: "God saves the world through Israel and the perfect Israelite; thus the Bible is incoherent and salvation impossible without Israel. We propose that the history of salvation is ongoing: the people of Israel and

---

1. Blaising and Bock, *Progressive Dispensationalism*, 49–50.
2. Lewis, *Short History of Christian Zionism*, 344.

their land continue to have theological significance."³ While, like Robinson, he disagreed with dispensationalism (McDermott does not believe Israel and the gentile nations run completely on separate tracks within redemptive history, as he defines dispensationalism), unlike Robinson, he correctly advocated for restoring a Jewish nation in the land of Israel and a return of the Jewish people to their land.⁴ This return of the Jewish people to their land and the restoration of a Jewish nation in the land of Israel are the first fruits of an ultimate prophetic fulfillment concerning the nation of Israel to come.⁵ To McDermott, New Christian Zionism is not merely a political Zionist movement, but is grounded in an exegetical and hermeneutical understanding of the biblical text (another area in which McDermott and Robinson varied). McDermott correctly advocated for the theological significance of Israel's land, an area at which he varied with Robinson.⁶ A dialogue between those who are interested in preserving Robinson's distinction theology and those within New Christian Zionism would also provide a useful contribution for future research.

Conclusion

Robinson's distinction theology provided a different and provocative answer on the fulfillment of Israel's promises in redemptive history. It was different from typical covenantal and dispensational answers on the same question, and thus provided a distinctive interpretation of the shape and framework of redemptive-historical biblical theology in Moore's biblical theology program that developed around Robinson's core course.

However, the reception of Robinson's distinction theology among those who followed him and expanded and popularized the biblical theology program at Moore varied. Those who became well-known teachers of biblical theology at Moore, like Goldsworthy and Dumbrell, show little to no knowledge or appreciation of Robinson's distinction theology, instead incorporating a traditional Reformed redemptive-historical biblical theology in line with Westminster scholar Geerhardus Vos into Moore's biblical theology curriculum.

---

3. McDermott, *New Christian Zionism*, 12.
4. McDermott, *Israel Matters*, xiv.
5. McDermott, *New Christian Zionism*, 27.
6. McDermott, *New Christian Zionism*, 320–21.

SUMMARY AND CONCLUSION

However, Goldsworthy later began to appreciate some aspects of Robinson's distinction theology (while not fully incorporating it into his biblical theology), and later biblical theologians at Moore brought a revival to Robinson's unique contribution in the biblical-theological discussion at Moore. Robinson's distinction theology could further shape the trajectory of a Moore School of Theology through the work of future scholars who continue appreciating or incorporating more of Robinson's unique position on the serious question he pursued: how to understand the place of Israel in redemptive history as one moves from the Old Testament to the New Testament (especially with respect to the fulfillment of Israel's promises) and advancing the understanding of redemptive-historical biblical theology beyond the typical Reformed view which he found to be inadequate. It would also be interesting to determine whether aspects of progressive dispensationalism or New Christian Zionism are brought into future discussions or conversations concerning Robinson's distinction theology into contributions at Moore College.

Afterword

I WANT TO TAKE a moment and thank you for investing your time to read my book. This book is my first major academic contribution and the capstone of my years of theological studies that resulted in my obtaining a PhD in systematic and biblical theology. I thoroughly enjoyed the journey through Donald Robinson's distinction theology concerning the role of Israel in redemptive history, as well as how other scholars at Moore Theological College carried forward, modified, or even rejected Robinson's unique theological position. While I am at variance with Robinson's (and most of his successors') conclusions, I have found Robinson to be a useful dialogue partner concerning the relationship between Jew and gentile in God's plan. I personally align closely with the position of my PhD supervisor, Dr. Craig Blaising, on progressive dispensationalism. I believe that Israel and the Jewish people (my fellow people) are still God's chosen people, and that God's promises to Israel will be fulfilled in a literal nation of Israel. I am a Christian Zionist, and I believe in the theological importance of the land of Israel in God's plan for the Jewish people. I also believe that a mass evangelization of the Jews will occur as more of them come to embrace faith in Jesus Christ, the Jewish Messiah, the Son of God and God the Son, in order to fulfill Rom 11:26, "so all Israel shall be saved." Like Dr. Blaising and Robinson, I do believe in the importance of an ecclesiological distinction between Jew and gentile in the church, but unlike Robinson, I also believe in an eschatological distinction between Jew and gentile in which Jewish Christians continue to be included in God's promises to his chosen people.

If you have read my book and have not yet professed faith in Jesus Christ, remember: "For all have sinned, and come short of the glory of God" (Rom 3:23), "For the wages of sin is death; but the gift of God is eternal life through Jesus Christ our Lord" (Rom 6:23), "For God so loved the world, that he gave his only begotten Son, that whosoever believeth in him should not perish, but have everlasting life" (John 3:16), "If we confess our sins, he is faithful and just to forgive us our sins, and to cleanse us from all unrighteousness" (1 John 1:9), and "That if thou shalt confess with thy mouth the Lord Jesus, and shalt believe in thine heart that God hath raised him from the dead, thou shalt be saved" (Rom 10:9). You can reach out and accept this free gift of salvation of the grace of Jesus Christ by faith and enter into a saving relationship with Jesus Christ as your personal Lord and Savior who died on the cross for your sins. If you believe what I have said, allow me to lead you in the following prayer:

> Father, I know that I am a sinner. My sin deserves judgment and eternal separation from you. But I also believe and know in my heart and now confess with my mouth that Jesus Christ died on the cross for my sins and paid my sin debt in full once and for all. I believe and know in my heart that Jesus Christ rose bodily from the grave. I accept his payment in full for my sins and invite him to enter my heart and become my personal Lord and Savior. I thank you for saving me, Jesus. Begin now to make me a new creation, born again, born from above, with a new spiritual birth walking in your will, your peace, and your presence. In the holy, wonderful, and precious name of Jesus I pray, Amen.[1]

If you prayed the above prayer and believe what you have prayed, you are now gladly a part of the family of God. You have an eternal home awaiting you in heaven, and a new spiritual life in Christ.

---

1. This prayer was inspired by the prayers and sermons of Dr. Adrian Rogers of Bellevue Baptist Church in Memphis, Tennessee, many of which can be found at lwf.org.

Bibliography

Ariel, Yaakov. "Israel in Contemporary Evangelical Christian Millennial Thought." *Numen* 59 (2012) 456–85. https://doi.org/10.1163/15685276-12341235.

———. "An Unexpected Alliance: Christian Zionism and Its Historical Significance." *Modern Judaism* 26 (2006) 74–100. https://doi.org/10.1093/mj/kjj005.

Athas, George. "Reflections on Scripture: Using the Distinction Between Jews and Gentiles as an Exegetical Key." In *Donald Robinson: Selected Works; Appreciation*, edited by Peter G. Bolt and Mark D. Thompson, 125–40. Camperdown, Aus.: Australian Church Record, 2008.

Augustine. *Expositions on the Book of Psalms*. Edited by A. Cleveland Coxe. Vol. 8 of $NPNF^1$. New York: Christian Literature, 1888. Logos.

———. "Letter 149." In *The Works of Saint Augustine: A Translation for the 21st Century*, edited by Boniface Ramsey, translated by Roland Teske, 2.2:360–77. Hyde Park, NY: New City, 2003. Logos.

Australian College of Theology. "About—History." Australian College of Theology, n.d. https://www.actheology.edu.au/about/history/.

Australian Fellowship of Evangelical Students. "National Training Event." afes, n.d. https://afes.org.au/national-training-event/.

Baker, David L. *Two Testaments, One Bible: The Theological Relationship Between the Old and New Testaments*. 3rd ed. Downers Grove, IL: IVP Academic, 2010.

Banks, Robert J. *Paul's Idea of Community: The Early House Churches in Their Cultural Setting*. Peabody, MA: Hendrickson, 1994.

Barnett, Paul W. *Apocalypse Now and Then: Reading Revelation Today*. Sydney: Aquila, 2001. https://archive.org/details/apocalypsenowtheooobarn/mode/2up.

Bass, Clarence B. *Backgrounds to Dispensationalism: Its Historical Genesis and Ecclesiastical Implications*. Grand Rapids: Eerdmans, 1960.

Beale, G. K. *A New Testament Biblical Theology: The Unfolding of the Old Testament in the New*. Grand Rapids: Baker Academic, 2011.

Blaising, Craig A. "Dispensation, Dispensationalism." In *Evangelical Dictionary of Theology*, edited by Daniel J. Treier and Walter A. Elwell, 248. Grand Rapids: Baker Academic, 2017.

———. "The Future of Israel as a Theological Question." *JETS* 44 (2001) 435–50. http://hdl.handle.net/20.500.12424/161669.

BIBLIOGRAPHY

———. "Premillennialism." In *Three Views on the Millennium and Beyond*, by Craig A. Blaising et al., edited by Darrell L. Bock, 155–208. Counterpoints. Grand Rapids: Zondervan, 1999.

Blaising, Craig A., and Darrell L. Bock, eds. *Dispensationalism, Israel and the Church: The Search for Definition*. Grand Rapids: Zondervan, 1992.

Blaising, Craig A., and Darrell L. Bock. *Progressive Dispensationalism*. Grand Rapids: Bridgepoint, 1993.

Blaising, Craig A., et al. *Three Views on the Millennium and Beyond*. Edited by Darrell L. Bock. Counterpoints. Grand Rapids: Zondervan, 1999.

Blomberg, Craig L. "Freedom from the Law Only for Gentiles? A Nonsupersessionist Alternative to Mark Kinzer's 'Postmissionary Messianic Judaism.'" In *New Testament Theology in Light of the Church's Mission: Essays in Honor of I. Howard Marshall*, edited by Jon C. Laansma et al., 41–56. Eugene, OR: Cascade, 2011.

Blomberg, Craig L., and Sung Wook Chung, eds. *A Case for Historic Premillennialism: An Alternative to "Left Behind" Eschatology*. Grand Rapids: Baker Academic, 2009.

Bolt, Peter G. *The Cross from a Distance: Atonement in Mark's Gospel*. New Studies in Biblical Theology 18. Downers Grove, IL: InterVarsity, 2004.

———. "The Family Correspondence of Thomas Moore, Esq., of Liverpool." In *Donald Robinson: Selected Works; Appreciation*, edited by Peter G. Bolt and Mark D. Thompson, 279–302. Camperdown, Aus.: Australian Church Record, 2008.

———. "God's Vision of Church." Sermon given on Vision Day at St. Matthias, Mar. 2, 1991. https://moorecollege.access.preservica.com/IO_33882718-ca58-48c3-a2e3-af19846ed2d4/.

———. *A Portrait in His Actions: Thomas Moore of Liverpool (1762–1840); Part 1: Lesbury to Liverpool*. Studies in Australian Colonial History 3. Camperdown, Aus.: Bolt, 2010.

Boyce, F. B. *Thomas Moore: An Early Australian Worthy*. London: Rowell and Sons, 1922. https://nla.gov.au/nla.obj-366919583/view?partId=nla.obj-366919924#.

Braga, Stuart. *A Century Preaching Christ: Katoomba Christian Convention, 1903–2003*. Sydney: Katoomba Christian Convention, 2003.

Brand, Chad, et al. *Perspectives on Israel and the Church: 4 Views*. Nashville: B&H Academic, 2015.

Campbell, Constantine. "Biblical Theology at Moore: Origins and Guiding Principles." Session at ETS Sixty-Third Annual Meeting, San Francisco, Nov. 17, 2011.

Campbell, J. Y. "The Origin and Meaning of the Christian Use of the Word *Ekklesia*." *JTS* 49 (1948) 130–42. https://doi.org/10.1093/jts/os-XLIX.195-196.130.

Chapman, David W., and Andreas J. Köstenberger. "Jewish Intertestamental and Early Rabbinic Literature: An Annotated Bibliographic Resource." *JETS* 43 (2000) 577–618. https://etsjets.org/wp-content/uploads/2010/06/files_JETS-PDFs_43_43-4_43-4-pp577-618_JETS.pdf.

Charlesworth, J. H., ed. *Jews and Christians: Exploring the Past, Present, and Future*. New York: Crossroad, 1990.

Childs, Brevard S. *Biblical Theology of the Old and New Testaments: Theological Reflection on the Christian Bible*. London: SCM, 1992.

CMJ UK. "Our History." CMJ UK, n.d. https://www.cmj.org.uk/our-history.

Cragoe, Thomas H. "W. H. Griffith Thomas." In *Handbook of Evangelical Theologians*, edited by Walter A. Elwell, 67–82. Grand Rapids: Baker, 1998.

Crutchfield, Larry V. *The Origins of Dispensationalism: The Darby Factor*. Lanham, MD: University Press of America, 1992.

Cullmann, Oscar. *Christ and Time: The Primitive Christian Conception of Time and History*. Translated by Floyd V. Filson. 3rd ed. Eugene, OR: Wipf & Stock, 2018.

Daley, Brian E. *The Hope of the Early Church: A Handbook of Patristic Eschatology*. Cambridge: Cambridge University Press, 1991.

Darby, J. N. "Considerations on the Nature and Unity of the Church of Christ." In *Ecclesiastical 1*, edited by William Kelly, 20–35. Vol. 1 of *The Collected Writings of J. N. Darby*. Repr., Sunbury, PA: Believers Bookshelf, 1971.

Davies, D. J. "The Interpretation of Scripture." MS in Rev. David J. Davies Papers, 1902–1935. MitchLib (Local Number: MLL MSS 3179) Box 1(1). Donald Robinson Library at Moore Theological College, Newtown, NSW, Australia.

Davies, Glenn. "William John Dumbrell: An Appreciation." In *Covenant and Kingdom: A Collection of Old Testament Essays by William J. Dumbrell*, edited by Gregory R. Goswell and Allan M. Harman, v–ix. RTRSS 2. Doncaster, Aus.: Reformed Theological Review, 2007.

Davies, John A., and Allan M. Harman, eds. *An Everlasting Covenant: Biblical and Theological Essays in Honour of William J. Dumbrell*. RTRSS 4. Doncaster, Aus.: Reformed Theological Review, 2010.

Davies, W. D. *The Gospel and the Land: Early Christianity and Jewish Territorial Doctrine*. Berkley: University of California Press, 1974.

Dickey, Brian. "Jones, Nathaniel." In *The Australian Dictionary of Evangelical Biography*, edited by Brian Dickey, 191–92. Sydney: Evangelical History Association, 1994.

Dickson, N. "Darby, John Nelson." In *Biographical Dictionary of Evangelicals*, edited by Timothy Larsen et al., 178–81. Downers Grove, IL: InterVarsity, 2003.

Diprose, Ronald E. *Israel in the Development of Christian Thought*. Rome: Instituto Biblico Evangelico Italiano, 2000.

Dockery, David S. *The Doctrine of the Bible*. Nashville: Convention, 1991.

Dodd, C. H. *The Parables of the Kingdom*. New York: Scribner, 1961.

Draxe, Thomas. *The Worldes Resurrection, or the generall calling of the Jewes* [. . .]. London: Eld, 1608.

Dubois, Marcel. "Jews, Judaism and Israel in the Theology of Saint Augustine: How He Links the Jewish People and the Land of Zion." *Imm* 22 (1989) 162–214.

Dumbrell, William J. *Covenant and Creation: An Old Testament Covenant Theology*. London: Paternoster, 2013.

———. "The Covenant with Abraham." *RTR* 41 (1982) 42–50.

———. *The End of the Beginning: Revelation 21–22 and the Old Testament*. Eugene, OR: Wipf & Stock, 2001.

———. *The Faith of Israel: A Theological Survey of the Old Testament*. Grand Rapids: Baker Academic, 2002.

———. *Galatians: A New Covenant Commentary*. Blackwood, Aus.: New Creation, 2006.

———. *Hebrews: A New Covenant Commentary*. North Paramatta, Aus.: Redeemer Baptist, 2009.

———. *John: Gospel of the New Creation; A New Covenant Exposition*. Caringbah, Aus.: New Covenant, 2006.

———. "Paul and Salvation History in Romans 9:30—10:4." In *Out of Egypt: Biblical Theology and Biblical Interpretation*, edited by Craig G. Bartholomew et al., 286–312. Scripture and Hermeneutics 5. Grand Rapids: Zondervan, 2004.

———. *Revelation: Visions for Today; A New Covenant Commentary*. Eugene, OR: Wipf & Stock, 2017.

———. *Romans: A New Covenant Commentary*. Eugene, OR: Wipf & Stock, 2005.

———. *The Search for Order: Biblical Eschatology in Focus*. Eugene, OR: Wipf & Stock, 2001.

Durnbaugh, Donald F. *Fruit of the Vine: A History of the Brethren, 1708–1995*. Philadelphia: Brethren, 1996.

Eichrodt, Walther. *Theology of the Old Testament*. Edited by Peter Ackroyd et al. Translated by J. A. Baker. 2 vols. OTL. Philadelphia: Westminster, 1961–67. Logos.

Ellis, E. Earle. *Paul's Use of the Old Testament*. Grand Rapids: Eerdmans, 1957.

Fackler, M. "Scofield, Cyrus Ingerson." In *Who's Who in Christian History*, edited by J. D. Douglas and Philip W. Comfort, 616. Wheaton, IL: Tyndale House, 1992.

Feinberg, John S., ed. *Continuity and Discontinuity: Perspectives on the Relationship Between the Old and New Testaments; Essays in Honor of S. Lewis Johnson, Jr.* Westchester, IL: Crossway, 1988.

Fellowship for Biblical Studies. "History." Fellowship for Biblical Studies, n.d. https://www.fbs.org.au/history.

Flew, R. Newton. *Jesus and His Church: A Study of the Idea of the Ecclesia in the New Testament*. Eugene, OR: Wipf & Stock, 2009.

———. "Some Outstanding New Testament Problems: IV. Jesus and the Kingdom of God." *ExpTim* 46 (1935) 214–18. https://doi.org/10.1177/001452463504600505.

Fredriksen, Paula. "*Secundum Carnem*: History and Israel in the Theology of St. Augustine." In *Augustine and World Religions*, edited by Brian Brown et al., 21–36. Augustine in Conversation: Tradition and Innovation. Lanham, MD: Lexington, 2008.

Fuller, Daniel P. *Gospel and Law: Contrast or Continuum? The Hermeneutics of Dispensationalism and Covenant Theology*. Grand Rapids: Eerdmans, 1980.

Furse-Roberts, David. "The Victorian Evangelical Shaftesbury: A Son of the Clapham Sect or a Brother of the Recordites?" *Chm* 128 (2014) 119–32. https://biblicalstudies.org.uk/pdf/churchman/128-02_119.pdf.

Galli, Mark, and Ted Olsen, eds. "John Nelson Darby." In *131 Christians Everyone Should Know*, 98–101. Nashville: B&H, 2000.

Geldbach, Erich. "Plymouth Brethren." In *P-Sh*. Vol. 4 of *The Encyclopedia of Christianity*, edited by Erwin Fahlbusch et al., 246–47. Grand Rapids: Eerdmans, 2005.

Gentry, Peter J., and Stephen J. Wellum. *Kingdom Through Covenant: A Biblical-Theological Understanding of the Covenants*. 2nd ed. Wheaton, IL: Crossway, 2018.

Gerrish, Jim. "Christians Remember Zion." Church & Israel Forum. https://www.churchisraelforum.com/favorites-13/.

Gibson, Richard J. "Biblical Theology at Moore: Teaching Biblical Theology." Session at ETS Sixty-Third Annual Meeting, San Francisco, Nov. 17, 2011.

———, ed. *Interpreting God's Plan: Biblical Theology and the Pastor*. London: Paternoster, 1997.

Giles, Kevin. *What on Earth Is the Church? An Exploration in New Testament Theology*. Downers Grove, IL: InterVarsity, 1995.

Goldsworthy, Graeme. *According to Plan: The Unfolding Revelation of God in the Bible*. Downers Grove, IL: InterVarsity, 1991.

———. *Christ-Centered Biblical Theology: Hermeneutical Foundations and Principles*. Downers Grove, IL: IVP Academic, 2012.

———. "Finding the Gospel in the Whole Bible: An Interview with Graeme Goldsworthy." In *Modern Reformation* 20 (2011) 40–45. https://www.modernreformation.org/resources/articles/finding-the-gospel-in-the-whole-bible.

BIBLIOGRAPHY

———. *Gospel and Kingdom.* London: Paternoster, 2001.
———. *The Gospel in Revelation.* London: Paternoster, 2001.
———. *Gospel-Centered Hermeneutics: Foundations and Principles of Evangelical Biblical Interpretation.* Downers Grove, IL: IVP Academic, 2012.
———. *Jesus Through the Old Testament: Transform Your Bible Understanding.* Abington, UK: Bible Reading Fellowship, 2017.
———. "The Kingdom of God as Hermeneutic Grid." *SBJT* 12 (2008) 4–15. https://cf.sbts.edu/equip/uploads/2010/02/sbjt_121_goldsworthy.pdf.
———. "Lecture 1: The Necessity and Viability of Biblical Theology." *SBJT* 12 (2008) 4–18. https://cdn.sbts.edu/media/publications/sbjt/sbjt_2008winter2.pdf.
———. "Lecture 2: Biblical Theology in the Seminary and Bible College." *SBJT* 12 (2008) 20–34. https://cf.sbts.edu/equip/uploads/2015/10/SBJT-V12N4.Goldsworth2.pdf.
———. "Lecture 3: Biblical Theology in the Local Church and the Home." *SBJT* 12 (2008) 36–50. https://cf.sbts.edu/equip/uploads/2015/10/SBJT-V12N4.Goldsworth3.pdf
———. *Preaching the Whole Bible as Christian Scripture: The Application of Biblical Theology to Expository Preaching.* Grand Rapids: Eerdmans, 2000.
———. *The Son of God and the New Creation.* Short Studies in Biblical Theology. Wheaton, IL: Crossway, 2015.
Grass, Tim. *F. F. Bruce: A Life.* Grand Rapids: Eerdmans, 2012.
Hall, Sarah Lebhar. "Anglicans and Israel: The (Largely) Untold Story." In *Understanding the Jewish Roots of Christianity: Biblical, Theological, and Historical Essays on the Relationship Between Christianity and Judaism,* edited by Gerald R. McDermott, 169–83. Studies in Scripture and Biblical Theology. Bellingham, WA: Lexham, 2021.
Hammond, T. C. *In Understanding Be Men: A Synopsis of Christian Doctrine for Non-Theological Students.* London: Inter-Varsity Fellowship, 1936.
———. *Inspiration and Authority: The Character of Inspiration and the Problems of Authority.* InterVarsity Papers 3. London: Inter-Varsity Fellowship, n.d. First published in *Evangelicalism,* edited by J. R. Howden. London: Thynne & Jarvis, 1925.
Hankins, B. "Scofield, Cyrus Ingerson." In *Biographical Dictionary of Evangelicals,* edited by Timothy Larsen et al., 589–91. Downers Grove, IL: InterVarsity, 2003.
Hannah, John D. "The 'Thomas' in the W. H. Griffith Thomas Memorial Lectureship." *BSac* 163 (2006) 3–17. https://www.galaxie.com/article/bsac163-649-01.
Hays, Daniel J., et al. *Dictionary of Biblical Prophecy and End Times.* Grand Rapids: Zondervan, 2007.
Hebert, A. G. *Christ the Fulfiller: Three Studies on the Biblical Types, as They Are Presented in the Old and New Testaments.* Sydney: Anglican Truth Society, 1957.
Hechler, William. *The Restoration of the Jews to Palestine.* N.p., 1884.
Herzl, Theodor. *The Jewish State.* Translated by Sylvie D'Avigdor. New York: American Zionist Emergency Council, 1946. https://www.jewishvirtuallibrary.org/quot-the-jewish-state-quot-theodor-herzl.
Hoch, Carl B., Jr. "The New Man of Ephesians 2." In *Dispensationalism, Israel and the Church: The Search for Definition,* edited by Craig A. Blaising and Darrell L. Bock, 98–126. Grand Rapids: Zondervan, 1992.
Hoffecker, W. Andrew. "Darby, John Nelson." In *Evangelical Dictionary of Theology,* edited by Daniel J. Treier and Walter A. Elwell, 228–29. Grand Rapids: Baker Academic, 2017.
Horner, Barry E. *Eternal Israel: Biblical, Theological, and Historical Studies That Uphold the Eternal, Distinctive Destiny of Israel.* Nashville: B&H Academic, 2018.

BIBLIOGRAPHY

Hort, Fenton John Anthony. *The Christian Ecclesia: A Course of Lectures on the Early History and Early Conceptions of the Ecclesia, and Four Sermons.* London: McMillan, 1897.

Horton, Michael. *God of Promise: Introducing Covenant Theology.* Grand Rapids: Baker, 2006.

Hunt, Keith, and Gladys Hunt. *For Christ and the University: The Story of InterVarsity Christian Fellowship of the U.S.A./1940–1990.* Downers Grove, IL: InterVarsity, 1991.

Hutchinson, M. "Guinness, Howard Wyndham." In *Biographical Dictionary of Evangelicals*, edited by Timothy Larsen et al., 272–74. Downers Grove, IL: InterVarsity, 2003.

Irenaeus. "Against Heresies." In *The Apostolic Fathers, Justin Martyr, Irenaeus*. In *ANF*, edited by Alexander Roberts and James Donaldson, 1:563–66. Buffalo: Christian Literature, 1885. Logos.

Jensen, Michael P. *Sydney Anglicanism: An Apology.* Eugene, OR: Wipf & Stock, 2012.

Jensen, Phillip. "Israel's Future." City Night Church, Mar. 25, 2007. Talk 21 of 32 in Romans 2006-7 The Bible Talks. https://phillipjensen.com/resources/israels-future/.

JewishHistory.org. "Crash Course." JewishHistory.org, n.d. https://www.jewishhistory.org/crash-course/.

Jewish Virtual Library. "Zionist Congress: First Zionist Congress and Basel Program (August 1897)." https://www.jewishvirtuallibrary.org/first-zionist-congress-and-basel-program-1897.

Johnson, Douglas, ed. *A Brief History of the International Fellowship of Evangelical Students.* Lausanne: IFES, 1964.

Joint Commission on Church Union. *The Faith of the Church* [. . .]. Melbourne: Joint Board of Graded Lessons of Australia and New Zealand, 1959. https://ctm.uca.edu.au/lay-ministries/wp-content/uploads/sites/6/2015/08/JCCU-1959-The-faith-of-the-church.pdf.

Jones, Nathaniel. *The Teaching of the Thirty-Nine Articles: A Plain Exposition of the Doctrines of the Church of England, with Their Scripture Proofs.* Sydney: Madgwick and Sons, 1904.

Judd, Stephen. "Davies, David John." In *The Australian Dictionary of Evangelical Biography*, edited by Brian Dickey, 88–89. Sydney: Evangelical History Association, 1994.

Judge, Edwin A. "Contemporary Political Models for the Interrelations of the New Testament Churches." *RTR* 22 (1963) 65–76.

Justin Martyr. "Dialogue of Justin with Trypho, a Jew." In *The Apostolic Fathers, Justin Martyr, Irenaeus*. In *ANF*, edited by Alexander Roberts and James Donaldson, 1:194–270. Buffalo: Christian Literature, 1885. Logos.

Kerr, William Nigel. "Scofield, Cyrus Ingerson." In *Evangelical Dictionary of Theology*, edited by Daniel J. Treier and Walter A. Elwell, 787–88. Grand Rapids: Baker Academic, 2017.

Kinzer, Mark S. *Postmissionary Messianic Judaism: Redefining Christian Engagement with the Jewish People.* Grand Rapids: Brazos, 2005.

Klinger, Jerry. "Reverend William H. Hechler—The Christian Minister Who Legitimized Theodor Herzl." *Jewish Magazine*, July 2010. http://jewishmag.com/145mag/herzl_hechler/herzl_hechler.htm.

Klink, Edward W., III, and Darian R. Lockett. *Understanding Biblical Theology: A Comparison of Theory and Practice.* Grand Rapids: Zondervan, 2012.

Knox, D. Broughton. "The Church and the People of God in the Old Testament." *RTR* 10 (1951) 12–20.

BIBLIOGRAPHY

———. "D. B. Knox: The Authority of the Bible." Australian Church Record, Jan. 26, 2017. https://www.australianchurchrecord.net/d-b-knox-the-authority-of-the-bible/.

———. *D. Broughton Knox: Selected Works*. Edited by Tony Payne et al. 3 vols. Sydney: Matthias Media, 2000–2006.

———. "The Date of the Epistle to the Galatians." *EvQ* 13 (1941) 262–68. https://biblicalstudies.org.uk/pdf/eq/1941-4_262.pdf.

———. *The Doctrine of Faith in the Reign of Henry VIII*. London: Clarke, 1957.

Köstenberger, Andreas J., and Peter T. O'Brien. *Salvation to the Ends of the Earth: A Biblical Theology of Mission*. New Studies in Biblical Theology 11. Downers Grove, IL: IVP Academic, 2001.

Krabbendam, Hendrik. "Hermeneutics in Preaching." In *The Preacher and Preaching: Reviving the Art in the Twentieth Century*, edited by Samuel T. Logan Jr., 212–45. Phillipsburg, NJ: Presbyterian and Reformed, 1986.

Kraus, C. Norman. *Dispensationalism in America: Its Rise and Development*. Richmond, VA: John Knox, 1958.

Kuhn, Chase R. *The Ecclesiology of Donald Robinson and D. Broughton Knox: Exposition, Analysis, and Theological Evaluation*. Eugene, OR: Wipf & Stock, 2017.

Ladd, George Eldon. *The Blessed Hope: A Biblical Study of the Second Advent and the Rapture*. Grand Rapids: Eerdmans, 1980.

Lake, Meredith. *Proclaiming Jesus Christ as Lord: A History of the Sydney University Evangelical Union*. Sydney: Evangelical Union Graduates Fund, 2005.

Lawton, William. "The Winter of Our Days: The Anglican Diocese of Sydney, 1950–1960." *Lucas: An Evangelical History Review* 9 (1990) 11–31. https://drive.google.com/file/d/1YVtHwfyaVMVhXDVaNHqXa6LGsZcQHbrJ/view.

Lewis, Donald M. "Evangelicals and Jews Together? Exploring the Roots of Christian Zionism." *Crux* 45 (2009) 2–9.

———. *The Origins of Christian Zionism: Lord Shaftesbury and Evangelical Support for a Jewish Homeland*. New York: Cambridge University Press, 2010.

———. *A Short History of Christian Zionism: From the Reformation to the Twenty-First Century*. Downers Grove, IL: IVP Academic, 2021.

Lillback, Peter A. "Covenant Theology." In *New Dictionary of Theology: Historical and Systematic*, edited by Martin Davie et al., 225–27. 2nd ed. Downers Grove, IL: IVP Academic, 2016.

Loane, Edward, ed. "Richard Johnson: An Unlikely Hero." In *Historical Studies and Series Index*, 14–35. Vol. 4 of *Donald Robinson: Selected Works*. Camperdown, Aus.: Australian Church Record, 2018.

———. "Richard Johnson Faithful Minister." In *Historical Studies and Series Index*, 8–13. Vol. 4 of *Donald Robinson: Selected Works*. Camperdown, Aus.: Australian Church Record, 2018.

———. "Thomas Moore and the Early Life of Sydney." In *Historical Studies and Series Index*, 36–73. Vol. 4 of *Donald Robinson: Selected Works*. Camperdown, Aus.: Australian Church Record, 2018.

———. "Thomas Moore of Moore Bank 1762–1840: The Father of Liverpool, Benefactor of Mankind." In *Historical Studies and Series Index*, 74–82. Vol. 4 of *Donald Robinson: Selected Works*. Camperdown, Aus.: Australian Church Record, 2018.

Loane, Marcus L. *A Centenary History of Moore Theological College*. Sydney: Angus and Robertson, 1955.

BIBLIOGRAPHY

Maass, Enzo. "Forgotten Prophet: William Henry Hechler and the Rise of Political Zionism." *Nordisk Judaistik* 23 (2002) 157–93. https://doi.org/10.30752/nj.69594.

Mangum, Douglas, and Douglas Estes, eds. *Literary Approaches to the Bible.* Lexham Methods Series 4. Bellingham, WA: Lexham, 2016.

Mangum, Douglas, and Josh Westbury, eds. *Linguistics and Biblical Exegesis.* Lexham Methods Series 2. Bellingham, WA: Lexham, 2016.

McDermott, Gerald R. "Can Evangelicals Support Christian Zionism?" *Evangelical Review of Theology* 43 (2019) 253–62.

———. *Israel Matters: Why Christians Must Think Differently About the People and the Land.* Grand Rapids: Brazos, 2017.

———. *The New Christian Zionism: Fresh Perspectives on Israel and the Land.* Downers Grove, IL: IVP Academic, 2016.

McIntosh, John Alan. "Anglican Evangelicalism in Sydney 1897–1953: The Thought and Influence of Three Moore College Principals—Nathaniel Jones, D. J. Davies and T. C. Hammond." PhD diss., University of New South Wales, 2014. https://doi.org/10.26190/unsworks/16666.

Merkley, Paul C. "Zionists and Christian Restorationists." *Proceedings of the World Congress of Jewish Studies* (1993) 93–100. https://www.jstor.org/stable/23536830.

Nelson, Warren. "Hammond, T(homas) C(hatteron)." In *The Australian Dictionary of Evangelical Biography*, edited by Brian Dickey, 150–52. Sydney: Evangelical History Association, 1994.

Netanyahu, Benzion. *The Founding Fathers of Zionism.* Jerusalem: Balfour, 2012.

New College. "Rev Dr Stuart Barton Babbage AM." *New'n'Old* (Spring 2012) 32. https://newcollege.unsw.edu.au/downloads/File/pdf/NewNOld-Spring2012-WEB.pdf.

Newton, Kenneth John. "A History of the Brethren in Australia with Particular Reference to the Open Brethren." PhD diss., Fuller Theological Seminary, 1990.

Niagara Bible Conference. "Declaration of Doctrinal Belief of Niagara Bible Conference." *Truth* 20 (1894) 509–11.

Noble, Thomas A. *Tyndale House and Fellowship: The First Sixty Years.* Downers Grove, IL: InterVarsity, 2006.

O'Brien, Peter T. "The Church As a Heavenly and Eschatological Entity." In *The Church in the Bible and the World: An International Study*, edited by D. A. Carson, 88–119. Eugene, OR: Wipf & Stock, 2002.

O'Brien, Peter T., and David G. Peterson, eds. *God Who Is Rich in Mercy: Essays Presented to Dr. D. B. Knox.* Homebush West, Aus.: Lancer, 1986.

Origen. "Commentary on John, Book 1." In *Origen*, edited and translated by Joseph W. Trigg, 103–49. ECF. London: Routledge, 1998.

———. *On First Principles.* Translated by G. W. Butterworth. Gloucester, MA: Peter Smith, 1973.

Packer, J. I. "Basic Christian Doctrines 36: The Nature of the Church." *Christianity Today* (1962) 886–87. https://www.christianitytoday.com/1962/06/basic-christian-doctrines-36-nature-of-church/.

———. *Concise Theology: A Guide to Historic Christian Beliefs.* Carol Stream, IL: Tyndale, 2001.

———. *"Fundamentalism" and the Word of God.* Grand Rapids: Eerdmans, 1958.

———. "Introduction: On Covenant Theology." In *Revelations of the Cross*, 9–21. Peabody, MA: Hendrickson, 2013.

———. *Knowing God.* Downers Grove, IL: InterVarsity, 1973.

———. "The Nature of the Church." In *Basic Christian Doctrines: Contemporary Evangelical Thought*, edited by Carl F. H. Henry, 241–47. New York: Holt, Rinehart, and Winston, 1962.

———. "One Body in Christ: The Doctrine and Expression of Christian Unity." Chm 80 (1966) 16–26.

Pakula, Martin. "A Biblical Theology of Israel in the New Testament." In *Donald Robinson: Selected Works; Appreciation*, edited by Peter G. Bolt and Mark D. Thompson, 105–12. Camperdown, Aus.: Australian Church Record, 2008.

Palu, Ma'afu. "The Significance of the Jew-Gentile Distinction for Theological Contextualization." In *Donald Robinson: Selected Works; Appreciation*, edited by Peter G. Bolt and Mark D. Thompson, 141–52. Camperdown, Aus.: Australian Church Record, 2008.

Parkes, James. *The Foundations of Judaism and Christianity*. Chicago: Quadrangle, 1960.

Parsons, H. M. "Dispensations." *Truth* 11 (1885) 460–66.

———. "The Dispensations and the Second Coming of our Lord." *Truth* 11 (1885) 314.

Peterson, David G., and John W. Pryor, eds. *In the Fullness of Time: Biblical Studies in Honor of Archbishop Donald Robinson*. Homebush West, Aus.: Lancer, 1992.

Powell, Russel. "Moore Veteran Called Home." Sydney Anglicans, Oct. 3, 2016. https://sydneyanglicans.net/news/moore-veteran-called-home.

Read, Jeff. "That You May Not Be Conceited." In *Donald Robinson: Selected Works; Appreciation*, edited by Peter G. Bolt and Mark D. Thompson, 13–123. Camperdown, Aus.: Australian Church Record, 2008.

Regent College. "Remembering Dr. William J. Dumbrell." Regent College, Oct. 3, 2016. https://www.regent-college.edu/about-us/news/2016/remembering-dr-william-j-dumbrell.

Richards, Malcolm. "The New Israel: Taken Over by Jesus." Lecture given at Moore Theological College, July 21, 2020. https://moore.edu.au/resources/the-new-israel-taken-over-by-jesus-acts-242-47-432-516/.

Richardson, Peter. *Israel in the Apostolic Church*. SNTSMS 10. Cambridge: Cambridge University Press, 1969.

Roberts, Vaughan. *God's Big Picture: Tracing the Storyline of the Bible*. Downers Grove, IL: InterVarsity, 2002.

Robertson, O. Palmer. *The Israel of God: Yesterday, Today, and Tomorrow*. Phillipsburg, NJ: P&R, 2000.

Robinson, Donald. "Adventures in Jewish-Christian Relations." In *Assembling God's People*, edited by Peter G. Bolt and Mark D. Thompson, 191–94. Vol. 1 of *Donald Robinson: Selected Works*. Camperdown, Aus.: Australian Church Record, 2008.

———. "Biblical Theology in Sydney." In *Historical Studies and Series Index*, edited by Edward Loane, 202–19. Vol. 4 of *Donald Robinson: Selected Works*. Camperdown, Aus.: Australian Church Record, 2018.

———. "Biblical Understanding of Israel—The Geographical Entity: Some Prolegomena." In *Assembling God's People*, edited by Peter G. Bolt and Mark D. Thompson, 179–90. Vol. 1 of *Donald Robinson: Selected Works*. Camperdown, Aus.: Australian Church Record, 2008.

———. "The Church in the New Testament." In *Assembling God's People*, edited by Peter G. Bolt and Mark D. Thompson, 212–21. Vol. 1 of *Donald Robinson: Selected Works*. Camperdown, Aus.: Australian Church Record, 2008.

———. "'The Church' Revisited: An Autobiographical Fragment." In *Assembling God's People*, edited by Peter G. Bolt and Mark D. Thompson, 259–71. Vol. 1 of *Donald Robinson: Selected Works*. Camperdown, Aus.: Australian Church Record, 2008.

———. "The Circumcision of Titus and Paul's 'Liberty'." In *Assembling God's People*, edited by Peter G. Bolt and Mark D. Thompson, 110–29. Vol. 1 of *Donald Robinson: Selected Works*. Camperdown, Aus.: Australian Church Record, 2008.

———. "The Distinction Between Jewish and Gentile Believers in Galatians." In *Assembling God's People*, edited by Peter G. Bolt and Mark D. Thompson, 130–51. Vol. 1 of *Donald Robinson: Selected Works*. Camperdown, Aus.: Australian Church Record, 2008.

———. "'Israel' and the 'Gentiles' in the Gospel of Mark." In *Assembling God's People*, edited by Peter G. Bolt and Mark D. Thompson, 28–44. Vol. 1 of *Donald Robinson: Selected Works*. Camperdown, Aus.: Australian Church Record, 2008.

———. "Israel and the Gentiles in the New Testament." In *Assembling God's People*, edited by Peter G. Bolt and Mark D. Thompson, 7–27. Vol. 1 of *Donald Robinson: Selected Works*. Camperdown, Aus.: Australian Church Record, 2008.

———. "Jew and Gentile in the New Testament." In *Assembling God's People*, edited by Peter G. Bolt and Mark D. Thompson, 409–29. Vol. 1 of *Donald Robinson: Selected Works*. Camperdown, Aus.: Australian Church Record, 2008.

———. "Jew and Greek: Unity and Division in the Early Church." In *Assembling God's People*, edited by Peter G. Bolt and Mark D. Thompson, 79–109. Vol. 1 of *Donald Robinson: Selected Works*. Camperdown, Aus.: Australian Church Record, 2008.

———. "Origins and Unresolved Tensions." In *Interpreting God's Plan: Biblical Theology and the Pastor*, edited by Richard J. Gibson, 1–17. London: Paternoster, 1997.

———. "Romans 9:7." In *Assembling God's People*, edited by Peter G. Bolt and Mark D. Thompson, 45–46. Vol. 1 of *Donald Robinson: Selected Works*. Camperdown, Aus.: Australian Church Record, 2008.

———. "The Salvation of Israel in Romans 9–11." In *Assembling God's People*, edited by Peter G. Bolt and Mark D. Thompson, 47–63. Vol. 1 of *Donald Robinson: Selected Works*. Camperdown, Aus.: Australian Church Record, 2008.

———. *Donald Robinson: Selected Works*. Edited by Peter G. Bolt et al. 5 vols. Camperdown, Aus.: Australian Church Record, 2008–2018.

———. "We Are the Circumcision." In *Assembling God's People*, edited by Peter G. Bolt and Mark D. Thompson, 170–78. Vol. 1 of *Donald Robinson: Selected Works*. Camperdown, Aus.: Australian Church Record, 2008.

———. "Who Were 'The Saints'?" In *Assembling God's People*, edited by Peter G. Bolt and Mark D. Thompson, 160–69. Vol. 1 of *Donald Robinson: Selected Works*. Camperdown, Aus.: Australian Church Record, 2008.

Rosenzweig, Franz. *The Star of Redemption*. Notre Dame: Notre Dame Press, 1921.

Rosner, Brian S. "Biblical Theology." In *New Dictionary of Biblical Theology: Exploring the Unity and Diversity of Scripture*, edited by T. Desmond Alexander et al., 3–10. Downers Grove, IL: IVP Academic, 2000.

———. "Biblical Theology at Moore: Reflections on One Scholar's Research." Session at ETS Sixty-Third Annual Meeting, San Francisco, Nov. 17, 2011.

Rowdon, H. H. "Dispensational Theology." In *New Dictionary of Theology: Historical and Systematic*, edited by Martin Davie et al., 258–59. Downers Grove, IL: IVP Academic, 2016.

Ryrie, Charles Caldwell. *Dispensationalism Today*. Chicago: Moody, 1965.

Salier, W. H. "Jew and Gentile in John." In *Donald Robinson: Selected Works; Appreciation*, edited by Peter G. Bolt and Mark D. Thompson, 95–103. Camperdown, Aus.: Australian Church Record, 2008.

Samuel Marsden Archives. "Griffith Thomas, W. H." Donald Robinson Library. http://atom.library.moore.edu.au/index.php/griffith-thomas-w-h.

Sandeen, Ernest R. *The Roots of Fundamentalism: British and American Millenarianism 1800–1930*. Chicago: University of Chicago Press, 1970.

Scofield, C. I. *Rightly Dividing the Word of Truth (2 Tim. 2:15): Ten Outline Studies of the More Important Divisions of Scripture*. Philadelphia: Philadelphia School of the Bible, 1921.

Shiner, Rory James Wilson. "An Appreciation of D. W. B. Robinson's New Testament Theology." In *Donald Robinson: Selected Works; Appreciation*, edited by Peter G. Bolt and Mark D. Thompson, 9–62. Camperdown, Aus.: Australian Church Record, 2008.

———. "Reading the New Testament in Australia: An Historical Account of the Origins, Development and Influence of D. W. B. Robinson's Biblical Scholarship." PhD diss., Macquarie University, 2017. http://hdl.handle.net/1959.14/1268511.

Soulen, R. Kendall. *The God of Israel and Christian Theology*. Minneapolis: Fortress, 1996.

———. "Post-Supersessionism." In *A Dictionary of Jewish-Christian Relations*, edited by Edward Kessler and Neil Wenborn, 350–51. Cambridge: Cambridge University Press, 2005.

Spencer, Stephen R. "Dispensationalism." In *The Encyclopedia of Christianity*, edited by Erwin Fahlbusch et al., 1:854–55. Grand Rapids: Eerdmans, 2005.

———. "Scofield, C(yrus) I. (1845–1921)." In *Dictionary of Major Biblical Interpreters*, edited by Donald K. McKim, 906–10. Downers Grove, IL: IVP Academic, 2007.

Stoffer, Dale R. *Background and Development of Brethren Doctrines, 1650–1987*. Philadelphia: Brethren Encyclopedia, 1989.

Stott, John. *Basic Christianity*. Downers Grove, IL: InterVarsity, 2008.

———. *The Cross of Christ*. Downers Grove, IL: InterVarsity, 1986.

———. *The Message of Romans: God's Good News for the World*. The Bible Speaks Today. Downers Grove, IL: InterVarsity, 2001.

———. *One People: Helping Your Church Become a Caring Community*. Old Tappan, NJ: Revell, 1982.

———. "The Place of Israel." In *Zion's Christian Soldiers? The Bible, Israel and the Church*, 164–72. Downers Grove, IL: InterVarsity, 2007.

———. *Understanding the Bible*. Grand Rapids: Zondervan, 1972.

Sydney College of Divinity. "Professor Peter Bolt." Sydney College of Divinity, n.d. https://scd.edu.au/team-members/professor-peter-bolt/.

Thiselton, Anthony C. *The Thiselton Companion to Christian Theology*. Grand Rapids: Eerdmans, 2015.

Thomas, W. H. Griffith. "Great Facts About Our Lord's Coming." *Sunday School Times* 65 (1923) 792–93.

———. *St. Paul's Epistle to the Romans: A Devotional Commentary*. Grand Rapids: Eerdmans, 1946.

Thompson, Mark D. "Donald William Bradley Robinson." In *Donald Robinson: Selected Works; Appreciation*, edited by Peter G. Bolt and Mark D. Thompson, 3–8. Camperdown, Aus.: Australian Church Record, 2008.

———. "Knox/Robinson for Today." Briefing, Dec. 20, 2011. http://thebriefing.com.au/2011/12/knoxrobinson-for-today/.

BIBLIOGRAPHY

Trumbull, Charles Gallaudette. *The Life Story of C. I. Scofield*. New York: Oxford University Press, 1920.

Vlach, Michael J. *The Church as a Replacement of Israel: An Analysis of Supersessionism*. Edition Israelogie 2. Berlin: Peter Lang, 2009.

Vos, Geerhardus. *Biblical Theology: Old and New Testaments*. Eugene, OR: Wipf & Stock, 2003.

———. "The Doctrine of the Covenant in Reformed Theology." In *Redemptive History and Biblical Interpretation: The Shorter Writings of Geerhardus Vos*, edited by Richard B. Gaffin Jr., 234–67. Phillipsburg, NJ: Presbyterian & Reformed, 1979.

Vreté, Mayir. "The Restoration of the Jews in English Protestant Thought 1790–1840." *JMES* 8 (1972) 3–50. https://doi.org/10.1080/00263207208700192.

Ward, Roland S. "A Passion for God and a Passion for Jews: The Basis and Practice of Jewish Mission 1550–1850." *RTR* 70 (2011) 1–24. https://rtrjournal.org/index.php/RTR/article/view/8/0.

Webb, Barry G. *The Message of Zechariah: Your Kingdom Come*. The Bible Speaks Today. Downers Grove, IL: InterVarsity, 2003.

———. "The Role of OT and of Biblical Israel—School of Theology 1987. Church and Society." Lecture given at Moore Theological College, Jan. 1, 1987. https://moorecollege.access.preservica.com/IO_19975a1a-5290-4af9-9a65-f0o10cc993d5/.

Wegner, Paul D. *A Student's Guide to Textual Criticism of the Bible: Its History, Methods and Results*. Downers Grove, IL: IVP Academic, 2006.

West, Janet "D. J. Davies: A Principal Embattled." Moore College Library Lecture, 1988. https://moorecollege.access.preservica.com/IO_e52cfb5d-3193-47db-9b0d-3404594795da/.

Williamson, Paul R. "Abraham, Israel and the Church." *EvQ* 72 (2000) 99–118. https://biblicalstudies.org.uk/pdf/eq/2000-2_099.pdf.

———. "Covenant." In *Dictionary of the Old Testament: Pentateuch; A Compendium of Contemporary Biblical Scholarship*, edited by T. Desmond Alexander and David W. Baker, 139–55. IVP Bible Dictionary Series. Downers Grove, IL: IVP Academic, 2002.

———. "Covenant." In *New Dictionary of Biblical Theology: Exploring the Unity and Diversity of Scripture*, edited by T. Desmond Alexander et al, 419–29. Downers Grove, IL: IVP Academic, 2000.

———. *Sealed with an Oath: Covenant in God's Unfolding Purpose*. New Studies in Biblical Theology 23. Downers Grove, IL: InterVarsity, 2007.

Windsor, Lionel J. "About Me." Forget the Channel, n.d. https://www.lionelwindsor.net/about/about-me/.

———. "Curriculum Vitae." Forget the Channel, n.d. https://www.lionelwindsor.net/about/curriculum-vitae/.

———. "The Formation of Gentile Christ-Believing Identity Vis-à-Vis Israel in Ephesians and Barnabas." *Biblica et Patristica Thoruniensia* 11 (2018) 377–90. https://doi.org/10.12775/BPTh.2018.019.

———. *Paul and the Vocation of Israel: How Paul's Jewish Identity Informs His Apostolic Ministry, with Special Reference to Romans*. BZNW 205. Berlin: De Gruyter, 2014.

———. *Reading Ephesians and Colossians After Supersessionism: Christ's Mission Through Israel to the Nations*. Eugene, OR: Cascade, 2017.

BIBLIOGRAPHY

Witsius, Herman. *The Economy of the Covenants Between God and Man.* 2 vols. Grand Rapids: Reformation Heritage, 2021.

"World Council of Churches." In *The Oxford Dictionary of the Christian Church*, edited by F. L. Cross and Elizabeth A. Livingstone, 1777–78. Oxford: Oxford University Press, 2005. Logos.

Yeats, J. M. "'To the Jew First': Conversion of the Jews as the Foundation for Global Missions and Expansion in Nineteenth-Century British Evangelicalism." *SwJT* 47 (2005) 207–23.

Zoccali, Christopher. "What's the Problem with the Law? Jews, Gentiles, and Covenant Identity in Galatians 3:10–12." *Neot* 49 (2015) 377–415. https://muse.jhu.edu/article/638905.

www.ingramcontent.com/pod-product-compliance
Lightning Source LLC
Chambersburg PA
CBHW050812160426
43192CB00010B/1730